John Keble, Robert F. (Robert Francis) Wilson

Outlines of Instructions or Meditations for the Church's Seasons

John Keble, Robert F. (Robert Francis) Wilson

Outlines of Instructions or Meditations for the Church's Seasons

ISBN/EAN: 9783337162740

Printed in Europe, USA, Canada, Australia, Japan

Cover: Foto ©ninafisch / pixelio.de

More available books at **www.hansebooks.com**

OUTLINES

OF

INSTRUCTIONS OR MEDITATIONS

FOR

The Church's Seasons,

BY

JOHN KEBLE, M.A.

EDITED, WITH A PREFACE, BY

R. F. WILSON, M.A.

"Declaratio Sermonum Tuorum illuminat et intellectum dat parvulis."
Ps. cxix. 130.

Oxford and London:
JAMES PARKER AND CO.
1880.

PREFACE.

SOME years ago Mr. Keble's MS. Sermons were entrusted to us, with a view to our making selections from them for publication. This has been done, and eleven Volumes have been published, under the superintendence of Dr. Pusey, who wrote a Preface to the Volume for Lent, which was the first published, though now standing fourth of the ten Volumes which form the series for the Christian Year. Vol. XI. being a miscellaneous collection.

But together with the mass of Sermons (dating from the year 1815 to 1865, thus reaching over half a century), and other MSS. sent to us, there were a large number of scraps of paper of all sorts and sizes, backs of letters, of parish notices, &c., &c., past counting, but weighing, when put together, over five pounds. These had been found, when Mr. Keble's papers had to be removed from Hursley Vicarage, scattered about in all kinds of places, and had been carefully collected by his nephew, the Rev. J. Keble, jun.[a], from whom we received them.

[a] These sketches bring vividly before me the recollection of days long ago, how he used to sit at the round table in the little Hursley Vicarage drawing-room, bending over his book or paper, in the midst of conversa-

They were at first set aside, while we were occupied with the work of selecting the Sermons, and preparing them for the press; but when that began to draw to a close, the loose papers were looked into, and the more they were considered, the more valuable they appeared; varying extremely in character, there was in them that combination of exceeding simplicity with deep and accurate theology, and wonderful familiarity with Holy Scripture, which is such a marked characteristic of his Sermons; and many of them had an originality peculiarly his own, which their very shortness and abruptness seemed to bring out, even more forcibly than if they had been filled out into finished compositions.

A number of them were copied, and shewn to Dr. Pusey, who entirely approved of their publication, and kindly looked over and compared with the originals, by far the larger number of those which form the contents of the present Volume. Specimens of them have since been occasionally submitted to others, in whose judgment we had confidence, and in every case the expressions of approval have been strong and uniform. In more than one instance the opinion was even given, that these outlines would be, to some, of more value than finished Sermons.

It has been thought that they may be of use in two ways; first as notes or sketches for Sermons; this was no doubt the purpose for which they were originally

tion grave or gay, in which he would from time to time take part, taking off his spectacles, looking up, and breaking in with "please say that again, I did not quite hear."—R. F. W.

written, and as it may be interesting and instructive, especially to young preachers, to see how the Author himself expanded his notes, a few have been introduced into the Volume, of which the working out will be found amongst the series of Sermons for the Christian Year, alluded to above:—thus No. xxvi. of these outlines will be found worked out into Sermon 16, Vol. III.; No. xxvii. in Sermon 18 of the same Vol.; No. xciv. seems to have been expanded into two Sermons, viz. 20 and 21 in Vol. I.; No. cii. will be found in Sermon 20, Vol. IX. But there are only a few of these, for, during the last years of his life, he preached chiefly from notes, and seldom wrote out his Sermons—and most of the papers selected for this Volume belong to that later time—they have thus a special interest, as being the substance of John Keble's latest theological teaching.

But besides their value as helps to those who have to teach others, they will, if I am not mistaken, be found to have a yet higher value for private and devotional use, as helps to Meditation. Most persons find this one of the most difficult, if not *the* most difficult of their religious exercises; and to some minds, who may not be able to adapt themselves to the more formal, and, so to speak, technical methods of meditation recommended by spiritual writers, it is thought that these outlines may be of great use. Some are more especially suited to this purpose than others, but all may be profitably turned to account in this way.

It remains to say a few words as to the form in

which these Outlines have been printed. It has been already said that the originals vary extremely—some are clear and legible, others hardly decypherable; in the facsimiles printed at the end of this Preface a specimen of each kind is given, from which it will be seen that in some cases the labour and responsibility of decyphering them has not been light. Some few, such as that on Ps. li., are so clearly and beautifully drawn out, that they might have been printed exactly as they were written; but these are rare exceptions; with the far larger number, justice as well to the Author, as to the reader, made *some* arrangement necessary, and it seemed best that it should be uniform throughout.

In the form which has been adopted, our object has been to keep close to the original, carefully avoiding any thing which might fix our own meaning upon it, but rather leaving it open to those who may use the notes, either as helps to preaching or to meditation, to follow out the trains of thought in their own way. Numbers, letters, and other marks evidently intended by the Author for his own guidance, have been omitted for the same reason, viz., in order to give greater liberty in the use of them.

The Volume does not profess to be a complete series for every day in the Christian Year. The papers which have been selected for printing have been arranged in the order of the Church's Seasons, and something will be found for most of the Sundays and Saints' Days, as well as for all the greater Festivals; but inasmuch as the series is not quite complete, it has been thought better not to specify the Sundays in the Seasons of Advent, Epiphany, Lent, Easter, and after Trinity. Those which obviously belong to special Sundays, are so marked in the Table of Contents.

A set of papers have been added at the end on the Penitential Psalms. They are believed to have formed the basis of a course of instructions on those Psalms, delivered in Lent, 1856, one of which, namely that on the first half of Ps. xxxii., will be found in Sermon 26, Vol. IV., of the Sermons for the Christian Year. Unfortunately this one, with an imperfect fragment on Ps. vi., is all that has been found of what, one cannot help feeling, would have been a most valuable series. It is possible that the rest were never written, but hardly likely, considering the completeness and finish of this one. Mr. Keble not unfrequently lent his Sermons to his friends. If this notice should meet the eye of any one who knows any thing about this set of Sermons on the Penitential Psalms, may I hope that he will communicate with me, or with the Rev. T. Keble, Vicar of Bisley.

These notes are rather different from the rest, and do not lend themselves so easily to the same kind of arrangement. They have been printed exactly as they stand in the originals, and placed at the end, in order to avoid breaking the continuity of the rest, and as being suitable for instruction or meditation at any season of the year.

With these few words of introduction and explanation these outlines are commended to English Churchmen, with the hope that they may be found to be among not the least valuable of their Author's precious legacies to the Church, in which he so loyally laboured, and to whose service the best energies of his whole life were so unsparingly given.

R. F. WILSON.

ROWNHAMS,
August 27, 1880.

The two Instructions of which facsimiles are given here, will be found at page 7, and at page 188. The first is for Advent, No. iii. "The Sign of the Son of Man;" the second is for Whitsunday, No. lxxxi. "The Penitent's Whitsuntide."

S. Mat, 24. 30. Τότε φανησεται, κ.

1. When ye Jews req.d a sign, X'd d. No. they [? X
Were of the wrong sort — it wd go yn more harm yn good
2. But when the D. [looked asking for] asked, he gave many signs —
false Xts, war, troubles, persecutions, divisions. &c &c
in the Ch. Wars often ye com: men false *Prophets;
a darkness — this Sign [ye X] — the Son of
Man — the gathering of all by J. Angels.
3. The ancients thought it be the sign of ye X. [
certainty yt + was from an early date in this the
-ing the Sign of X. The + height of ye Sun, when
-dead is by yt the + darkened & eclipsed (so acts 26.)
"We are to understand how the sign of ye + Christ, yt all his
may see him "whom they pierced, & the sign of his
Victory." (Orig.)

                                        to his disciples
λ. as in S. Mat. X. 38. "Whosoever taketh not &c. XV. 24. If
any man will come after me" &c. [to ye apo.) S. Luke 14.
27. (to ye multitudes.) "& is "lifting up" ye S. of Man."
(in S. John) to his disciples in c. 8. & in c. 12 — his
his direct predictions, verified contrary to likelihood, of his
dying, not come true, S. John XVIII
4. It was ye symbol of his doctrine as spoken in preaching
S. P. 1 Cor. ch. how + &c is to ym who perish foolishness &c. & to

UNIV. OF
CALIFORNIA

Ps. LI. 10...13.   Nov S. 1863.

This Ps. is our Ps. ...
We are as David ....
Our sins as his sins ...
Our hope as his hope ...
(W.d that our repentance were like his) –.

But now N.B. those verses of his Prayer especially make ... from me ....

See, he asks not only pardon but conversion ....
(not even comfort, for he wd. have his sins ever before him)
but he wants God's Rescue & good Spt. restored
                                                         to him
May we not say, Here is a penit. sinner &c
                 one
espying his Whitsuntide?

  Good F. & Atonem.t
  Easter D. & Justifn.   } are not enough
  Asc. D. & Intercession
, nor White. & Sanctifn. also   unless he have a
̶T̶h̶e̶r̶e̶ ̶m̶u̶s̶t̶ ̶b̶e̶ ̶r̶e̶a̶s̶o̶n̶a̶b̶l̶e̶ ̶h̶o̶p̶e̶   reasonable hope of
himself sharing in it

He wants to be free fm. ye Power as well as the
punishm.t of Sin – of his own sins

He wants the H.S. qu. own.   Comforter

CONTENTS.

			PAGE
I.	Advent.	*The Lord's Coming*	1
II.	,,	*The Bridal Procession*	5
III.	,,	*The Sign of the Son of Man*	7
IV.	,,	*The Book of Life*	9
V.	,,	*Death*	11
VI.	,,	*The Use of Reproach*	13
VII.	,,	*The Vision of Isaiah*	15
VIII.	,,	*The Live Coal from the Altar*	18
IX.	,,	*The Happy Remnant*	21
X.	Third Sunday.	*Preliminary Warnings*	25
XI.	,,	*The Warnings of the Clergy*	28
XII.	,,	*The under Shepherds of the Lord*	30
XIII.	Fourth Sunday.	*Making the most of the Divine Presence*	32
XIV.	Christmas.	*The Christian Birth*	35
XV.	S. Stephen.	*S. Stephen a Pattern for Young Men*	39
XVI.	S. John.	*The Light of God in Christ*	41
XVII.	,,	*The Witness of Age and Experience*	43
XVIII.	The Holy Innocents.	*The Example of Little Children*	47
XIX.	Epiphany.	*Worship*	49
XX.	,,	*Obedience*	51
XXI.	,,	*Patience*	53
XXII.	,,	*Faith*	56
XXIII.	Septuagesima.	*Thankfulness*	58
XXIV.	Sexagesima.	*Confession*	60
XXV.	,,	,,	61
XXVI.	,,	*Probation*	63
XXVII.	Quinquagesima.	*Clothing*	65
XXVIII.	,,	*Love*	67
XXIX.	Ash-Wednesday.	*Lent a Time of Penance*	69
XXX.	Lent.	*Moses in the Mount*	71
XXXI.	,,	*No Time for Delay*	73

			PAGE
XXXII.	Lent.	*Retirement and Silence*	75
XXXIII.	,,	*Watching and Working*	77
XXXIV.	,,	*Sin a Possession*	79
XXXV.	,,	*Sin a Leprosy*	82
XXXVI.	,,	*Sin a Blindness*	84
XXXVII.	,,	*Sin a Palsy*	86
XXXVIII.	,,	*Sin a Deafness and Dumbness*	88
XXXIX.	,,	*Sin a Death*	90
XL.	,,	*Escape for thy Life*	92
XLI.	,,	*The Lenten Ember-tide*	93
XLII.	,,	*True Forgiveness*	95
XLIII.	Holy Week.	*Ecce Homo*	97
XLIV.	Palm Sunday.	*The Form of a Servant*	101
XLV.	,,	*The Model Man*	103
XLVI.	,,	*The Decree of Sacrifice*	105
XLVII.	,,	*The Tears of Jesus*	108
XLVIII.	,,	*The Time of Visitation*	110
XLIX.	,,	*A Word to Frequent Communicants*	112
L.	Monday in Holy Week.	*The Day of Cleansing*	114
LI.	,,	,, *The Sinner's Wounds*	116
LII.	Tuesday.	*Spiritual Perplexity*	118
LIII.	Wednesday.	*Christ's Mind towards Judas*	120
LIV.	,,	*The Attraction of Jesus in His Passion*	122
LV.	Thursday.	*The Attraction of Jesus in the Holy Eucharist*	126
LVI.	,,	*The Sacrifice of the Eucharist*	129
LVII.	,,	*The Legacies of Christ*	131
LVIII.	Good Friday.	*The Attraction of Jesus in His Crucifixion*	134
LIX.	,,	*The Finished Work*	136
LX.	,,	*The Price of our Blessings*	137
LXI.	Easter Eve.	*The Price of our Hopes*	140
LXII.	Easter.	*The Mystery of Easter*	142
LXIII.	,,	*The Glory of the Despised Name*	144
LXIV.	,,	*The Chosen Witnesses*	147
LXV.	,,	*Easter Illumination, &c.*	149
LXVI.	,,	*The Touch of Faith*	151
LXVII.	,,	*The Miracle of Hindrances to Sin*	153

			PAGE
LXVIII. Easter.	*The Responsibility of Belonging to God*	.	155
LXIX. ,,	*The Unruly Will*	.	158
LXX. Rogation Tide.	*Failures in Prayer*	.	161
LXXI. ,,	*The Prevailing Intercessor*	.	163
LXXII. ,,	*The Typified Intercession fulfilled*	.	164
LXXIII. ,,	*Waiting in Prayer*	.	166
LXXIV. Ascension Day.	*Ascension Joy*	.	168
LXXV. ,,	*The Power of the Ascended Christ*	.	171
LXXVI. ,,	*The Kingdom and the Priesthood*	.	174
LXXVII. ,,	*Praise the Key-note of the Ascension*		177
LXXVIII. ,,	*Moses a Type of Christ*	.	178
LXXIX. ,,	*Elijah a Type of Christ*	.	182
LXXX. Whitsunday.	*Thanksgiving the Grace of Whitsunday*		185
LXXXI. ,,	*The Penitent's Whitsuntide*	.	188
LXXXII. ,,	*The Whitsuntide Self-examination*	.	190
LXXXIII. ,,	*The Holy Ghost our Advocate*	.	192
LXXXIV. Trinity Sunday.	*Our Incorporation in the Blessed Trinity*	.	194
LXXXV. After Trinity.	*The Christian Sacrifice.* I.	.	196
LXXXVI. ,,	,, II.	.	200
LXXXVII. ,,	,, III.	.	203
LXXXVIII. ,,	*Failure in God impossible*	.	206
LXXXIX. ,,	*The Tokens of having been with Jesus*		209
XC. ,,	*Christ's Love, our Coldness*	.	213
XCI. ,,	*Our Lord's Will for His Servants*	.	214
XCII. ,,	*Obedience better than Sacrifice*	.	217
XCIII. ,,	*National Calamities*	.	220
XCIV. ,,	*The Long-suffering of God*	.	222
XCV. ,,	*The Service of Good-will*	.	224
XCVI. ,,	*The Field of our Hidden Treasure*	.	226
XCVII. Tenth Sunday.	*The Woman of Sarepta*	.	228
XCVIII. Eleventh Sunday.	*The Pharisee and the Publican*	.	230
XCIX. Fourteenth Sunday.	*The Secret of Ingratitude*	.	234
C. Eighteenth Sunday.	*Fearlessness under Warnings*	.	236
CI. Nineteenth Sunday.	*Absolution*	.	240
CII. ,,	*Self-loathing*	.	242

		PAGE
CIII.	After Trinity, Twenty-first Sunday. *Pardon and Peace*	244
CIV.	Twenty-third Sunday. *The Citizenship of the Christian*	246
CV.	Twenty-fifth Sunday. *The Divine Use of Distress*	248
CVI.	Last Sunday. *Enduring Love*	251
CVII.	,, *The Land of Blessing*	253
CVIII.	S. Andrew. *Conversion*	256
CIX.	S. Thomas. *Love the Key of Faith*	258
CX.	S. Paul. *The Test of Conversion*	260
CXI.	The Purification. *Holy Exactness*	262
CXII.	,, *The union of Offering with Purity*	264
CXIII.	S. Matthias. *The Eternity of Hell*	265
CXIV.	The Annunciation. *How?*	267
CXV.	SS. Philip and James. *Strictness and Severity*	269
CXVI.	S. Barnabas. *Kindliness and Stedfastness*	271
CXVII.	S. John Baptist. *Energy and Strength*	273
CXVIII.	S. Peter. *The Apostolic Church*	275
CXIX.	S. Michael, &c. *The Ministry of the Angels*	278
CXX.	S. Luke. *S. Luke an "Image" of our Lord*	280
CXXI.	,, *The Good Physician and the Good Patient*	282
CXXII.	SS. Simon and Jude. *Railing Words*	284
CXXIII.	,, *The Peril of Knowledge without Love*	286
CXXIV.	All Saints. *The Note of Holiness*	288
CXXV.	,, *Fellowship with the Saints*	291
CXXVI.	,, *The Saints' nearness to Christ*	293

THE PENITENTIAL PSALMS.

I.	Psalm vi.		297
II.	,,	xxxii.	301
III.	,,	xxxviii.	305
IV.	,,	li.	310
V.	,,	cii.	312
VI.	,,	cxxx.	313
VII.	,,	,,	315
VIII.	,,	cxliii.	317

I.

Advent.

THE LORD'S COMING.

"The coming of the Lord draweth nigh."—S. JAMES v. 8.

WHEN you are on a journey,
You watch the marks of your progress,
As they appear or disappear.
Such and such a hill is now in view:
We are so much nearer the end of our journey.
Or if it be a voyage,
Or a job of work, or what not?
Such reminders are welcome:
We love to find that we are getting on.
Or when you expect a visitor,
And either long to see him, or are afraid of not being ready.
So each holy season is welcome as it comes;
And, with special emphasis, this holy season of Advent.
Of what it is the token, you know—
Of the coming of our Lord.
If you believe anything, you believe that He will come,
To be our Judge.
Just consider—that He will come.
Who? The Lord.
What awe! what wonder!
To do what? To judge.
When any work is to be inspected, whoever is to inspect,

It makes the workman anxious.
But here it is Christ who is to be the Judge:
God—who knows all,
Man—who can feel for all.
Once before He came to save;
Now He comes again to judge.
To judge whom? Us.
To judge us—you—me—all,
Even as He died for all.
And He will come soon—before you are aware.
Observe the signs of His coming:—
The Gospel preached:
Yet the Son of Man hardly finding faith on the earth.
Some of us think much of politics,
And of the great doings of this world;
But what of them all in that Day?
Perhaps the world may go on long after our time;
But what of that to us?
He will come to you and me at our deaths;
And that is sure to be soon.
Think when you last looked into a grave,
Or heard a knell for the dead.
Consider steadily that, in a short time,
You will be where that person is.
And this world will be to you what it is to him.
And this also is the Lord's coming to you.
You will be aware of Christ's Presence then,
In quite a different way from what you are now.
You will be, as it were, alone with Him.

You will know for certain what His Mind is towards you.
Christ, then, is at hand.
Are you getting ready for Him?
Are your robes washed?
Are your talents improved?
Are your lamps lighted and trimmed?
Are you at all intent on these things?
Nay: do you care in the least about them?
Are you better than you were last Advent?
"There is time enough yet." Who told you that?
Christ tells you plainly, "There is not an hour to spare."
He says, "Behold, I come quickly."
It is quite another voice that says,
"Where is the promise of His coming?"
You are left watching; and you say one to another,
"Take thine ease, eat, drink, and be merry."
But your Master's word is,
"Let your loins be girded about, and your lights burning."
Death is at hand, and judgment after death.
Do you not see it?
Do you not hear the passing-bell,
For persons as young and younger than yourself?
You may hide your eyes,
As they say some foolish birds do;
But the hunters are on you just the same.
You may look another way;
But He is nearer to you, moment by moment.
You yourself cannot stand still;
Much less can you turn back.

Along the broad way or the narrow,
You must go on to meet your Judge.
And whatever it seems now,
You know that, when the journey is over,
It will seem to you like railway-speed.
What is the use of forgetting this,
And behaving as if you were to be always here?
Why not rather make much of your Lord's warning,
And use it continually,
Against all troubles and temptations?
Why be fretful?
"The coming of the Lord draweth nigh;"
And then all this will be over.
Better " stablish your hearts."
Why be lustful?
"The Day is at hand;" and you must give account
Of what you have been doing in the darkness.
Why be covetous?
The fire is at hand, which will burn it all up.
Why be lazy?
The Lord is nigh: what if He should find you so?
His reward is with Him, and it is worth working for.
Time is very short: Eternity very long.
And to each one of us is allowed
A very little of that short time,
To provide for that endless Eternity.
Too little, only that we have
An Almighty Saviour to plead for us,
And an Almighty Spirit to help us.

By Their Help, if you will use it, you are safe.
But if you trifle with it, what is to become of you?
Where will you be in that Day?

II.

THE BRIDAL PROCESSION.

"*Lord, Lord, open to us.*"—ST. MATT. xxv. 11.

THIS is especially the Advent Chapter.
It opens with, "Then shall the Kingdom."
"Then" marks the Second Coming of our Lord.
It will be, in the Kingdom of Heaven—the Church,
As if there should be a Wedding.
See how the Christian Dispensation resembles a Wedding.
There is a Bridegroom,
And a Bride,
A Marriage Feast,
A place ordained for it,
Virgins invited to the Feast.
The time, in the night: but also uncertain.
Lamps therefore wanted.
And oil to trim the lamps.
And each one to have a lamp, and a vessel with oil.
And each one to join the Bridegroom and the Bride,
In the Procession.
This is our condition;
We have our lamps lighted;
And we come forth, to meet the Bridegroom.

But He is tarrying,
And it will probably be with us,
As with so many others before us,
We shall be asleep when He comes.
But such as we are, in going to sleep,
Such shall we be, when we awake.
We shall awake indeed;
The Trumpet will leave no choice in that.
But if, before that summons shall come,
Our lamps should have gone out,
Or should have all but gone out,
It will be too late for us, then,
To procure oil wherewith to trim them.
Neither Saint nor Angel will be able to help us;
The Holy Spirit will have withdrawn Himself;
The Bridegroom will pass by,
And we, with lamps gone out,
Shall knock at the door in vain.
He will say, "I know you not."
Therefore, bring oil in your vessels,
With your lamps.
Bring the Grace of God,
To keep up and to realize your outward profession.
Bring holy desires
To sanctify your good works.
Bring good works
To mature and embody your holy desires.
That the shutting of the door,
Which to the foolish will be despair,
May be to you everlasting security.

III.

THE SIGN OF THE SON OF MAN.

"Then shall appear the sign of the Son of Man in Heaven."—S. MATT. xxiv. 30.

WHEN the Jews required a sign,
Christ said, No, they were of the wrong sort:
It would do them more harm than good.
But when the disciples, Andrew being one, asked,
He gave many signs:
False Christs,
Wars,
Troubles,
Persecutions,
Divisions,
An evil power within the Church,
Worse afflictions than ever,
More false prophets,
Darkness,
"The Sign of the Son of Man,"
The gathering of all by the Angels.
The ancients thought the sign of the Son of Man to be
The sign of the Cross.
"The Cross brighter than the sun,
"Which indeed is by the Cross darkened and eclipsed[a]."
"We are to understand here the sign of the Cross,
"That the Jews may see Him whom they pierced,

---

[a] S. Chrysostom, Acts xxvi.

"And the sign of His victory [b]."
Certainly from an early date in His Ministry
The Cross was the sign of Christ.
To His messengers He said, "He that taketh not his cross [c]."
To His disciples, "If any man will come after Me,
"Let him ... take up his cross [d]."
To the multitudes, "Whosoever doth not bear his cross [e]."
To Nicodemus, the "lifting up" of the Son of Man [f].
The same expression repeated to the Jews [g],
In His direct predictions of His Crucifixion;
Verified contrary to likelihood,
That His saying might come true,
Signifying what death He should die.
It was the symbol of His doctrine, adopted in preaching;
"For the preaching of the Cross
"Is to them that perish foolishness [h]."
So the sign came to be visibly used,
In Baptism, Confirmation, and everywhere;
And the Saints loved it dearly.
S. Peter, S. Andrew, S. John were attracted to Him,
As "the Lamb of God that taketh away the sin of the world."
And S. Paul especially, "God forbid that I should glory,
"Save in the Cross [i]."
So it has been ever since;
And we see it with our eyes;
The Cross prevailing

[b] Origen.   [c] S. Matt. x. 38.   [d] S. Matt. xvi. 24.
[e] S. Luke xiv. 27.   [f] S. John iii. 14.   [g] S. John viii. 28; xii. 32.
[h] 1 Cor. i. 18.   [i] Gal. vi. 14.

Against the Roman banners and the Greek wisdom.
How could the token of a shameful death
Have ever got such honour in a natural way?
And besides, it was so remarkably foreshewn.
Depend on it, whenever you see it,
On a spire, an ornament, anywhere,
You see a sign
Of the coming of the Son of Man,
And of the end of the world.

IV.

THE BOOK OF LIFE.

"Another book was opened, which is the Book of Life."—REV. xx. 12.

THERE are three books which are to be opened:
The Book of the Law,
By which we are to be judged;
The Book of our deeds,
Which is the record of evidence concerning us;
And the Book of Life,
Concerning Which it is written in the text,
Whosoever was not found written in the Book of Life
Was cast into the lake of fire.
This Book had been mentioned many times in Scripture before.
To Moses [k]:
To David [l]:

---

[k] Exod. xxxii. 32, 33.   [l] Ps. lxix. 28.

To Daniel [m]:
To Malachi [n]:
To the Seventy [o]:
Of the Faithful [p]:
To the Church at Sardis [q]:
Of Apostates [r]:
Of our Lord [s]:
Of dwellers in Heaven [t]:
That Day will be like a Royal Visit,
With an amnesty,
And those who are left out condemned.
We have reason to believe that our names,
One and all, were once in this Book,
As Satan's name was once among the good Angels.
They may have been blotted out [u].
If they are not there now, our sin is in fault [x].
What are the tokens of our names being there?
Mourning for iniquity [y]:
Misgivings for our own sins [z]:
Serious talk [a]:
Labouring with such as S. Paul [b]:
Overcoming temptation [c]:
Not worshipping the world [d]:
Sacrifice, as of our Lord [e]:
"In the head of the Book it is written of Me [f]:"

[m] Dan. xii. 1.   [n] Mal. iii. 16.   [o] S. Luke x. 20.   [p] Phil. iv. 3.
[q] Rev. iii. 5.   [r] Rev. xiii. 8; xvii. 8.   [s] Heb. x. 7.   [t] Rev. xxi. 27; xxii. 19.   [u] Rev. iii. 5; xiii. 8.   [x] Exod. xxxii. 33.   [y] Ezek. ix. 4.
[z] Ps. lvi. 8.   [a] Mal. iii. 16.   [b] Phil. iv. 3.   [c] Rev. iii. 5.
[d] Rev. xiii. 8; xvii. 8.   [e] Heb. x. 7.   [f] Ps. xl. 7.

And therefore it is the "Lamb's Book of Life."
To which we may add one more sign:
Walking by faith.
Try yourselves by these signs in time,
That you may not be tried and condemned
In Eternity.

V.

DEATH.

"Now it is high time to awake out of sleep."—ROM. xiii. 11.

THIS means, of course, that if we wait longer,
It will most likely be too late.
Because death will be here,
And then no more can be done.
The Bridegroom with His friends will go in;
And what if we are left out?
Consider: it is now but an *if*,—a presage;
Before long it will be a reality.
When we were boys, we used to fancy
How it would be when we grew to be men.
And so of all other great changes:
Service, marriage, new homes, and the like.
And shall we not dwell on death,
Which is more certain than all?
Now we read of it; we hear of it; perhaps we see it.
It is well we should think:
A little while, and it will be our own case.

Only that we cannot really know what death is.
We may know a good deal of those other things;
But with all men's growth in knowledge,
Death is as great a mystery as ever.
Of things after death, by God's mercy, much is told us.
But what death is, is still a secret.
For what we do know of it,
Let us practise ourselves in time.
We know it will take us among the things out of sight:
Therefore let us walk by faith, not by sight,
We know there is no repentance in the grave:
Therefore let us repent in time.
We know it will bring us before the Judge:
Therefore let us be prepared with our accounts.
We may not plead "Not guilty;"
But we may plead a full pardon,
If we have been truly contrite;
If we have forsaken all sin in heart and spirit;
If we have denied ourselves for Christ's sake;
If we have taken in earnest to good works,
Especially to alms-deeds:
Then shall we find that, as He hath helped us hitherto,
Through trials which seemed beforehand intolerable,
So will He help us in this also.
But it will, most likely, be a sore trial.
Let us pray for ourselves,
And for one another.

II.

THE USE OF REPROACH.

*"Let him curse, because the Lord hath said unto him,
Curse David."*—2 SAM. xvi. 10.

This is the right way of preparing for Judgment:
To call ourselves to a sharp account in time.
"Judge yourselves, that ye be not judged."
Anything that helps us in this,
Helps to make us ready,
And should be welcomed.
Shimei's conduct to David is an example.
He reproached him with guilt towards Saul,
But most untruly.
Yet in calling him "a bloody man,"
He said the truth without knowing it;
And David took it home,
Not as Shimei, but as God, meant it.
Here is an instance of a third preliminary court,
Which Providence opens in this world,
To prepare us for the great Account.
There is the court of Conscience,
And the court of Scripture.
Here we have the court of Satan.
Shimei's words were Satan's words.
God made them His own,
By sending a dart from His Spirit with them,
To pierce David's conscience.
Thus he uses Satan, the Adversary,

The Accuser of the brethren,
To promote His saving Work.
So it was in the case of Job:
Once, twice, Job was accused,
And came off the more glorious.
So it was in the case of Joshua [g].
The resistance to the second Temple,
Was a type of resistance to Christ by the Pharisees;
And to the Church by Satan's agents always.
As Christ and the Church turn it to good,
So may you and I,
If we will rightly use reproach.
You and I are not like Christ and the Church.
There is sure to be more or less ground
For what is said unkindly of us;
If not in any one particular instance, yet in some others.
Think of it thus:
If you are blamed, or ill thought of,
For what you do right,
Say, "I deserve it all, and worse,
"If he did but know."
If you are not so tried,
Use yourself to consider
What an enemy could most effectually bring against you,
If he knew.
That is the charge which Satan is preparing against you
At that Day.
See that you prepare for it:

[g] Zech. iii.

That you have a full pardon to plead.
Do not let him dishearten you with the thought
That it were vain, your trying to be good.
But use it to keep you lowly and watchful.

VII.

THE VISION OF ISAIAH.

"I saw the Lord, sitting upon a throne, high and lifted up, and His train filled the temple."—ISAIAH vi. 1.

ISAIAH is the great Prophet of the Gospel;
His calling is, therefore, particularly recorded.
What was the manner of it?
It was the year of King Uzziah's death:
That king who had spoiled noble beginnings
By his sacrilege;
Who was, therefore, punished in the temple.
Isaiah took particular interest in Uzziah [h]:
Therefore we may judge that he repented [i].
About the time of the king's death,
Isaiah—being in that temple
Which he had profaned,
And the Lord had vindicated,
Saw, in vision, the whole Gospel.
He saw the Lord's Presence [k];

---

[h] 2 Chron. xxvi. 22. [i] Compare ver. 20. [k] Rev. xxi. 3.

He saw the provision
For making sinners worthy of that Presence;
He saw the success of that provision;
Many called, but only a few chosen.
He saw the Lord—our Lord Jesus Christ;
Whether the other instances in the Old Testament
Are rightly so construed or not,
Of this one there can be no doubt[l],
He saw Him sitting on His Throne,
High and lifted up;
Therefore the vision relates to the time
After the Ascension,
When He had begun to take to Himself His great Power,
And to reign.
He saw His skirts—His Saints—His living robe
Filling the temple.
The Church on earth is full of Him [m].
The head and crown of His Saints are the Seraphim.
How are they qualified?
With reverence, modesty, obedience.
How do they serve Him? Chorally.
In their mutual love:
In the joint creed of the Trinity:
In the general diffusion of His Name.
How did Creation and all bear witness[n]!
How could Isaiah's feeling be other
Than what he next describes?
"Woe is me! for I am undone;

---

[l] S. John xii. 41.   [m] S. John i. 26.   [n] Heb. xii. 26—28.

"Because I am a man of unclean lips,
"And I dwell in the midst of a people
"Of unclean lips°."
Yet what he saw was but a shadow
Of the things among which we live.
This is the very doctrine of Christ's first Coming.
What if we should suddenly awake,
And find it so,
When it will be too late to suit ourselves to it?
Mark this, ye trifling ones,
Who think to play life away:
Ye easy-going ones,
Who think to sleep it away:
Ye covetous ones,
Who think to make the most of life in getting:
Ye sensual, in enjoying yourselves.
Ye are " of unclean lips,"
And your people " of unclean lips."
What will ye do,
When your eyes shall be opened in an instant,
And rest on the King, the Lord of Hosts?

° Exod. vi. 12, 30.

VIII.

THE LIVE COAL FROM THE ALTAR.

"Lo, this hath touched thy lips; and thine iniquity is taken away, and thy sin purged."—ISAIAH vi. 6, 7.

THE Prophet was full of fear and confusion,
Suddenly made aware of the glorious Presence,
From Which there could be no escape.
For It filled the Temple.
It was all Holiness;
And he and his people all uncleanness.
Also he had become aware of the glorious Service.
But how could such as he join in It,
Those who led It being such as they were?
Your Judge on His throne invites you
To bear your part,
Not in a like, but in the same, glorious Service,
To the Trinity,—the Thrice-Holy God.
The Seraphim, since their creation,
Have carried on this Service;
And the Saints, since their conversion.
It will be your joy and glory,
If you come worthily to It.
I will suppose that you wish, you long to do so;
But you feel yourself unworthy;
Your lips have been unclean,
And you have not sanctified them with prayer;
You have polluted them with oaths;

With lies, foul talk, slander, irreverence;
And you are in bad company,—
"I dwell among a people of unclean lips."
And you are afraid of still being tempted.
Well, what was Isaiah's remedy?
He bemoaned himself to the Lord,
Full of religious fear;
So must you.
But on the Altar was That which prepared him;
By purification, not without pain;
By touching his lips;
It was brought to him by a Heavenly Messenger,
With a word of Absolution.
This was his remedy: do you apply it.
How may a Christian do so?
The Trinity is too aweful;
But remember the Incarnation of God in Christ;
And His Sacrifice upon the Cross;
And how to apply that Sacrifice.
Tell Him your misery,
And He, by His Seraph—His Church,
Will offer to make you partaker of That which is on the Altar;
The living, life-giving Sacrifice.
That holiest Thing is like fire,—
A glowing precious stone or metal,—
Both God and Man.
Fire, to change what can be changed,
Into Its own likeness,
But to consume and spoil what cannot be changed.

Laid on the unclean lips,
If you be willing, It will purge:
If you be unwilling, It will burn.
A great risk! but your only chance;
Except you can do without Christ.
Of course, being fire, there will be pain;
But what of that?
Come, then, but with deepest reverence;
For even the Seraphim hid their faces,
And touched not with their hands.
Come with the same sort of mind
That you would wish to come with,
If you were going to be ordained, as many now are,
Whom this Chapter particularly suits.
He says, "Whom shall we send, and who will go for us?"
They answer, "Here am I, send me."
Well, but does He not say the same to you,
In your place and station?
You have *some* work to do for Him:
You cannot do it without Him:
This is the place to find Him:
And this—this very "Now,"
Is the time to begin looking after Him,
More earnestly than ever you have done.

IX.

THE HAPPY REMNANT.

"A remnant shall be saved."—ROM. ix. 27.

WHAT was it that enabled Isaiah
To remain in God's Presence,
And to join in His Service?
The live coal on his lips from the Altar.
What enables sinful man now,
To endure the same Presence,
And to join in the same Service?
The touch of Christ's sacrificed Manhood,
Especially in Holy Communion [p].
But as the coal was painful,
So the Cross cannot be without pain, and self-denial.
"If we suffer, we shall also reign with Him [q]."
"If so be that we suffer with Him,
"That we may be also glorified together [r]."
And so the Prophet found,
When he offered himself, upon God's Revelation,
To bear the Message of the Trinity.
The mercy of it was sadly embittered,
By the prediction that it would be a failure.
For that is the meaning of what follows.—
"Go and tell this people,
"Hear ye indeed, but understand not;
"And see ye indeed, but perceive not.

[p] Jer. i. 7; Ezek. xi. 2; Dan. x. 10, 16.   [q] 2 Tim. ii. 12.
[r] Rom. viii. 17.

"Make the heart of this people fat,
"And make their ears heavy, and shut their eyes;
"Lest they see with their eyes, and hear with their ears,
"And understand with their heart, and convert, and be healed[s]:"
Judah would go on provoking God,
Until she was laid waste, and led captive;
But yet there would be a Remnant[t].
All this was but a shadow
Of the more aweful prediction,—
Of the sadder obstinacy—of the greater forsaking—
Of the more blessed Remnant,
In our Lord's time.
And that time, itself, was but a shadow
Of how it will be in the last days.
It comes, in fact, to our Lord's question,—
"When the Son of Man cometh,
"Shall He find faith on the earth?"
And "many are called, few chosen."
A fearful vision!
But we must needs face it:
Else why was it recorded?
It is a sad thought about Christmas,
That Christmas after Christmas should come and go,
And seem to leave the world at least no better than it was.
How may we improve this thought?
Not by thinking of our neighbours,
"I am no worse, but a little better."
Depend on it, there is not one of them so bad,

---

[s] Isa. vi. 9, 10.   [t] Chap. x. 20—22; xxxvii. 31.

But he thinks the same of you.
Nay, rather, think how bad sin must be,
What a deep taint—how dangerous!
How good our Lord Jesus Christ, the Saviour, is,
Who bears with it, and seeks to cure it.
How certain that there will be a Remnant,
And that you are freely chosen out, to be one of It,
If you do not make the choice void,
By your perverseness.
Do you wish to have the comfort of ensuring this?
Then behave as if it were true,
And you will ensure it.
Follow up this thought a little:
How if you had heard Him call from Heaven,
Call you by your name, A.B., and say,
" I have chosen you out of the world,
" To be a member of Myself :
" Therefore keep your hand back from this,
" Turn your eyes away from that."
Would it not move you to obey?
How if you heard Him say,
" I will have *you* to be saved :
" You were in My Mind, in Mine Incarnation,
" And on My Cross.
" I have never forgotten you ;
" Ah! why should you be so easily led to forget Me?"
If you heard Him say this to some one whom you dearly love,
Would it not engage your gratitude?
Well, He says it to all.

Do you not really think the time past may suffice,
To have wrought the will of the evil one?
Ask those who are really trying,
If it does not make them happier.
Ask them what they would take now,
To go back to the devil's service.
Think of the world burning under your feet,
What it will be to be left, to burn with it,
While you see the happy Remnant ascending,
And perhaps then praising God,
For having made them serious,
In those very thoughts,
Which you, even now, are inclined to scorn.
Enter on your Christmas with these thoughts,
And I dare promise you it will be a happier one,
Than, if you have been careless, you have ever spent before.

X.

Preliminary Warnings.

"Also I set watchmen over you, saying, Hearken to the sound of the trumpet."—Jer. vi. 17.

There are two great Gifts of God,
Whereby He would prepare us for His second Coming:
One is the Bible;
The other is the Church.
We acknowledge them on two Advent Sundays.
But as the Bible is of no use,
Unless men read it, pray over it, and practise it;
So neither is the Church,
That is, the Ministry of the Word and Sacraments,
Unless we take its warnings.
Consider the parable of the Watchman or Sentinel:
We are as in an enemy's country;
And our Commander has posted Sentries on the walls [u].
They have their trumpets—the Gospel, in each mouth,
To give warning when they see the sword coming—
Coming openly, or by stealth.
If we give warning, and you take it—well.
What if we give no warning?
You must not think to lay the whole blame upon us.
Because the word "watch" is said "unto all [x]."
It is small comfort for you,
That your blood is required of us.

[u] Isa. lxii. 6; Ezek. iii. 17.   [x] S. Mark xiii. 37.

Neither can you say that you perish unjustly;
Since whatever *we* are,
The Church is a Watcher that makes itself heard,
At least in the plain Creeds,
And in the ten Commandments.
But what if you have taken the warning already;
Have you any need, then, to listen to the Watchman?
Cannot you get on, then, without the Church's trumpet?
No,—for even the righteous need to be warned,
That they may not fall away.
Also that they may be thoroughly prepared
For the Coming of the Judge,—
Better and better, as the End draws on.
They want the Sacraments,
Every one of which, with the preparation, is a great warning.
Therefore leave off blaming the Watchmen,
Either for negligence or for importunity,
And rather look to yourself,
What you have been doing with their warnings.
Have you not stopped your ears?
Or got out of hearing?
Or listened to something else?
Made a noise, as one might say,
On purpose to drown the trumpet?
Have you not, in effect, said to the Watchman,
"Well, your duty is done; now just let us alone."
And when he did let you alone,
You would fain excuse yourself by saying,—
"He never spoke to me."

Consider, and lay it to heart, while there is yet time.
As you deal with these preliminary warnings,
So will it be with you,
When the final Warning, the last Trumpet, shall be blown.
Imagine one who has made much of these warnings;
How he will "look up, and lift up his head."
Imagine one who has scorned them as mere words;
To him they will come back,
As burning fires—fearful realities.
Often it is so, even in this world.
You will find, at last, that in hearing us—that is, the Church,
You heard Christ.
In despising us, you despised Christ.
But may it please Him to give you a better mind,
"While it is yet called to-day."
That we may "give account of you with joy,
"And not with grief."

XI.

The Warnings of the Clergy.

"Whom we preach, warning every man, and teaching every man, in all wisdom, that we may present every man perfect in Christ Jesus."—Col. i. 28.

How good of our Lord to send Heralds before,
That we may not be taken unawares;
And such also as will help us to get ready!
As S. John the Baptist before His first Coming;
And the clergy now.
They are like persons trusted with children,
While the Father is away.
We know what a care it is,
To rear children, or even dumb creatures;
How much more to rear souls!
This is implied in the word "perfect."
You are out at nurse,
And your Father will come and claim you.
"Where is My flock that I gave thee?"
What a thought for Pastors!
And the trust is renewed for each one of you.
How can we help trembling
When we think of our vows?
And you—how serious this should make you!
For it shews how precious your souls are.
And it leaves you the more without excuse,
If you cast your souls away.

It will be no comfort in that Day
To be able to throw some blame on us.
Miserable for us—but no comfort for you!
Think how it will be;
For we shall certainly know each other.
The unbelievers in the days of the Flood, will see Noah.
Lot's sons-in-law will see Lot.
Pharaoh will see Moses.
Saul will see Samuel, and Jonathan too.
Demas will see S. Paul.
And every one of you will see his own Pastor.
Bear, therefore, with remonstrance.
Pray that we may be brave, and not slothful.
Above all, care for yourselves.
Now we look for the Day of Account;
But presently It will be here.
How shall we then wish that we had done more for you!
And you,—that you had made better use of what little we did.

XII.

The under Shepherds of the Lord.

"He shall feed His flock like a Shepherd, He shall gather the lambs with His arm, and carry them in His bosom, and shall gently lead those that are with young."—Isaiah xl. 11.

At this time God puts us all in mind, both Priests and people,
  Of the care He has taken of His flock,
  In providing Shepherds under Himself:
    As in old time, Joshua and Eleazar;
  And, as in the Christian Church, Apostles,
    And those whom they ordained.
    In the Gift which He gave them [y];
The Gift of a peculiar Presence of the Holy Ghost,
    Full of awefulness—and of blessing.
    Observe that they are called "Angels."
  For awefulness,—the case of Judas is enough.
    Judas is the type of bad clergy;
  And the end of Judas is a type of their end.
    Of your charity, then, pray for us.
    But now rather consider His great mercy,
    In this Apostolical Succession of men,
Whereby He visibly feeds His flock, like a Shepherd.
    How great is the blessing you may judge,
      By the types in the Old Testament.

[y] See 1 Tim. v. 22, and 2 Tim. i. 6.

The Jewish Priesthood was a great blessing,
How much greater the Christian Priesthood!
Not merely for outward order,
Though outward order is a great thing;
But for the very security of our Spiritual Being.
For, by these His under Shepherds,
Our Lord pledges Himself to feed His flock.
He means them to be to us,
What nurses are to the children of a loving mother.
To gather the lambs of the flock,
As in Baptism, Catechizing, and other care.
To carry them in His Bosom,
As by instruction and guidance,
By protection and help;
To wait on the weary and the heavy-laden,
As "gently leading those that are with young."
To feed the flock, spiritually, with His Word,
Sacramentally with His Body and Blood.
Thus, as He lived and died for you,
So He waits on every one of you,
Grudging you no good thing.
Would that we and you could learn
To think of one another, always thus.
The flock, to see Christ in the Shepherd;
The Shepherd, to see Christ in each one of the Sheep.
Hard lessons, both,
Considering our infirmities, and yours;
Requiring much faith;
But it may be had for asking, and trying.

Ask we then, and strive,
For ourselves and for one another;
And may God give us His blessing,
Though we so little deserve it.

XIII.

MAKING THE MOST OF THE DIVINE PRESENCE.

"*Thou, O Lord, art in the midst of us, and we are called by Thy Name; leave us not.*"—JER. xiv. 9.

WHAT a sad confession we make
In the Collect for the last week in Advent!
That "through our sins and wickedness,
"We are sore let and hindered,
"In running the race that is set before us."
It is just like Isaiah's record of sins separating from God[1].
As if one should say, "Thy Scriptures have failed,
"Thy Church hath failed,
"All seems darkening as the day comes on:"
There is but one thing to fall back upon—
Our Lord's own Presence.
For we know the fault is in us, not in Him.
"The Lord's Hand is not shortened that it cannot save;
"Neither His Ear heavy that it cannot hear[2]."
The Collect prays for this Presence;
The Gospel assures us of It;
The Epistle bids us take comfort by It.

---

[1] Isa. lix.   [2] Ibid. ver. 1.

As the people of God, before and during the Captivity,
Lamented that He should be as a Stranger,
As a Champion perplexed [b].
So the worst could not bear to give up His Presence,
Nor can they now.
The best can desire no more.
Only realize it: are you trying to do so?
Are you taking His hints?
Such as, the name Christian;
The Sunday rest;
The Christmas and other holidays.
By these and other signs,
He is still with us.
But most in the Sacrament of His Body and Blood;
: Blessed are such as know it!
But is there no sound of Μεταβαίνωμεν [c]?
No danger, no symptom of His departure?
From the Nation—for its unbelief?
From the Parish—for its worldliness?
From the Congregation — for its irreverence?
Let each look at home,
And most into his own soul.
Is He not making as if He would depart?
O detain Him; as at Emmaus,
Before it is too late.
Do not wait, as Saul did,
Catching at His skirts in vain.

Jer. xiv. 8, 9: see also Dan. ix. 17, 18, and 1 Sam. xii.
[c] 'Let us depart.'

Do you ask, "How are we to keep Him?"
Do not make yourselves strange to Him,
Make much of Him in every way;
Do not pretend to love Him,
While you fail to honour Him.
He is come to sup with you this Christmas;
Mind how you receive and entertain Him.
Turn out all bad company.
If He seem to have withdrawn Himself,
Seek Him diligently [d].
You will surely find Him [e].
Can you find it in your heart to deal rudely with Him,
When He comes with His sweet and secret whisperings?
Take care lest the common Proverb
Be fulfilled in you very awfully:
"He that will not when he may,
"When he will, he shall have nay."

[d] See Cant. v. 6. [e] Compare vi. 3 and Isa. lv. 6.

XIV.
Christmas.

The Christian Birth.

"Unto you is born this day in the City of David, a Saviour which is Christ the Lord."—S. LUKE ii. 11.

This day is the Birth day of our best Friend,
So far we all know and understand,
Of Christmas Day.
And it teaches us much of our duty.
I wish we all attended even to such things as these;
To be glad and rejoice at His Birth,
Not at little things about ourselves.
To be bountiful,
To try to make people happy,
Especially His friends.
To present our best to Him, that is, ourselves.
Not to absent ourselves from His Feast,
Nor to insult It by coming unworthily.
Nor in any way to displease Him wilfully
On His own Day.
But there must be more than this,
To make entire Christian Festival.
We must think of Christ's three Births;
One: from all Eternity,
Whereby He is the Word of the Father;
The "only-begotten Son [f];"

[f] Collect.

The "brightness of His Glory [g];"
"The express Image of His Person [g];"
"By Whom also He made the worlds [g]."
"In the beginning was the Word [h]."
A second: of the Virgin Mary, as now,
Whereby He is the Son of Man.
"Given us . . . to take our nature upon Him;
"To be born of a pure Virgin [f];"
"This day have I begotten Thee [g];"
"Let all the Angels of God worship Him [g];"
"God hath anointed Thee with the oil of gladness [g];"
"And the Word was made Flesh [h]."
A third: also by the Holy Spirit,
Of each one of us [i].
"That we being regenerate,
"And made Thy children by adoption and grace,
"May daily be renewed [f]."
"As many as received Him, to them gave He power
"To become sons of God [h]."
For we, too, have more birth days than one,
And our second birth day
Is a third kind of Birth day to Him.
Our being "born again"—born in Him,
Born of God—made members of Him,
Is the same thing as His being born in us.
Therefore as He said of all men,
"I will declare Thy Name unto My Brethren,"

[f] Collect.   [g] Epistle.   [h] Gospel.
[i] S. Mark iii. 34; S. Matt. xii. 48—50.

So of all Christians He said,
"Behold My mother."
Christians are His mother
By His being formed in them.
In this sense our Baptism Day
Is a Birth day to Him as well as to us.
And being born in us His will is to grow in us,
To the measure of the Stature of the Fulness of Christ.
Which is the same thing
As our growing up unto Him in all things.
Try yourself:
Are you getting more like Him,
In Devotion and in Dutifulness,
In Lowliness and in Meekness,
In Charity and in Purity?
If not, your better nature, Christ in you,
Will dwindle away;
And then your only remedy will be,
To get Christ re-formed in you [k].
Blessed the Penitent who can exemplify this.
More blessed he who is God's instrument,
As S. Paul was,
To bring it about in others.
He is Christ's Parent in a very precious sense [l].
Strive to have it so.
No other way to a happy Christmas,
To a happy family meeting.
And it is the way to that,

[k] Gal. iv. 19.   [l] 1 Cor. iv. 15.

Of which all Christmas, and all family meetings, are types,
Our blessed re-union in Heaven.
Whatever your case may be at present,
. The real consolation of this good time is here—
"I will see you again,
"And your heart shall rejoice,
"And your joy no man taketh from you."

XV. S. Stephen's Day.

S. STEPHEN A PATTERN FOR YOUNG MEN.

"*I have written unto you young men, because ye are strong, and the Word of God abideth in you, and ye have overcome the wicked one.*"—S. JOHN ii. 14.

Christ's taking part in our Nature,
In order that He might die,
Ought to be a remedy against the slavish fear of death.
A Christian believing it,
And ordering his life accordingly,
Will be constantly practising how to die.
And so when death comes,
He will meet it composedly,
As one who has learned his lesson.
Even the heathen knew a little of this.
These three holy days are instances of it;
They are instances of happy deaths,—
Happy through the following of Christ.
For which the soul has been prepared,
By the life's practice.
Consider how S. Stephen died;
Devoting himself to his Master,
As Christ to His Father.
Praying for his murderers,
As our Lord in His word, "Father forgive them."
It was a victory over his enemies,

Visible and invisible.
His name, "a Crown," is a token of Victory.
He is therefore a pattern
For young persons, of whom S. John writes,
"Young men, ye are strong, and His word abideth in you.
"And ye have overcome the wicked one."
You have natural energy;
Use it for Christ.
You like to be real and decisive;
Let His Word abide in you.
You like Victory;
Overcome the wicked one.
These things were carried out,
In S. Stephen's death.
Wish, pray, strive,
That they may be carried out in yours.

XVI.
S. John the Evangelist.

The Light of God in Christ.

"This then is the message which we have heard of Him, and declare unto you, that God is Light, and in Him is no darkness at all."—1 S. John i. 5.

It appears by the services of this day,
That the Church connects, in a peculiar way,
The idea of Light with S. John the Evangelist.
Why is this?
The Gospel gives the key to it.
He was "the disciple whom Jesus loved.'
And Jesus is "the true Light,"
For He is the only-begotten Son,
By Whom the Father declareth Himself.
The Father is the Fountain of Light:
"God is Light,
"And in Him is no darkness at all."
The Son is "the brightness of the Father's glory,
"And the express Image of His Person."
And so, "He lighteneth every man
"That cometh into the world."
And in proportion as they are nearer to Him,
They get the more light.
S. John was nearest of all the Apostles
To the Son of God;

For he was the beloved disciple,
And he lay in His Bosom.
Therefore as Moses, when he saw God on the Mount,
So S. John, caught the Glory,
And shewed It to his brethren;
Declaring the Divinity of our Lord,
More expressly than the other Evangelists.
Therefore he is among them as the Eagle,
And he is called especially "the Divine."
The object then of the Collect to-day is plain,
That this doctrine of S. John,
The doctrine of our Lord's two Natures,
May never cease in the Church;
But may throw its light
Over all that is said and done there,
Whether by each one of us in particular,
Or by the Body to which we belong.
That it may be to us in this world,
As a light shining in a dark place—
The light of day, .
At the far end of a dreary cavern,
Increasing more and more unto the perfect Day.
The light of everlasting life
In Him Who is Life.
And how may this be?
How may we secure this light?
Surely in the way that S. John first attained it.
By abiding close to Him
Who is the Fountain of Light.

Seeking to lean on His Bosom;
To repose on Him in all troubles;
And to find Him in everything,
As S. John was ever first to recognise His Presence[m]:
And that especially in His Sacraments.
And to keep ourselves pure;
"Blessed are the pure in heart,
"For they shall see God."
This is the foundation of all.
Without it, all seeming trust,
Illumination, devotion,
Is but the device of the Enemy.
May we have grace to remember this,
Those of us who seem to feel ourselves drawn towards God.

XVII.

THE WITNESS OF AGE AND EXPERIENCE.

"*That which we have seen and heard declare we unto you, that ye also may have fellowship with us: and truly our fellowship is with the Father, and with His Son Jesus Christ."—*
1 S. JOHN i. 3.

WELL is it appointed that of the two Saints,
Who come nearest to our Lord's Birth day
One should be the first,

[m] S. John xxi. 7; Rev. i.

And the other the last,
    As far as we read,
Of that generation, to die in His service;
    One in youth, and by violence;
The other quietly, in extreme old age.
Plainly then those outward circumstances
    Are all one to Him and to His love.
As S. Stephen shewed how past generations
    Were connected with our Lord,
So S. John, especially, the future.
Thus he describes the Apostolic office:
"That which was from the beginning,
    "Which we have heard,
"Which we have seen with our eyes,
    "And our hands have handled,
    "Of the Word of Life,
"That which we have seen and heard,
    "Declare we unto you."
Are they not loving and majestic words?
    A man must have seen, heard, and felt
        Our Incarnate Lord,
Before he can truly declare Him.
S. John, having seen, heard, and felt Him,
    Declares Him to others.
What was his object in so doing?
To make others as happy as himself.
In this he is just contrary to the devil,
Who made himself miserable by separating from God;
    And who wants to make us miserable also.

And S. John declared our Lord
To other ages also.
Dying latest, and writing in extreme old age,
He was a visible link
Between our Lord and the next age;
As his writings are between Him and all ages.
They are a message
Breathed from the very Bosom of God.
And our Lord has aged disciples in every generation,
Performing, in their measure, the same office.
How much ought we to make of them,
And of their words[n]!
How surely will the time come,
When we shall regret having indulged ourselves
In disregarding them.
How thankfully should we encourage ourselves
By their precept and example,
In loving one another,
And in walking in the light.
There is no surer test
Of a wise and improving Christian,
Than unfeigned respect and love
For those who have grown old in God's service;
Whether rich or poor;
Remembering them and minding their warnings.
Even as no one thing would be more effective,
In making a Church or a Generation orthodox,

[n] See the account of S. Matthias, Acts i. 21, 22; and S. Paul, 1 Cor. ix. 1.

Than earnest faith in our High Calling and Communion,
As taught especially by S. John,
In the doctrine of the Sacraments,
And as witnessed by his followers
In all Antiquity.

XVIII. Holy Innocents' Day.

The Example of Little Children.

" Ye are of God, little children, and have overcome them; because greater is He that is in you than he that is in the world."—
1 S. John iv. 4.

He who taught us to say always "Our Father,"
Loved to speak to us as little children.
And He taught His beloved Disciple
To do the same.
In all His true followers,
He sees that character,
Which He praised in the little ones,
Whom He took up in His arms and blessed.
You may think that it is only their simplicity,
Which makes them innocent;
But it is more; it is a strong sense of duty.
You may often see this in baptized children,
If care has been taken to teach them loving obedience
As in not venturing where they ought not;
In not touching nor tasting anything without leave;
In governing their very looks,
In Church or at meals.
What is it that enables them to do so?
It is the Holy Ghost within them.
If they go on so,
They will surely overcome the world;

For these things are but types,
Of the more serious trials to come.
As, going into the way of temptation;
As, not waiting to consider right and wrong;
As, keeping no guard over the senses.
As these things make all the difference in children,
So they make all the difference in Christians.
The little children must not say,
They cannot help being naughty;
Neither must we.
The strong man armed need not be too mighty,
Either for us or for them.
For here is One stronger than he.
The very sight of little children
Should teach us a better mind;
As also should the thought of being spoken to so lovingly,
By Jesus' beloved Disciple,
And by Jesus Himself.
Do you not long to hear the word,
From His own blessed Mouth?
Persevere a little, and you shall hear it.

XIX. Epiphany.

Worship.

"O come let us worship, and fall down, and kneel before the Lord our Maker."—PSALM xcv. 6.

To-day every thing preaches, in Heaven and in earth;
And all preach the same thing;
"Come and worship."
The Shepherds preach;
For they have not done telling of Christmas night.
Bethlehem preaches;
For it shows Him born of a Virgin,
And born where the Prophet said He should be.
The Angels preach,
By the memory of their carol.
The Star preaches in the East;
And the Wise men preach, on their journey,
From beginning to end.
And, what is very remarkable,
The Scribes too, and Herod, preach;
The former unconsciously;
The latter unwillingly.
For Herod, like Caiaphas and others,
Was guided to use words of inquiry,
Which might well teach us our duty.
What can a person, seeking the Pearl of great price, say,
More to the purpose than what he said?

"Search out the Child;
" And that diligently;
" And bring your neighbours word;
" That they may come,
" And worship Him also."
Will you not learn a lesson from him?
You know, by all this witness,
That Christ is at Bethlehem.
Will you not seek Him out there?
And do what you can in reason to let others know?
By word and conversation,
By charity, by faith, by purity.
Let them "take knowledge of you,
" That you have been with Jesus."
That they may not only admire, but come;
And not only come, but worship.
And not, as the Magi, worship and depart,
But go on worshipping,
Through this world, and for ever;
Casting their crowns before the Throne,
As the Wise men before the Infant Jesus.
What can you wish for more, in time and in Eternity?

XX.

OBEDIENCE.

"And He went down with them, and came to Nazareth, and was subject unto them."—S. LUKE ii. 51.

THERE is not a plainer lesson in all the Bible,
Than what the Services of to-day teach,
In respect of the duty of Obedience,
And the reason for it.
Obedience is, simply, doing as you are bid;
The first Commandment—
That is, the first you learn to practise.
And you must go on practising it, all your life.
As under instruction;
As in service, and in ordinary labour;
As in any profession;
As in a family;
As subject to law, and to the rules of Society.
Only go on, from this earthly obedience
To believe in your Father and Mother in Heaven [o],
And you have the principle of Christian Obedience,
Most easy to understand: but hard to keep.
For this was the very Fall in Eden;
The very meaning of the word sin is lawlessness [p];
Men will have their own way.
It will be your ruin—you know it will;

[o] Gal. iv. 26.   [p] ἁμαρτία, ἀνομία.

And yet you will go on and take it,
If you are at all left to yourselves.
Therefore, the good God invites you to submit yourselves;
He binds you to Him in Baptism;
He calls you to bind yourselves to Him again,
In Confirmation, and by all His Ordinances.
But when people, especially the young, hear of this rule,
Of perfect Obedience—of not having their own way,
The flesh rises against it;
The world ridicules it;
And the devil is at hand, to give the greatest force to all.
The duty is plain;
The danger no less so;
How is the one to be done—the other to be avoided?
Why, just as soldiers do their work.
Follow your Captain, and do as He does.
It is no shame, but the greatest glory,
To tread in the steps of the great King.
It is no loss, but the surest Victory,
To fight under the banner of the Almighty.
And what is all His human Being,
But obedience to God?
"Lo, I come to do Thy will [q]."
What were His Childhood and Youth,
But Obedience to His Parents?
You think it knowing and manly,
To have a mind and will of your own.
His wisdom, seen in the Temple, led Him to be subject;

[q] Heb. x. 7; Ps. xl. 7.

Not only for a little while, till He was grown up,
But all along, it was His way,
For thirty years.
There He was, a poor Carpenter, obeying orders;
Working for His bread.
This same Jesus is with you now, watching you.
Are you not ashamed to make much of yourselves,
To make much of your own will,
In His Presence?

XXI.

PATIENCE.

"*Mine hour is not yet come.*"—S. JOHN ii. 4.

LET us seek a lesson from our Lord's own Mouth
During the weeks of Epiphany.
The first week—that we must be about our Father's business.
The second—that we must keep our Father's time.
Consider His saying in the Text.
How did He speak it?
Not in disrespect to His mother [r].
But in regard of time, as He said to His Apostles,—
"Of that day, and that hour, knoweth no man,
"No, not the Angels which are in Heaven,
"Neither the Son, but the Father [s]."

[r] See S. Luke ii. 51.   [s] S. Mark xiii. 32.

And again, as He corrected the mistake of the Jews,
"It is not for you to know the times or the seasons,
"Which the Father hath put in His own power [t]."
As He set us the example all along,
There is a time for all things,
The knowledge of which the Father keeps to Himself;
And His time must be ours.
So that in this sense, as well as in respect of sufferings,
Patience is a great part of our calling.
"In your patience possess ye your souls [u]."
"Let patience have her perfect work [x]."
"Ye have need of patience [y]."
"He that believeth must not make haste [z]."
Christ's way is taught by His first miracle at Cana—
Always to keep the best till last.
A hard doctrine,
Especially to the young,
Who are too like Esau—
Ready to barter future hopes for present pleasures.
You want to be free, before your time,
Like the Prodigal son.
You want to know the world, like Eve.
See what misery comes, even in this world.
Take an example from Cana itself,
How many marriages are made miserable,
Or penitential instead of purely innocent,
For want of keeping our Lord's rule.

[t] Acts i. 7.   [u] S. Luke xxi. 19.   [x] S. James i. 4.   [y] Heb. x. 36.
[z] Isa. xxviii. 16.

Use yourself now in your young days,
To keep that rule dutifully;
To keep it in little things;
As in times of fasting;
Fridays well spent would make Sundays happier.
As in times of leaving off work;
Remember the fourth Commandment.
As in respect of taking liberties;
Wait till you have asked.
And this may take a higher meaning—
Every morning, let the world alone
Till you have prayed;
Do the same at every meal;
And every evening;
And with every serious undertaking.
Thus giving your days to Christ,
You will find Christ's day yours.
And this is no counsel of perfection,
But simply what we all have promised in our Baptism;
To renounce the world;
To live by faith;
To love God best.

XXII.

Faith.

"Go thy way, and as thou hast believed so be it done unto thee."—S. Matt. viii. 13.

Here is another Rule or Principle,
Laid down by our Lord,
In healing the Centurion's servant;
And repeated to the two blind men [a].
But it was the general rule of all His miracles;
And not least, of those in the Epiphany Gospels;
Of the Lepers:
Of the Centurion:
Of the disciples in the boat.
The possessed persons were like little children,
For whom it is enough, that they put no bar in the way;
The devils "believed and trembled."
But the Centurion had much faith,
And obtained not only healing but praise.
The disciples had but little faith,
They were just saved from the wreck,
Much and little—compared with their privileges.
The Centurion was like those, who have few advantages,
Yet in deep humility cling to our Lord,
And trust Him with those dear to them,
At whatever distance He seems to be.

[a] Chap. ix. 27.

The disciples were like ordinary Christians,
Who know they have Christ "on board," with them,
Yet are excited and disquieted, at earthly troubles.
Now you have all professed faith;
In Baptism and in Confirmation,
It is said to each one of you,
"Go thy way, and as thou hast believed,
"So be it done unto thee."
How has it been with you?
How is it now?
Have you ever put yourself out of the way,
To come to our Lord?
Or, having Him with you in the boat, all the time
Did you then only seek Him,
When you were in alarm?
Have you loved God's people, and God's worship,
As the Centurion did?
Have you these signs?
Are you in a way to have them?
Take care:
It is no use trifling with God Almighty.

XXIII.

𝔖𝔢𝔭𝔱𝔲𝔞𝔤𝔢𝔰𝔦𝔪𝔞.

THANKFULNESS.

"*All Thy works praise Thee, O Lord, and Thy Saints give thanks unto Thee.*"—Ps. cxlv. 10.

SEPTUAGESIMA is a mingled time;
A time of joy for Creation;
Mingled with grief and fear for what may come of it.
Therefore the "Alleluia" is used to cease in the Church;
And mourning is put on.
But the first note struck, is that of joy for Creation [b];
And this note again is double;
Joy of the Works; and of the Saints.
The unconscious; and the conscious [c].
The Works praise Him by obeying His Laws,
And fulfilling His purposes;
Which even the Heathen and the bad spirits admire;
And man offers the joy for them.
The Saints—who are they?
Not simply the Holy ones, ἅγιοι,
But the ὅσιοι, holy and dear;
As joined to Christ, Who is essentially ὅσιος [d].
Well, these Saints are evermore praising God;
Not only by being the occasion of praise to Him;
But by actually offering Praise, as a Sacrifice;

[b] See Job xxxviii. 7, and "Benedicite."   [c] Ps. xix., xcviii., cxlviii.
[d] Heb. vii. 26, Rev. xv. 4, and xvi. 5.

Being invited to do so by Him,
By the Voice from the Throne[e];
And taught "Alleluia,"
As they are taught the Lord's Prayer.
And also by thanking Him for it all,
As for a personal favour to themselves[f]:
"We give thanks to Thee for Thy great Glory."
But because they are not only ἅγιοι, but ὅσιοι,
Fallen and Redeemed ones,
Their thanksgiving is tempered, on earth,
With shame and fear;
It sounds wistful and plaintive;
As the unconscious praise of the creature tells also of "travail[g]."
In Paradise, it will be all Hope and Rest.
In Heaven, it will be fulness of Thanksgiving,
Because it will be "fulness of Joy."
Pray then, and strive to be thankful,
As well as obedient.
If there is a Heaven on earth,
It is in the heart of such a man.

[e] Rev. xix. 5.   [f] Rom. viii. 28.   [g] Rom. viii. 22.

XXIV. Sexagesima.

CONFESSION.

"And the Lord God called unto Adam, and said unto him, Where art thou?"—GEN. iii. 9.

THIS calling of Adam turns our attention to Confession;
Therefore to-day we will consider the preparation for it.
For indeed there is great reason to have fear about it,
 That many make their confessions as a mere form.
  They say, "Of course we are miserable sinners,
   "All men are so;
  "But we own it, and we hope God will be merciful."
   I fear it is so in Church,
    Because I know it is so out of Church;
    So it was with Pharaoh, Ahab, and others.
Now this is a very sad thing: how is it to be mended?
One way of mending it would be, for people to consider,
 What they do, when they confess.
  What God is;
  What sin is;
  How God hates sin;
  What the end of it must be;
  How we must come to hate it,
  If we are to be happy in Him.
  How we must not only fear punishment,
   But hate sin.

This is to be done by considering sin,
With its aggravations, in each instance.
This will be a long business,
And a very imperfect one,
If not done at short intervals.
Therefore we come back to our old rule,
Of which too much can hardly be said—
Very particular self-examination every evening.
That *our* book may answer to God's Book.
That, judging ourselves, we may not be judged.
That accepting Fatherly chastisement,
We may be admitted hereafter to Fatherly Love.

XXV.

Confession.

"*But the woman, fearing and trembling, knowing what was done in her, came and fell down before Him, and told Him all the truth.*"—S. Mark v. 33.

Confession is the second ingredient in Repentance;
It is Repentance in word;
And it is quite necessary [h];
But it goes very much against the grain.
So we see in children;
What a trouble it often is, to make them confess,

[h] 1 S. John i. 9.

Even when they have no chance of severe punishment.
As wise parents do their best,
To bring their children to confession;
So God our Father wills to bring us,
By such ways as these:—
When the mischief of our sins breaks out,
As in the case of Achan;
When the wise and good suspect us,
As in that of Gehazi;
When other sins like our own shock us,
As in the case of David;
When Church Services come to us with power,
As in the case of those who were baptized by S. John;
And with some, who are represented by the woman of the Gospel,
When He has healed them,
And gives them to understand
That it would be for His glory to confess it[1].
As for us—the more we are hindered
From confessing publickly, or formally,
The more should we be on our guard,
Not to lose the substance of confession;
As by owning faults to those whom we have wronged,
And asking pardon for them.
By confessing, or not denying the truth,
When we are charged with it.
By abstaining from all endeavours to seem better than we are.
By patiently enduring reproach in other kinds,

---

[1] See Acts xix. 18.

After Christ's own example.
He who shall truly try this way, may have good hope,
That, though our Saviour may hide His Face for a time,
He will one day turn round to him,
In the presence of all His Saints,
And say to him, as He said to this poor woman,
"Go in peace, and be whole of thy plague."

XXVI.

PROBATION.

"And the Lord said, My Spirit shall not always strive with man, for that he also is flesh; yet his days shall be an hundred and twenty years."—GEN. vi. 3.

CONSIDER these points—
The completeness of corruption on the earth;
God repenting of His Bounty;
Giving notice to Noah;
Still striving with man;
Yet in time ceasing to do so;
Telling man how long time he should have.
The case is like our own.
We read of a sort of Paradise in the Church,
When first set up;
We see how things are fallen from it now;
We trace it to the same cause,—Lust.
We know that God strives with us;

We know that He will in time repent;
We know that it cannot be above so many years;
We see the Ark of Refuge building;
We may yet come in, and take part in the work.
Beware not to urge our being flesh as a reason to delay this.
It tells the contrary way.

XXVII. Quinquagesima.

CLOTHING.

"Unto Adam also, and to his wife, did the Lord God make coats of skins, and clothed them."—GEN. iii. 21.

THE merciful dealing of Almighty God with His creatures
Which we may observe in the sentence concerning man's work,
Finds its parallel, in the teaching of Holy Scripture,
Concerning his clothing.
Here too we have his original condition,
Like that of little children [k];
His shame after the fall;
His vain efforts to hide it,
Mere legal and outward decency [l];
God's gift of clothing;
A token of our fall, and shame, and punishment;
Therefore not to be abused, for luxury or pride.
A token also of mercy,
As in the other parts of the sentence;
A pledge that He would hide our souls' nakedness by-and-by.
And this He did, by taking our nakedness on Himself,
As in His Birth;
As when He was stripped,
To be scourged, and to be crucified.
The same thing He taught in another way,
By taking on Him the likeness of our sinful flesh;

[k] Gen. ii. 25. [l] Gen. iii. 7.

As Jacob clothed himself with skins, to be like Esau.
And this, that He might clothe us with Himself,
Sacramentally here,
Gloriously hereafter.
We may, if we will, strip ourselves like maniacs;
Too many have done so;
Perhaps some of you have done so, more or less;
But it is not too late.
A Lenten time is coming;
Jesus is at hand.
You may come to Him,
And He will cast out the Devil entirely;
And when Easter comes,
You shall be found at His Feet,
"Sitting, and clothed, and in your right mind."
He will clothe you,
And you shall "walk with Him in white [m]."

[m] Rev. iii. 4, 5; xix. 8: 2 Cor. v. 2—4.

XXVIII.
LOVE.

"Charity never faileth."—1 COR. xiii. 8.

God is Love; and God never faileth;
Neither therefore doth Love.
All powers, advantages, accomplishments, pass away;
Prophecy, Tongues, Knowledge, all pass away;
Love may be without these;
And these without Love.
In any case, these fail,
As the stars will fall,
And a ship may be wrecked,
And flowers must fade.
But Love, being of God, partaketh of His Eternity.
It is constant.
Other graces are of this world, and end with it.
This is true even of Faith and Hope;
They are most precious and necessary;
But they relate to an imperfect condition.
Love in perfection, is the fulfilment of them all;
And, in rudiment, Love is the life of them here;
Therefore we must never fail in Love,
Though a person become unlovely, provoking, wicked,
Though he thwart us, or use us ill,
In property, in feeling, in character,
And though no return of love be made.

So it is in marriage;
So it is in the case of mothers and children;
So, above all, it was with our Lord on earth;
So it is with the Saints, who are one with Him.
When love seems impossible, think of Him;
And how you have yourself tried Him.
Think of the delight of loving everlastingly;
And that, if we are to have a reasonable hope of such love,
We must practise it here.
And that from morning till night.
Love towards all, little and great;
In spite of weariness,
In spite of disgust,
In spite of ill-usage, and seeming uselessness.
But mind : you cannot love by merely wishing to love,
Nor by merely praying to love;
Love must grow in you by an indirect process,
By obedience.

XXIX.
Ash-Wednesday.

LENT A TIME OF PENANCE.

"*If we would judge ourselves, we should not be judged.*
1 COR. xi. 31.

What is Lent?
We all know it is a time of fasting;
And we know what fasting is.
But what is the religious use of Lent?
It has many; but now to speak of one only—
How do Parents manage their children?
Withholding their food is a very common punishment.
Sometimes good children of themselves decline food,
When they feel they are unworthy.
Now we are all children in respect of holy things;
And we have need to deal with ourselves as such.
Why not punish ourselves,
As a kind discreet parent would punish us,
By starving ourselves more or less?
Thus the fasting of Lent would be penal;
Inflicted by ourselves, on ourselves,
For past sins, and sinful inclinations.
Not as if we could satisfy God's Justice,
But to express to Him our sense of what we deserve;
That we are not worthy to partake of His good gifts;
To signify our surrender of ourselves,
To bear whatever He may judge best.

Also, as is done with children,
To set a mark on the wrong things;
And to keep us from them hereafter.
And all this especially in respect of the appetites,
Which are thereby mortified.
Fasting is a punishment;
A penance for inordinate eating and drinking;
And for the sins of the body occasioned thereby.
But there are other sins which need punishment;
And therefore there are other mortifications,
Which are proper for Lent.
Vanity about clothes, persons, cleverness, popularity,
Is punished by retirement.
Evil or conceited ways of speaking, are punished by silence.
Covetousness is punished by Almsgiving,
And by declining gainful projects.
Sloth is punished by watching and by work.
And self-love, generally, is punished by self-denial,
By denying our own tastes secretly.
And in all these penal exercises,
We have two great encouragements.
First, from the examples of such as David and Ahab;
Next, from the promise,
"If we would judge ourselves, we should not be judged."
Therefore it cannot be said that it is presumptuous,
To inflict penalties on ourselves;
As it might have been said,
If we had no Scriptural warrant for doing so.
And as to the manner,

We have the directions of the Church,
About which we may ask those appointed to tell us.
Under these cautions, we may so use our Lent,
That it may be to us a time of salutary punishment.
A warning from God, accepted by us;
Which is the meaning of the number forty.
For we shall find, on consideration of certain numbers,
That they are often a key,
To the interpretation of Holy Scripture.
As three, twelve, seven.
So, if one wished to know about Lent,
One might get a good clue,
From the mystical number Forty.
And what is the very first use of this number?
It is to express penal warning,
As at the Deluge.
That came too late;
May it please God that this be not too late for us.

XXX.
Moses in the Mount.

"*And he was there with the Lord forty days and forty nights; he did neither eat bread, nor drink water.*"—Exod. xxxiv. 28.

As the number forty is connected with punishment,
By the history of the Flood;
And with punishment and probation together,

By the history of the Israelites in the wilderness;
So is it associated with high contemplation,
By the first forty days which Moses spent in the Mount.
These days were spent in fasting also,
And in two respects were like our Lord's Lent, and ours.
For however our Lord's Lent may be regarded,
So far as He represented us sinners,
As a penal exercise,
It seems more natural to believe,
That it was chiefly a time of Communing with His Father,
As ours should also be.
But of this Holy Scripture tells us nothing.
Let us go back to Moses;
What were his subjects of contemplation
In the earlier Fast?
They were, first, the two Tabernacles:
In the first of which was the Ark,
The Mercy Seat with the Cherubim,
And God communing with His People.
In the second, the Table, the Candlestick, the two Altars [n].
Next, the Vail between the two Tabernacles.
Thirdly, the Vestments of Aaron:
Ephod, Breast-plate, Robe, Mitre.
Fourthly, the Sacrifices of Consecration:—three kinds, in all;
Sin-offering, Burnt-offering, Peace-offering.
Fifthly, certain Preparations:—
Such as, Ransom, Laver, Oil, Incense, Workmen, Sabbath.
Lastly, the Decalogue.

[n] See Heb. ix.

What must our care be?
To wean ourselves from the world,
And to muse on Christ's Mediation;
Represented by the Tabernacles and the Vail.
The Church's participation in It;
Represented by the Vestments and Sacrifices.
Our portion with the Church;
Represented by the Preparations and the Decalogue.
To know and do these things,
There must be self-denial and humility.

XXXI.

No Time for Delay.

"For the time past of our life may suffice us."—1 S. PET. iv. 3.

Yes indeed: enough and more than enough have we given,
To the world, the flesh, and the devil.
Is it not true that even to this day we have gone on,
Perhaps very sinfully, at all events very imperfectly?
Consider your childhood;
How irreligious, too often!
How selfish; how false; how unthankful; how slothful!
Consider when you grew up;
How, too likely, you gave yourself up improperly,
To the passions and fancies of that time of life.
Consider how you have slighted warnings;
How unworthy your repentance has been.

What have you to say, at this moment,
Why sentence of death should not be passed on you?
Yet God spares you, and gives you another chance;
Bringing you again to this holy Season.
The time past of our life is enough for us to have done wrong:
Why put off Conversion any longer?
Make up your mind to suffer for Christ's sake,
To suffer something unpleasant in one way or another.
Do not shrink from pain;
The pain of Self-examination.
Nor from the pain of Confession,
If need be to man, but certainly regularly to God.
Nor from that of Amendment;
Nor from Restitution;
Nor from forgiving others;
Nor from Perseverance;
Nor from enduring suffering as Penance;
Nor from ill-usage;
Nor from spiritual disappointment;
Nor from the sense of other people's sin and folly.

XXXII.

Retirement and Silence.

"*He sitteth alone, and keepeth silence, because He hath borne it upon Him.*"—Lam. iii. 28.

Our Lord's Lent was spent in the Wilderness,
Either in solitude,
Or amongst the wild beasts, or devils.
This is another point in His Penance for us to copy.
For, in truth, that time was His Penance;
Endured to set us an example of the same.
He, like us, knew the delight of sympathetic society.
"Jesus loved Martha, and her sister, and Lazarus [o]."
"Having loved His own which were in the world,
"He loved them unto the end [p]."
"I have called you friends [q]."
"I will see you again [r]."
He knew also the pain of separation.
"Ye shall leave Me alone [s]."
Very often in the Psalms, He complains of this separation.
"My kinsmen stood afar off [t]."
"I looked for some to have pity upon Me,
"But there was no man.
"Neither found I any to comfort Me [u]."

[o] S. John xi. 5.   [p] xiii. 1.   [q] xv. 15.   [r] xvi. 22.
[s] xvi. 32.   [t] Ps. xxxviii. 11.   [u] lxix. 21.

"Thou hast put away mine acquaintance far from Me,
"And made Me to be abhorred of them [x]."
"My lovers and My friends hast Thou put away from Me,
"And hid Mine acquaintance out of My sight [y]."
"I am even as it were a sparrow that sitteth alone [z]."
He was alone in the Types which prefigure Him;
Joseph, Moses, Elijah,
Daniel, who was left alone to see the vision [a].
And our Lord was worse than alone;
He was in gross unworthy companionship.
Among the wild beasts [b], or with bad men, or devils.
What should then be a sinner's course?
Silence to all save himself and his God.
And so also—He "became dumb;"
He waited *"still"* upon His Father;
He made as if He had nothing to say.
How much more should we be silent in our guilt!
Thou hast sinned in company,
Learn to do without company at all.
Thou hast dealt rudely with thy God,
Be content to be rudely dealt with.
Thou hast forsaken Him,
Be content to be forsaken.
Thou hast sinned in talk,
Be content to keep silence.
Thou hast sinned in selfish ways,
Be content, nay, be glad, to be overlooked,

[x] Ps. lxxxviii. 7.   [y] ver. 18.   [z] cii. 7.   [a] Dan. x. 7.
[b] Ps. xxii. 12, 16.

To be disappointed—forgotten.
The less thou art able to retire at fixed times,
Be the more watchful to do so at occasional times.
Thou hast sinned in boasting,
Be sometimes silent even from good words.
Thou hast sinned by cowardice,
Force thyself to speak—in truthfulness to confess.
Accept bereavements, separations, estrangements,
As opportunities of penance assigned by Him.
That He may open thy mouth at last,
To shew forth His Praise,
And nothing but His Praise.

XXXIII.
Watching and Working.

"*Couldst thou not watch with Me one hour?*"—S. Mark xiii. 37.

Bodily and mental weariness,
And so far shrinking from work,
Seem to be the effects of the Fall.
Compare the command "to dress and to keep[c]"
With the sentence "in sorrow and in sweat[d]."
This is part of the punishment of sin;
Therefore our Lord took it upon Himself with the rest[e].

[c] Gen. ii. 15.   [d] Gen. iii. 17, 19. See also Eccles. i. 3, and 13—18; ii. 17, 23; xii. 12: Hooker's Ecc. Pol. i. 280.   [e] S. John iv. 6: S. Matt. viii. 24.

And herein also He denied Himself;
He would work for His bread thirty years,
And He would have no place to lay His Head.
In His ministry, He had no leisure, so much as to eat;
The Gospels tell us how He made time for prayer;
"In the morning, rising up a great while before day,
"He departed into a solitary place, and there prayed."
"He went out into a mountain to pray
"And continued all night in prayer to God."
On three special occasions He thus made time for prayer,
After the Miracle of the five loaves [f];
At the Ordination of His Apostles [g];
And before the Transfiguration [h].
During the last week of His life, He took no rest,
His nights were spent in the Mount of Olives [i].
His principle being to "finish His work [j]."
Take then religiously your portion of hard work;
Ye that have to live by it, make much of it;
As likening you to your Lord.
Ye that have to employ yourselves,
Take care to do so dutifully, thoroughly, cheerfully.
Be patient when it is irksome,
Or when your leisure is interrupted,
Offer all as a Sacrifice of voluntary self-denial, to God.
And give up some of your rest to Him,
If you can do so discreetly,

---

[f] S. Mark vi. 46.   [g] S. Luke vi. 12.   [h] S. Luke ix. 28.
[i] S. Luke xxi. 37.   [j] S. John iv. 34; v. 17, and ix. 4.

Observe, the Scripture speaks of "watching [k]."
And the Church has ordained Vigils.
And we know, in all practical matters,
How needful something of the kind is.

XXXIV.

SIN A POSSESSION, OR MADNESS OF THE SOUL.

"*Now shall the Prince of this world be cast out.*"—S. JOHN xii. 31.

Do you remember the question put to Christ,
"What shall we do that we may work the works of God?"
It was put to Him in scorn, once;
But afterwards both to Him[l], and to His Messengers[m], in earnest.
Shall we not take care this Lent to put it to Him in earnest?
For every work has its time;
And every time has its work;
And God's Will is done,
When we order our works accordingly.
This is the time of Lent.
What is the work of Lent?
In one sense, Fasting;

---

[k] Ps. cxxxiv.; lxiii. 6; cxix. 148; xxii. 2 (our Lord's agony): 2 Cor. vi. 5; xi. 27: Eph. vi. 18.

[l] Acts ix. 6.   [m] Acts ii. 37, and xvi. 30.

In another sense, Prayer;
In a third sense Meditation, and Religious thought.
But all have one and the same object in view—
Turning from our sins,
That we may turn to God in earnest.
And since all sin is the work of the Devil,
Turning from sin is destroying his work;
That is, "casting out the Prince of this world."
Well therefore, does Lent begin as it does,
With a rehearsal of Christ's Victory over the Devil.
As if it began with a Proclamation, by sound of Trumpet,
"Now is the Prince of this world cast out."
And to take away all doubt of this inward Miracle—
A doubt but too natural to our corrupt hearts,
Behold a series of outward Miracles!
Every one of them a token and pledge,
Of a much greater inward Miracle;
Every one of them an encouragement
To go on in the work of Lent.
What is the spiritual encouragement, here,
From our Lord's casting out devils?
It shows the fact, and it teaches the manner, of victory—
Of Christ's Victory, in the heart, over all sin,
As it is a Possession, or Madness;
And especially over spiritual sins.
What are spiritual sins?
Pride;
Rebellion;
Envy;

Malice, Lying, and evil Speaking.
These make people blind, and deaf, and dumb;
And, in another way, lustful.
They cannot bear the sight of our Lord;
They cannot give up their mischief.
Compare the case of the Pharisees, and of Judas,
And see how wretched, even in this world,
Such sins make their victims.
The Victims of such sins must be brought to our Lord,
By Prayer and the Intercession of friends.
But when the case is not so bad,
Men must learn to pray for themselves.
We must all learn to do so,
For these sins are very blinding.
Ever suspect yourself of them;
Watch, as well as pray against them.
Learn to think much of our Lord;
To become really acquainted with Him.
Then you will be ashamed to praise yourself in your heart;
Ashamed to judge and speak hardly of others;
Ashamed to be sullen, fretful, unkind.
When you catch yourself in such things,
You will fear the deadly sins, of malice, envy, lying.
Learn not only to bear with the sweet and gentle,
With the pure and devout,
But really to honour them,
And to wish yourself like them.
When you have got so far,
You have made a great step towards the " Mind of Christ."

You will help them ;
And they will pray for you ;
And by degrees, the Devil will go quite out of you.

XXXV.
Sin a Leprosy of the Soul.

"And Jesus moved with compassion, put forth His Hand, and touched him, and saith unto him, I will, be thou clean."
S. Mark i. 41.

We have seen how sin is like a Possession ;
How the work of Lent is meant to be Christ's Voice,
Saying, "Hold thy peace, and come out of him."
Now let us see how sin is like Leprosy ;
And the work of Lent, His Voice,
Saying, "I will, be thou clean."
The cure of Leprosy was one of His common Miracles,
But Holy Scripture only gives two cases in detail ;
In His first circuit through Galilee,
One Leper seeks our Lord ;
Kneels—falls prostrate—owns His Power ;
Doubts only His will.
In His last journey from Galilee,
Ten Lepers meet Him ;
They stand afar off—they cry out.
To the first He says, at once, "I will, be thou clean."
To the last, "Go show yourselves to the Priest :"
Thus He puts them on their trial.

The Leprosy is a very loathsome disease;
It is spreading;
It is infectious;
It is hereditary;
It is incurable by man;
Therefore, God Himself took it in hand.
The Priest is the judge of it [n].
The Leper must obey the Priest.
He wears signs of mourning [o];
He cries "unclean;"
He covers his lips;
He dwells alone.
The Priest is also the judge of the Leper's cure [p].
By certain appointed ceremonies,
The cure is referred wholly to Christ;
Here, and in other places, it is claimed by Him.
The old Discipline of the Church was the reality of this claim.
Lent is a fragment of it:
Are we so using it?

[n] Lev. xiii.　　[o] Ibid. ver. 45, 46.　　[p] Lev. xiv.

XXXVI.
FOR THE ANNUNCIATION.

SIN A BLINDNESS OF THE SOUL.

"*He put clay upon mine eyes, and I washed, and do see.*"
S. JOHN ix. 15.

SIN is like a Possession or Madness;
And it is like Leprosy.
The Madness is cured by Christ,
When He says with Power,
"Hold thy peace, and come out of him."
The Leprosy is healed by Christ,
When He says, "I will, be thou clean."
Scripture teaches that sin is also a Blindness;
And for that also there is a Word of Power;
"Receive thy sight."
But observe that this complaint of Blindness,
As well as Leprosy, and most others,
Our Lord was accustomed to heal
By Touch as well as by Word[q].
And He added Spittle in some cases[r].
But in the text, besides all this, He made clay;
He anointed with the clay;
He bade the blind man wash.
Now what was the meaning of all this?

---

[q] S. Matt. ix. 29; xx. 34: S. Mark viii. 22.   [r] S. Mark viii. 23; vii. 33.

Consider the blind man begging at the Temple gate;
He was an Image of Adam,
Turned out of Paradise,
And blind to spiritual things.
Consider our Lord spitting on the ground,
And making clay of the spittle,
That was an Image of the Incarnation.
What was the anointing with the clay?
It represented the application of His Incarnation,
By His Spirit, to our souls.
The washing in Siloam, was like Naaman's in Jordan,
It represented, first Baptism, and then Repentance.
Thus the whole history belongs to this Festival,
The Day of the Incarnation of our Lord,
Which almost always occurs in Lent;
As indeed the thought of it is most necessary,
To the work of Lent.
For how can we be cured,
But by Him Who is the Healer of sin?
You must, at least, have faith in Him;
You must try His remedies;
You must do nothing to counteract them.
You are blind;—how blind you do not know;
But unless you are as bad as the Pharisees,
You will own to some blindness.
"He that lacketh these things is blind,
"And cannot see afar off,
"And hath forgotten that he was purged from his old sins[1]."

[1] 2 S. Pet. i. 9.

If you can, in some measure, see
Into the Land which is very far off,
Yet your sight is dimmer than it should be;
You have, in some degree, forgotten this fact—
That you were " purged from your old sins."
The remedy must be There,
Where the first deliverance came from;
That is from Christ,
Who, as on this day, became Incarnate,
And it will come in the way of self-surrender;
As Mary received her Blessing.

XXXVII.
Sin a Palsy of the Soul.

"Rise, take up thy bed, and walk."—S. John v. 8.

As sin is a Possession, and a Leprosy, and a Blindness,
So it is also a Palsy;
For as in Palsy the senses do not obey the will,
So it is in man's fallen estate[t]:
Partly, by original sin diffusing itself through all;
But still more, by actual and habitual sin,
Whereby man has sold himself to do evil.
This kind of paralysis shows itself, especially,
In Irreligion.

[t] Rom. vii. 14—23; Gal. v. 17; Rom. vi. 19.

Persons feel as if they could not pray,
Nor care for Holy things.
Often it appears like partial paralysis,
In special sins; as in avarice;
Or in slothfulness;
In vain, false, boastful, censorious talk;
Or in profane, or corrupting talk.
What are you to do?
Consider the Paralytic of Capernaum[a];
He permitted his friends to bring him in;
And in that strange way—through the roof;
He rose when bidden;
And he glorified God.
What of the other at the Pool of Bethesda?
He had been ill thirty-eight years;
He was so helpless that all reached the water before him;
He had no friend;
There was no one to bring him to Jesus;
Nor to plead for him, as the Centurion did for his servant;
It would seem also, that he had been a great sinner.
So our Lord came to him.
But his faith was tried also by the effort;
As the faith of those who brought the sick was tried;
As the faith of the Centurion;
Of the Paralytic Æneas;
Of the lame man at the Temple gate;
Of those whose hands were withered.
There was always an effort required, and made.

[a] S. Mark ii. 3—5.

Do you make the same;
Both in general and in partial paralysis;
Drag yourself to Christ as you may;
Remember the widow's mite.
Never despair.
Never leave off trying.
"Stretch forth thine hand." "Take up thy bed."
Christ's people will go on praying for you;
And Christ Himself will never cease interceding.
And what you do for yourself, do also for others.

XXXVIII.

Sin a Deafness and Dumbness of the Soul.

"And looking up to Heaven, He sighed, and said unto Him, Ephphatha, that is, Be opened."—S. MARK vii. 34.

After Possession, Leprosy, Blindness, Palsy,
We may notice the deaf and dumb,
As special objects of Christ's Mercy.
Not now the possessed, but those naturally so.
We know what a denial deafness is,
How great a mercy, therefore, to cure it!
We ought to think the more of His mercy,
In sparing us this affliction.
But what is being spiritually deaf?
We may find the answer in the Proverb,—
"None so deaf as those who will not hear."

We are all such, by nature;
"Even as the deaf adder that stoppeth her ears."
Our deafness is not *cured* by Baptism,
But the better principle is infused.
If the natural evil is encouraged,
Too soon it will prevail,
And men will become habitually deaf.
And if deaf, they will be dumb;
For as it is in nature, so it is in grace.
So we find it in the sullen and obstinate;
And very distressing it is.
Think of its making even our Saviour sigh.
He only can heal it;
Bring it to Him;
Be not down-hearted, nor yet too severe.
There is also a deafness to His Word,
And a dumbness in Prayer.
But if you are conscious of either,
And if you have the least wish to be healed,
Be sure He thinks of it more than you do,
And longs more to have it healed.
At any rate you can *listen*, and *stammer;*
Trust Him for the rest.

XXXIX.

SIN A DEATH OF THE SOUL.

"Lazarus, come forth."—S. JOHN xi. 43.

WE must all die;
We shall all stand in need of Christ,
And of His miraculous Mercy, to raise us to life again.
And what is more, we all know that It will come.
The Voice that called Lazarus out of the grave,
The Same will call us out.
And what then?
That will depend on our condition,
In respect of the other death,
The death of the soul;
To which also we are alike subject.
Of which the death of the body is both the penalty,
And also the type.
From the death of the soul we must be raised
Even in this world;
That life of the soul may be perfected, in the other world,
But it cannot begin There.
Do not say, "I have nothing to do with this;
"It is only for a few great sinners."
Nay; death is the natural condition of all souls;
Without special Grace all must fall into it.
Special Grace has indeed been constantly offered;
But have you used it?

If not, it is very likely you are dead again.
Death is so generally the condition of men—
Of people calling themselves Christians,
That the Church prays for Life,
As for a Grace needful for all.
To be raised "from the death of sin,
"To the Life of Righteousness."
You had better examine how it is with you.
Have you Breath,—to pray by His Spirit?
Have you Consciousness,—to know yourself?
Have you Sensation,—to know God?
Have you Motion—towards God?
Have you not been burying yourself,
In some dark place, where God's Light is not?
Has not the world been lying on you,
Like a great stone?
Has not the flesh been corrupting you more and more?
Have not bad habits been swathed round you?
Have not your senses been wrapped up,
As in a napkin?
In the napkin of selfishness;
Making you useless for the things of God;
Well, you and your friends must get our Lord to come,
To stand·by and call you by name.
He will have you loosed,
And you shall sit down with Him,
And never die any more.

XL.

Escape for thy Life.

"Escape for thy life; look not behind thee, neither stay thou in all the plain; escape to the mountain."—GEN. xix. 17.

WHAT was the state of things in Sodom, that morning?
Much like the ordinary state of things in this world,
As we see it now.
What was the Coming of the Angels like?
Like the Mission of the Church of Christ:
Remonstrating;
Persecuted;
Miraculously preserved;
Full of warning;
One sort of people mocking;
Another sort lingering.
Is not this the case of most of us?
The word then is the same now,
"Escape for thy life [x]."
Remember, it is for our life;
Not to indulge any regrets;
Nor to take liberties;
Nor to continue wilfully imperfect—
Not to stay "in the plain;"
But ever to tend upwards to "the mountain."

[x] S. Luke ix. 62.

Allowance will be made for infirmities,
As for the "little city" of Zoar.
How inexcusable, then, if we turn back,
As Lot's wife "looked back from behind" her husband.

XLI.

THE LENTEN EMBER-TIDE.

"*I fell down before the Lord, as at the first, forty days and forty nights; I did neither eat bread nor drink water.*"—DEUT. ix. 18.

MOSES was obliged to be in the Mount,
For a second time of forty days and nights;
And, as before, fasting.
Not this time receiving the Tables,
But taking them up with him,
To be written upon by the Finger of God.
It was to be a time of entire solitude;
Not even the flocks and herds were to feed there.
There was to be a solemn Proclamation
Of the Covenant of Repentance, in the Name of the Lord.
It must be regarded as a time of special Intercession,
Intercession for the sins of the people—
In which it sets forth the Lent of the Church;
And Intercession for the sins of Aaron [y]—
In which it sets forth the Ember Week of Lent.

[y] Deut. ix. 20.

So should Lent be to us a holy Season of special retirement;
Of prayer for pardon of the sins of God's people;
More especially of the Priests;
And of those connected with ourselves,
As enumerated in the Litany.
So may we hope, for another year to be admitted to penance;
Even as the Children of Israel were told to "go forward."
But we must take with us the Commandments,
And lay them up in the Ark:
That is to say, we must seek Holiness,
Which must be first, That Which abides in the Person of Christ,
And from That, in His Body, the Church.
In the guardianship of the Levites,
We see the work of the Christian Ministry;
It is the token of the Presence of His Body.
Hope on then to the end, for you are prayed for;
But mind that you pray too;
And take with you both the Creed and the Commandments.

XLII.
TRUE FORGIVENESS.

"*Now therefore be not grieved, nor angry with yourselves, that ye sold me hither: for God did send me before you to preserve life.*"—GEN. xlv. 5.

  Joseph we know was a pattern of purity;
 Now he comes before us with a lesson of sweetness;
Not separating the sixth from the seventh Commandment,
   As the world encourages men to do.
    Observe this sweetness,
  In his filial love—" Doth my Father still live?"
   Why did he not speak before?
 Because he would be sure of seeing Benjamin;
   Also he would try their repentance;
  Also he would not let them vex themselves.
  Yet think how bad their conduct had been.
  For mere envy they had sinned against him;
And so many against one; and that one a mere boy;
   They had also sold him for a slave;
 And at the mean price of twenty pieces of silver;
Lastly, they would not hear when he besought them.
  How many, would have upbraided the wrong-doers,
   Even if they did forgive such wrongs;
  Or been haughty in their condescension.
   How few would have quite forgiven them!
   How is it with you under injustice?
  Have you no anger? no sullenness? no revenge?
    Is there no ἐπιχαιρεκακία?

Is nothing reserved, as too bad to be forgiven?
Is nothing really good for your enemies grudged?
True forgiveness, is continually professed,
Yet it may, one fears, be very rare.
Not so Joseph's forgiveness; he carried it out thoroughly;
It was the same after seventeen years as at the beginning[r].
What was the secret of it all?
He walked with God.
"How can I do this wickedness, and sin against God[a]?"
"God sent me—not you[b]."
"Am I in the place of God[c]?"
Men, when affronted, speak of God in a very different way.
They are apt to curse, or make a spiteful vow.
But "a Greater than Joseph is here," Who is yet figured by him.
Who is the First-born of the Beloved Wife, after barrenness;
Sold to the Heathens;
Left in the place of sinners;
Raised up and glorified;
Drawing His enemies to Him;
Forgiving and feeding them.
Do you then forgive, and ye shall be forgiven;
Forgive your neighbour for Christ's sake,
And God, for Christ's sake, will forgive you.

[r] Gen. l. 14—21.   [a] Ib. xxxix. 9.   [b] Ib. xlv. 8.   [c] Ib. l. 19.

XLIII.
𝕳𝖔𝖑𝖞 𝖂𝖊𝖊𝖐.

ECCE HOMO.

"*Being found in fashion as a Man.*"—PHIL. ii. 8.

SEE how profitably you may meditate daily,
During this most Holy Week,
On the words
"Ecce Homo."

PALM SUNDAY.
Ecce Homo.
Behold the Man!—the very God Incarnate!
Consider generally,
How "being in the Form of God"—yea, "equal with God,
"He made Himself of no reputation;
"And took the form of a Servant;
"And being found in fashion as a Man,
"Humbled Himself, and became obedient unto death,
"Even the death of the Cross."
That we might be delivered from death eternal.

HOLY MONDAY.
Ecce Homo.
Behold the Man!—"Man of the substance of His Mother."
Consider our Lord's relation to His Mother,

Causing Him to be really of our blood;
A Blood-relation to us all.
Laying the foundation of His example to us,
In His demeanour to her.

HOLY TUESDAY.

Ecce Homo.
Behold the Man! as Pilate meant the words.
See the scourges and blows; the mockery and insult;
The thorns, the robe, the reed.
Behold the Man! as the Jews took the words,
First the council, then the crowd;
The world's testimony;
Witnessing for Him, yet giving Him up.
Therefore no dependence ought to be placed on the world;
Nor on ourselves, so far as we only protest against sin,
Yet in act agree to it;
No rare case.

HOLY WEDNESDAY.

Ecce Homo.
Behold the Man! and Judas betraying Him.
Consider Judas making known the place
Where He might be found;
And shewing which of those in the garden was " the Man."
Consider the cause of this betrayal, and the consequence of it.
Consider the warning to us all;

But to those especially, who, for purposes of their own,
Put others in the way of sin;
Tempting them to any kind of wrong liberties;
So making their weak points known to the evil one.
Consider and repent; attend to warnings.
It was neglect of warnings that ruined Judas.
He was warned[d]; and so are we:
Our fall will be like the fall of the Angels,
If we scorn our warning.

HOLY THURSDAY.

Ecce Homo.

Behold the Man! Christ Jesus, offering Himself for us
To God the Father, eternally in Heaven.
And we offering continually to God the Father, on earth,
His Sacramental Body and Blood in Holy Communion.
"This do in Remembrance of Me."

GOOD FRIDAY.

Ecce Homo.

Behold the Man!—on the Cross.
We say the words to God;
God says the words to us.
We say the words to one another;
Let us take care to say them to our own hearts.
"Look unto Me, and be ye saved,
"All the ends of the earth."

[d] S. John vi. 70; xiii. 10, 18: S. Matt. xxvi. 24.

EASTER EVE.

Ecce Homo.

Behold the Man! as in the Cradle and on the Cross,
So in the Grave.
This is what man must come to.
The natural man may believe that there is an end here,
"Sealing the stone, and setting a watch."
But behold the Man Christ Jesus!
On Him are the marks of the New Man—
The Second Man—the Lord from Heaven.
He will rise;
For He only died because He so willed.
See His wounds;
In His Limbs—the sign of Atonement,
In His Side—the sign of Sacramental Grace.
Behold the Angels watching Him;
The soldiers can do nought against them.
By and by, your grave and mine will be empty;
And where will the tenant be?
All will depend upon those marks of the New Man;
And those marks will depend upon our life.

XLIV.

Palm Sunday.

THE FORM OF A SERVANT.

"Christ Jesus .... made Himself of no reputation, and took upon Him the form of a servant."—PHIL. ii. 5, 7.

THE Apostle had said, by the Holy Ghost, that Christ Jesus, being in the Form of God, thought it not robbery to be equal with God: that is, He made as if He did not count His Godhead dear unto Him—as a prize to be eagerly grasped or laid hold of.

For the word "robbery" here seems to mean much the same as the word "prey" in the Prophet Jeremiah[e]; where God promises to such or such a person, that his life should be unto him for "a prey," that is, for something which had fallen to his lot, which he would cling to, and make much of.

S. Paul says that our Blessed Lord, in His inconceivable love for us did, as it were, deal with His own Divine Nature, as though He cared not for It, as though He were putting It off, in order to save us; so very low was the condition to which He stooped, when He took upon Him to deliver man.

He was like a King, putting off His glorious apparel, and lowering Himself into the "horrible pit," into the "mire and clay," that He might raise up those who were plunged in the very depths of it, and set their feet upon the Rock.

[e] See ch. xxi. 9; xxxviii. 2; xxxix. 18; xlv. 5.

All this the Apostle tells us in saying, "He counted it not a prey that He was equal with God, but emptied Himself."
And now consider what he next says:
"He made Himself of no reputation,
"And took on Him the form of a Servant."
How did He take on Him the form of a Servant?
In that He made Himself a Creature;
For all things serve Him [f].
In that the creature so honoured was man;
Man, who had made himself a slave, instead of a son [g].
And this He expressed by typical action.
As, especially by washing His disciples' feet [h].
Observe His knowledge of Himself [i];
"That He was come from God, and went to God."
And His knowledge of us [k];
Even as He knew the heart of Judas.
"He laid aside His garments;"
This answers to "He emptied Himself [l]."
He "girded Himself," that is, He dressed as a slave;
And then He did a slave's work.
He told S. Peter that he should "know hereafter what He did,"
Know the mystery of His Action.
But observe how He was but bringing to a point,
What He had been doing all His life.
He had been a Slave, as it were, to His Father [m].

---

[f] Ps. cxix. 91; compare Rev. iv. 11. [g] See Heb. ii. 15, 16; Isa. lii. 3; S. John viii. 34; Rom. vi. 16, 20; 2 S. Pet. ii. 19.
[h] S. John xiii. 4. [i] Ib. 3. [k] Ib. 2. [l] ἑαυτὸν ἐκένωσεν.
[m] See S. John vi. 38; v. 30; iv. 34; xvii. 4; xix. 30.

He was among His Apostles, "as he that serveth [n]."
And we are to have the same mind.
Only think :—
In the least little bit of self-denying courtesy,
Of forbearance, helpfulness, bounty,
We may, if we will, practise ourselves in His Image;
And prepare ourselves for His Joy [o],
Which will be the joy of serving His Redeemed [p].

•

XLV.

THE MODEL MAN.

"*And being found in fashion as a man, He humbled Himself, and became obedient unto death, even the death of the Cross.*"
PHIL. ii. 8.

"HE took on Him the form of a Servant,"
By being "made in the likeness of men;"
For man, as such, is a servant or slave,
Both as a creature, and as a sinner.
And we may add that, whether man will or no,
He is forced to do God's Will.
In other words, man *must* work out God's purposes.
This explains why our Lord was circumcised;
In token of His being God's Servant,
And bound to do the whole Law.

[n] Rom. xv. 3.   [o] Heb. xii. 2.   [p] S. Luke xii. 37.

He was made a true Man, in the likeness of other men,
Though not such as they were ;
Since all the while, He was not only sinless,
But the most High God ^q.
Yet in flesh and blood He was "like to His brethren ^r."
And so He was "found in fashion,"
That is, He proved to be in outward appearance,
As another man, with "no form nor comeliness."
Being made as sinners are,
He humbled Himself as sinners ought.
See how He humbles Himself in His Passion ;
He is sold for a slave's price ;
As a sinner He seeks a place apart ;
He kneels, and prays as any sinner might ;
He falls on His Face ;
He shrinks from the Cup ;
He sacrifices His own Will ;
He is content to be strengthened by an Angel ;
He endures an Agony ; He sweats Blood ;
He seeks sympathy of His Disciples ;
He prays again and again, contrary to proud impatience ;
He expostulates with His persecutors ;
He permits, so gently, the worst indignities—
Judas to kiss Him ;
His Hands to be bound ;
The Jews to drag Him about ;
A servant to smite Him on the Face ;

^q Rev. vii. 11 ; xxii. 13.   ^r Heb. ii. 14.

False witnesses to prevail, as if He could not answer;
Spitting, blindfolding, buffeting, mocking.
But pause—before you go on to the Lord's Death.
Consider, have you been with Him in your life?
Have you prayed, like a sinner in agony?
Have you given up your own will?
Have you remembered others in your prayers?
Have you risen from prayer to help others?
Have you endured the contradiction of sinners?
Then may you hope, in what remains, to be like Him;
Abiding in Him, walking as He walked,
And dying, after your measure, as He died.
All this will depend on one thing—
Your obedience.

XLVI.

THE DECREE OF SACRIFICE.

"Lo, I come, in the Volume of the Book it is written of Me, to do Thy will, O God."—HEB. x. 7.

This is the time of Sacrifice;
The time when Christ especially sacrificed Himself;
And we are especially to sacrifice ourselves,
To Him, with Him, and through Him.
We know what Sacrifice is;
Giving up oneself, or something of one's own;
Giving up what one values to another.

But how then can there be Sacrifice to God,
Since all belongs already to Him?
As there may be Prayer to God, though He knows what we want;
And Confession to God, though He knows all our sins;
So there may be Sacrifice to God,
Because He has given us one thing of our own—
He has given us a Will.
If we give up our wills to God, that is our Sacrifice.
This Sacrifice was required of Adam;
He refused it, and we know the consequence;
The penalty was incurred; he was lost for ever;
His nature became corrupt, and therefore we were lost in him.
No creature in Heaven or in Earth, could find a remedy;
But the Creator did;
And this Remedy is the Gospel of Jesus Christ.
The Foundation of it all is laid in His Word,
"I come to do Thy Will, O God."
God the Son made Himself Man,
In order that He might have a human will,
Wherewith to submit Himself entirely to the Divine Will—
To His Father's Will from all Eternity,
And to His own Divine Will, as in the Agony of Gethsemane.
This was His purpose from Everlasting,
Hence it may be called the Decree of Sacrifice.
His purpose began to be fulfilled at His Incarnation;
But it was consummated at His Death.
Since then, He still sacrifices;
But no more with a suffering, blood-shedding Sacrifice.
Now He offers the Memorial of that Sacrifice.

The Services of this Holy Week teach us all this.
To-day His Incarnation is commemorated,
In the Collect and Epistle.
To-day also He set Himself apart for the Cross.
As the Lamb was set apart for the Passover, on the tenth day,
So He set Himself apart, for the Sacrifice of the Cross.
This was His work for this day.
Your work and mine should be the same;
For He came to be our Example,
As the Services of the Church shew.
He is the great Captain, going before, to suffer and to save you.
Will you not follow Him?—for shame?—for fear?
Knowing what must happen to him who turns back.
Will you not follow, for the sure victory?
Yea rather, for love and gratitude?
Here you are, in the world,
Where God has set you to do His Will.
And in the Church, where you have promised to do His Will,
Little as you may have thought of it.
And you are on the edge of the other world,
Where you cannot escape from His Will.
If His Will were always pleasant,
There would be no Sacrifice in obeying It;
No likeness to Christ, and no Reward.
As it is, every one may have a part in both.
Every child, man, or woman, may have a part in Christ's Cross;
And therefore, a part in His Crown.
This is your time; but it will very soon be gone.

XLVII.

THE TEARS OF JESUS.

"And when He was come near, He beheld the City, and wept over it."—S. LUKE xix. 41.

THE time is coming when we remember our Lord's Death.
Consider one by one some of the tokens of His love,
Of His true love towards us.
Consider His tears over Jerusalem.
First, the time—at the end of His Ministry,
On the first day of the last week.
Three years He had been seeking fruit[*],
As, on this very day, by the road-side,
And had found none.
And now He was setting Himself apart as the Victim,
According to the law of the Passover.
Next, the place—on the slope of the Mount of Olives;
Jerusalem in her glory, in sight,
The people magnifying Him;
But He knew by Divine foresight,
What would happen there a few nights after.
And so, He weeps;
Not for the earthly glory lost to Jerusalem;
Still less for His own sufferings;
But for her ruin, caused, as it was, by her own guilt.
But she was no nearer, nor dearer to Him, than we are.

[*] S. Luke xiii. 7.

We must understand Him to weep for our guilt;
As the Angels and He rejoice at our conversion.
Remember also, how it is said of us sinners,
That we crucify Him afresh.
And observe the special guilt,
Of not knowing the time of our Visitation.
That He speaks, and we will not hear;
That He knocks, and we will not let Him in.
As yet, it is not too late; but it will be too late soon.
Time passes on;
Our power diminishes;
He is provoked.
Think: is there not in us some one thing we know of,
For which He is, at this moment, as it were weeping over us?
O let us make haste, and amend it,
Lest we be as children unpitying to their parents.
Who will say a word for us then,
At the Last Day?

XLVIII.

THE TIME OF VISITATION.

"Because thou knewest not the time of thy Visitation."
S. LUKE xix. 44.

CONSIDER in this history, our Lord's true Humanity:
That He "came near;" that He "wept," as once besides;
For the City; for the People;
Why did He weep?
"Because thou knewest not the time of thy Visitation."
Consider what this "Visitation [t]" is:
Any remarkable interference of God;
As, to Sarah [u];
As, to the Children of Israel in Egypt [x];
As, to the Captives in Babylon [y];
As, to Zacharias [z];
As, to the Gentiles [a];
And as here, to Jerusalem.
His "Visitation" comes at set times [b],
Which are marked, and people ought to know them.
God gives signs;
And by them He reveals His secrets unto His Servants [c].
Now the signs to Jerusalem were many; and the time was clear;
So that the Jews were without excuse.

[t] Ἐπισκοπή.   [u] Gen. xxi. 1.   [x] Gen. l. 24.   [y] Ps. cvi. 4, and Jer. xxix. 10.   [z] S. Luke i. 68, 78.   [a] Acts xv. 14; 1 Pet. ii. 12.
[b] Καιροί.   [c] Amos iii. 7.

Like all times, it will have passed after a while;
And now it has passed, so far as Jerusalem is concerned;
Therefore He weeps.
But it was not then past, with respect to all individuals.
There was "a Remnant;" and each one might be of it,
And so it is now, though we know not for how long.
Only we know that to each one, "the time is short."
Over each one of you the Lord is pausing,
And does not yet strike;
And He mourns over you,
If you will not know "the time."
Will you not care for His tears?
Will you not care for your own soul? .
Will you not, now at least, look on, as He always does,
To the one fearful Visitation which is coming?
Look on to that first,
And then, look up to Him, "and be ye saved."
So this very day, this hour, this moment, shall be your "time,"
Shall be a blessed Visitation to you.

XLIX.

A Word to Frequent Communicants.

"He came near where I stood; and when he came, I was afraid, and fell upon my face."—Daniel viii. 17.

So it is—or ought to be—with us at certain times;
As when the Church has given her wonted notice,
To prepare for Easter Communion.
And the notice should bring many thoughts;
As, to those who have neglected Holy Communion;
So also, to those who are frequent Communicants.
There is a real danger to frequent Communicants;
The danger of unthoughtfulness;
And it must be guarded against,
By the general habit of reverence;
By devoting yourselves afresh after every Communion,
Instantly beginning your preparation for the next;
By using yourself to remember—
"At such a time It will be."
And when temptation comes,
By asking, "how can I communicate if I do this?"
When needing help, or when help comes,
By saying, "I must treasure this or that,
"For prayer or for thanksgiving at my next Communion."
By connecting with It what you read or hear;
By associating with It God's Providences.
Never fear making too much of It;

Consider Who, and What It is; how it gathers all in one.
How the Will of God appoints your Communions,
    As so many steps towards Heaven.
Do you have the same will, and it will be so.
You will be There before you can imagine it,
Wondering at the strangeness of your own Salvation.

L.
Monday in Holy Week.

THE DAY OF CLEANSING.

"And Jesus went into the temple, and began to cast out them that sold and bought in the temple, and overthrew the tables of the money-changers, and the seats of them that sold doves; and would not suffer that any man should carry any vessel through the temple."—S. MARK xi. 15, 16.

THE Holy Week answers to that solemn time,
Before a Christian's death.
Palm Sunday is like accepting the sentence;
Holy Monday is like setting your house in order.
Our Lord looked over the Temple on the Sunday;
On the Monday, returning to Jerusalem,
He passed sentence on the barren fig-tree;
A type, first of Judea,
Then of unfruitful Christians.
Coming into the Temple, what did He find?
The very same disorder which he had corrected,
Three years and a-half before.
He cleanses it again;
Only in some respects He speaks now,
More severely than before;
And thus He claims the Temple for His own.
He makes it part of the preparation for His Death,
That He should cleanse it.

He shews thereby how much He has at heart,
Our reverence for Holy Places.
He sets us an example of preparation;
Of putting our houses in order,
Both literally and spiritually.
Literally, by paying our debts;
By making our wills;
By arranging other things;
By correcting known mischiefs;
By providing for works of charity,
As "the blind and lame came to Him in the temple
"And He healed them."
Spiritually, He sets an example—
To governors, of cleansing the Church.
To each individual, of cleansing His inward house,
Even the soul, which is His House;
For He came to dwell in it at Baptism.
And though this soul, which is His,
May be never so sadly occupied by evil spirits,
Which have entered in and dwelt there since,
He can, and will, cleanse it for us,
If we seek and beseech Him in earnest.
Perhaps it is full of "money-changers,"
That is, of cares about getting money,
And of temptations,
Which would have us "sell the doves,"
That is, the consolations of the Holy Spirit,
For the things of this world.
We must turn all such spirits out;

We must not mind dealing rudely with them;
Even with our most cherished evil fancies.
And as our Lord, at this second time of cleansing,
Would not suffer even a vessel for earthly use,
To be carried through the Temple;
So, as our last hour draws on,
We ought to shut the door of our hearts against worldly cares,
Even when they are innocent.
So shall we lie down in peace,
And our bodies—His Temple—shall be raised,
Even as our Lord's Body was raised,
At the appointed time.

LI.

THE SINNER'S WOUNDS.

"*Thy arrows are very sharp.*"—Ps. xlv. 6, P.B.

THE Epistle sets Christ before us as a Great Warrior,
In a soldier's dress.
His garments red with blood.
What blood? His own Blood [d].
He treads that wine-press alone.
It is "the wine-press of the Wrath of God."
So dyed, He goes forth,
To overcome sinners with a soldier's weapons;

[d] Rev. xix. 13; S. Luke xxii. 44.

With His Sword, and with His Arrows,
His Sword—the Word of God,
His Arrows—the Reproofs of His Providence.
His Wounds are Life or Death, as people make them.
See in this week's history both Sword and Arrows;
His washing the Disciples' feet,
What an Arrow for S. Peter, for S. James, and for S. John!
For Judas especially, as he sat at meat,
What an Arrow was in the words,
"The hand of him that betrayeth Me is with Me on the table."
What an Arrow for S. Peter when He warned him!
What a Sword went forth when He said,
" He that eateth bread with Me,
" Hath lifted up his heel against Me."
What a very sharp Arrow when He gave the Sop!
When He struck to the ground those that came to take Him;
When He spoke so gently to Judas;
When He turned and looked upon S. Peter;
When He addressed the women;
When He consoled the thief;
What Arrows went out from Him!
He comes to us now in the same dress,
With the same weapons.
We cannot escape His wounds.
We may choose what they shall be to us,
Whether they shall be Life or Death.

LII.
Tuesday in Holy Week.

SPIRITUAL PERPLEXITY.

"My God, My God, look upon Me; why hast Thou forsaken Me?"—Ps. xxii. 1.

CONSIDER our Lord in His Self-denial,
   Denying Himself spiritual comfort;
   Condescending to be in perplexity,—
"I am come to send fire on the earth;
"And what will I, if it be already kindled [e]?"
Herein He did but shew Himself the same God,
   As all through the Old Testament,
Trying one thing after another, for the conversion of men.
"What could have been done more to My Vineyard,
   "That I have not done in it [f]?"
He "wondered that there was no Intercessor [g];"
"Wondered that there was none to uphold [h];"
"How shall I do for the daughters of My people [i]?"
"It may be that the House of Judah will hear [k]:"
"O Ephraim, what shall I do unto thee [l]?"
"O Judah, what shall I do unto thee?"
"How shall I give thee up, Ephraim [m]?"
   So in His earthly Ministry.

[e] S. Luke xii. 49, 50.   [f] Isa. v. 4.   [g] Ib. lix. 16.
[h] Ib. lxiii. 5.   [i] Jer. ix. 7.   [k] Ib. xxxvi. 3.   [l] Hos. vi. 4.
[m] Ib. xi. 8.

He "marvelled because of their unbelief[n];"
He likened them to "children sitting in the market[o]."
He condescended to be in agony, or strife of spirit;
"Now is My Soul troubled, and what shall I say[p]?"
Consider, above all, the Agony in the Garden;
How He condescended to feel as one forsaken;
As one who looked out in vain; whose voice was not heard;
When others had been, and were to be, refreshed,
   How no refreshment came for Him.
See how the Psalms which end in a minor key[q],
   Were thus fulfilled in Him.
   Comfort yourself with this Pattern,
   When your soul refuses comfort;
As it will sometimes, from bodily disease;
   Or from a morbid temperament;
Or from a way of feeling you have got into.
Consider the sayings of Divine Inspiration:
   "Why abhorrest Thou my soul?"
   "Hath God forgotten to be gracious?"
   "Tarry thou the Lord's leisure."
"Yet a little while, and He that shall come, will come."
   How much better to go on mourning,
   And even sinking, to the end,
   Than to fall asleep in false comfort,
   And to wake, and find it a dream.
   God preserve us all from that!

---

[n] S. Mark vi. 6.   [o] S. Luke vii. 31—34.   [p] S. John xii. 27.
[q] As Ps. lxxiv. and lxxxviii.

LIII.
Wednesday in Holy Week.

THE MIND OF CHRIST TOWARDS JUDAS.

"The Son of Man goeth as it is written of Him, but woe to that man by whom the Son of Man is betrayed; it had been good for that man if he had not been born."—S. MATT. xxvi. 24.

EXAMINE yourselves,
Whether you have the mind of Christ.
And especially to-day, whether you are of His mind,
Towards this unhappy Judas; and towards such as he was.
For this is the day of Betrayal.
It was His Will that Judas should be saved;
He shed as much Blood for him as for Peter;
Therefore hate no man.
He bore with Judas all along;
Therefore behave to no one as if you hated him.
He warned Judas;
Therefore think not lightly of the faults of any.
Do not suffer sin upon any.
See the persistent love of His warnings,
Again and again they were repeated to Judas.
"He that sitteth with Me at the table,"
"One of you shall betray Me,"
"He that dippeth with Me in the dish,"
"He it is to whom I shall give a sop,"
"That thou doest, do quickly,"
"Friend, wherefore art thou come?"
Yet, that none might pervert such love,

As if it could never reject the guilty,
He did, as it were, pass sentence upon Judas;
"Good were it for that man, if he had never been born."
This could not be,
If God's love made pardon a necessity—
A necessity that Judas should be accepted at last.
Sad though it be, we must receive the conclusion.
And this is the sentence of Incarnate Love—
In the middle of the Feast of Love—
In preparation for the Sacrifice of Love—
The final sentence passed on such as Judas.
What a thought for those brought very near to Christ,
Whom He is constantly warning in His love!
For the covetous, the sullen, the selfish,
For the obstinate in sin,
For all who deal scornfully with Holy Things!
Every such sin persisted in, will end in hardness of heart.
Thank God we are still in the way of warnings.
"Good were it for that man if he had not been born."
Therefore believe stedfastly in Hell;
And let it be known to others that you believe.
Never cease praying for others,
And setting them a good example.
And that your example may be in earnest,
Never lose the fear of Hell for yourself;
Never cease to hate the things which will bring you there.
Remember, not only "the wicked will be turned into Hell,"
But "all the people that forget God[1]."

[1] Ps. ix. 17.

LIV.

THE ATTRACTION OF JESUS IN HIS PASSION.

"And I, if I be lifted up from the earth, will draw all men unto Me."—S. JOHN xii. 32.

ALL sorts of men were to be drawn round the Cross,
Because "all had sinned;"
"There were none righteous, no not one."
In the evening, in the last time,
The whole congregation were to slay the sacrifice.
We all were to be redeemed.
The loving Saviour spread out His arms to all.
"As in Adam all die;
"Even so in Christ shall all be made alive."
"As by one man's disobedience many were made sinners,
"So by the obedience of One shall many be made righteous."
And therefore, when He speaks of being "lifted up,"
He purposely calls Himself the Son of Man.
But there is also an attraction of Grace,
As well as a drawing of Providence;
There is a secret virtue in the Cross,
To win all hearts not utterly reprobate.
And of this also it pleases Him to give examples,
In that great company of His followers.
Mary of Bethany was drawn;
She had felt the attraction beforehand;
Sitting at our Lord's Feet,
She had perhaps understood Him better than many;

And so made her offering, in the spirit of love,
Which strives to be kind to those whom it expects to lose.
    The Disciples at supper were drawn;
    S. Peter at the washing of their feet;
    All of them at the notice of betrayal;
    S. John leaning on Jesus' Bosom;
    S. Peter wishing to follow Him;
    And all professing not to deny Him.
    Each and all of them were drawn to Him.
    Pilate's wife was drawn;
Pilate's own misgivings prove that even he was drawn.
What a serious thought that so many should resist Christ,
    Resisting the attraction of which they are conscious.
    Probably Simon the Cyrenian was drawn;
    Since his sons became disciples.
    The penitent thief was drawn;
    His blessed mother and her sister were drawn;
    S. Mary Magdalene was drawn;
    The Centurion, and as men say, Longinus,
The Captain, and the soldier who pierced His Side were drawn;
    The multitudes were drawn;
    Those employed in His Burial were drawn;
    Little knowledge or faith had they in the Resurrection,
    But they held to Him for love.
    Some of all sorts were drawn to Him;
Therefore no outward circumstances need keep any from Him.
    We cannot come without His Father's drawing,
    But He offers here to draw us, if we will.
    Let us say, "Draw me: we will run after Thee."

He hath drawn us from our youth upward;
He hath drawn us "with the cords of a man."
What have we gained by resisting His gentle force?
Hear the words of one,
Who yielded himself at once to the attraction,
And who never broke from it, nor hung back.
"Yea doubtless, and I count all things but loss,
"For the excellency of the knowledge
"Of Christ Jesus, my Lord:
"For whom I have suffered the loss of all things,
"And do count them but dung,
"That I may win Christ, and be found in Him,
"Not having mine own righteousness which is of the law,
"But that which is through the faith of Christ,
"The righteousness which is of God by faith:
"That I may know Him,
"And the power of His Resurrection,
"And the fellowship of His sufferings,
"Being made conformable unto His Death;
"If by any means I might attain
"To the Resurrection of the dead.
"Not as though I had already attained,
"Either were already perfect;
"But I follow after,
"If that I may apprehend,
"That for which also I am apprehended of Christ Jesus.
"Brethren, I count not myself to have apprehended,
"But this one thing I do,
"Forgetting those things which are behind,

"And reaching forth to those things which are before,
"I press towards the mark
"For the prize of the high calling of God
"In Christ Jesus [a]."
Which of us, however fond of earthly things,
Would not own in his secret heart,
That he should be much happier, as well as better,
If he could give such an account of himself?
We have but to will it in earnest, and to pray,
And we shall be in the way to that happiness.
Does it seem too much to hope for?
Well might it seem so.
But we are not to indulge such misgivings;
We are not to doubt, for the word is sure;
And it is spoken to us among the rest:
He saith " *Whosoever* cometh;"
His word is to *All* that believe.
Mistrust Him not, my Brother, whoever thou art
Art thou not one of that "All?"
Be not afraid; only believe.

[a] Phil. iii. 8—14.

LV.
Thursday in Holy Week.

THE ATTRACTION OF JESUS IN THE HOLY EUCHARIST.

"And I, if I be lifted up from the earth, will draw all men unto Me."—S. JOHN xii. 32.

CONSIDER the special subject of this day;
One great result of our Lord's lifting up on the Cross—
The Sacrifice and Sacrament of the Eucharist;
How that blessed Mystery tends to draw all men,
To draw them in a special way to Christ.
But observe, in order to the efficacy of this Sacrament,
There was to be another lifting up from the earth,
His Resurrection and His Ascension,
Leading to His work of Intercession,
When He should have ascended to His Father;
"I ascend to My Father and your Father,
"To My God and your God [t]."
Such then being the idea of the Eucharist,
See how It draws all men to Him.
It draws us as a Remembrance appointed by Him;
It is endearing to be told by any, to remember;
Think of tokens and keepsakes among friends;
How much more to be told by Him!
It draws us, as the ordained Remembrance of His Death;
Love "to the end" is very attractive.
It draws us, as setting forth the particulars of His Death;

[t] S. John xx. 17.

Like mourners going over it in their minds.
It draws us, as honouring Him before men;
As people have gravestones and monuments.
It draws us as taking part in what He is now doing;
How much people think of help in prayer,
S. Paul many times asks for such help;
But our part in the Eucharist is much more.
It draws us the more, as what He is doing now,
He is doing it for us [n].
It draws us as bringing Him near,
Literally, though ineffably.
It draws us as preparing a Table for us,
Where He really gives us to eat His Flesh,
And to drink His Blood;
With more than Mother's love,
It draws us, as being a Seal of His own providing,
Of perfect union with Himself hereafter.
Therefore all who love the Lord, love the Holy Communion;
And have ever made It their chief happiness on earth.
And if any do not so value Holy Communion,
There is reason to fear about their loving Him.
If you do not *at all* care about Holy Communion,
Be sure you do not love Him.
If you do not *so* care as to overcome difficulties,
In order that you may come worthily,
You do not love Him enough.
He is only taking His turn, with other things,
With the things of this world, which occupy your heart.

[n] See S. Stephen's vision, Acts vii. 55.

At this Season, especially, He is "lifted up;"
And He would " draw" you " all" to Him.
Easter Day will be a great day of trial :
We shall see who come outwardly ;
But who they are who really come as they are drawn,
We shall not see till a future Day,
When He will appear, as He is, "lifted up ;"
And His Sign shall be with Him,
To " draw all men" unto Him, in another sense.
Think with yourself, " Christ is now drawing me,
" I am sure of it outwardly,
" I hope it may be so inwardly, by His Spirit.
" I know that I am lost if I do not come to Him.
" And I know that 'no man can come' to Him,
" Except He and His Father draw him.
" I may not reckon on being drawn hereafter,
" If I reject this call.
" I will therefore, please God, turn to Him at once;
" I will prepare myself,
" I will seek Him where I know He may be found ;
" I will long and pray that I may love Him, and obey Him ;
" And He will help me, for He died for me."

LVI.

THE SACRIFICE OF THE HOLY EUCHARIST.

"*This Cup is the New Testament in My Blood which is shed for you.*"—S. LUKE xxii. 20.

"*This Cup is the New Testament in My Blood, this do ye, as oft as ye drink it, in remembrance of Me.*"—1 COR. xi. 28.

AT the end of His Life-long Sacrifice,
Our Lord did, as it were, make His Will.
And His doing so was also an Act of Sacrifice.
His Will was to offer Himself, on the appointed morrow,
"A full, perfect, and sufficient Sacrifice,
"Oblation, and Satisfaction,
"For the sins of the whole world;"
And to "institute a perpetual Memory
"Of that His precious Death,
" Until His Coming again."
His Will was "not only to die for us,
" But to be our spiritual Food and Sustenance."
His Legacy, therefore, was Himself,
Under the form of Bread and Wine;
And, with Himself, all graces and blessings.
Being not merely a Covenant, but a Legacy,
His Will could not take effect till after His Death;
It was signed and sealed with Blood,
As was the old Covenant;
Therefore both were called διαθήκη.
So His Sacrifice on the Cross became a Peace-offering.

K

And as in the case of the Paschal Lamb,
They who presented it became partakers of it;
So, His Death, being the Sin-offering which purchased peace,
Was turned into a Peace-offering;
And is now re-presented in memory of that Peace,
And afterwards partaken of by the Faithful;
Thus, both sealing, and applying, the Covenant.
The Sacrifice is presented by our High Priest;
And in union with It,
All our prayers and thanksgivings are presented.
Consider then the Sacrifice of the Holy Eucharist;
How nearly it is connected with the Sacrifice of the Cross;
See how necessary is the First,
For the application of the Second.
The Holy Eucharist is His last Will;
How can you slight it?
It sums up His dying words to you;
How can you forget them?
It is the partaking of Himself;
How can you do without Him?
It is the Token of His Peace;
Will you still be enemies?
It is your part in the Sin-offering;
Would you rather remain unforgiven?
It is the recommendation of your prayers;
Would you rather they were not heard?
In all this we are not making too much of the Holy Eucharist;
For all turns upon the *worthy* receiving;
This, begun and persevered in, is a golden chain,
A Jacob's ladder, which cannot fail.

LVII.

THE LEGACIES OF CHRIST TO HIS PEOPLE.

"*This is the Blood of the Testament, which God hath enjoined unto you.*"—HEB. ix. 20.
"*He is the Mediator of the New Testament.*"—IB. v. 15.

THE New Testament—
Consider what that word means;
And how it applies to Christ's Gospel.
To-day let us consider Christ,
As making His Will in our favour.
He did so, especially, on that last evening of His mortal Life.
He is as a rich man at the point to die,
Who calls together whom he will;
And tells them how he will assign his property.
But our Lord can make no mistake;
Nor can His intentions be frustrated.
There is no room for misgiving.
In whose favour does He make His Will?
He Himself tells us—
In favour of those of whom He says to His Father
"Thou gavest them Me out of the world [x]."
There is no room for envy or jealousy;
Each may have all.
What are His legacies?

[x] S. John xvii. 6, 9, 20.

THURSDAY IN HOLY WEEK.

Take them in order from the four Gospels;
The Legacy of His Body,
Mystically and invisibly remaining with us;
He is gone—and yet He is here.
The Legacy of the Apostolical Succession.
The Legacy of the Comforter.
The Legacy of His Scriptures.
All these Legacies are sealed with His Blood,
And made effectual by His Intercession,
For the perfect union of His people with Himself.
This is your Inheritance;
And the security for It.
It is true, there are conditions;
There must be imperfection in reaching It;
Persecution and danger in the way to It;
The Testator gives you fair warning of this.
You see your Inheritance;
But you are not forced to accept It.
If you can find anywhere, a more loving Saviour,
A more merciful God, a higher Heaven,
You are free to choose.
One of those who were present,
When our Lord began to declare His last Will,
"Went out immediately,"
And sold his share for "thirty pieces of silver."
You may follow him, if you will;
You also may go away.
But God forbid that you should make such a choice!
God give you a heart devoted to Christ!

Ready now and always to say,
"Lord, to whom shall we go?
"Thou hast the words of eternal Life."
"Thou shalt guide me with Thy counsel."
"Whom have I in Heaven but Thee?
"And there is none upon earth that I desire
"In comparison of Thee.
"My flesh and my heart faileth,
"But" my Lord and my "God,"
Even JESUS CHRIST,
"Is the strength of my heart,
"And my portion for ever."

LVIII.
Good Friday.

THE ATTRACTION OF JESUS IN HIS CRUCIFIXION.

"And I, if I be lifted up from the earth, will draw all men unto Me."—S. JOHN xii. 32.

GOD draws men to the Cross,
First by His Providence, then by His Grace.
He began to do so at the very time of the Crucifixion;
Now the same process is going on continually.
It began formally at Pentecost;
And will not cease until the end of the world.
And still it is the same story,
On a large scale, or on a small;
Christ Crucified draws men's attention,
By His merciful Providence,
Whether or no they let Him draw their hearts,
By the power of His Grace.
So the unconverted Saul, and the Jewish Council were drawn;
And Cornelius, and Gallio were drawn.
The constant effect of persecution is to draw men;
So, still better, is the effect of the voluntary Cross.
We see these effects in our own time;
By wars and divisions on the one hand;
By works of charity on the other.
It is also part of His Providence,
To draw all *things*, as well as all men, to Himself.

So it is in the privacy of individual life,
Where any one shews his penitence or self-denial,
As they who in the early days of the Church, made sacrifices,
"Parted with their goods to all as every one had need;"
As Barnabas, who "laid" his estate "at the Apostles' feet;"
Or as many of the Ephesians, who "confessed
"And shewed their deeds."
People cannot ignore His drawing;
It preaches better than all our sermons;
It is more effectual, to win or to condemn.
So, by degrees, the outward conversion of the world goes on.
By-and-by it will be completed.
And then, quite literally, it will be true of all men,
That they are drawn to Christ crucified.
It is now a matter of faith;
Then it will be an object of sight.
And it will still be Christ "lifted up."
He will come from Heaven, for He has ascended Thither.
He will bear His Scars, for He was wounded on the Cross,
And "the Sign" of Him, they say, will be the Cross.
Then all men will be drawn to Him;
The wicked, by force, to receive their sentence;
The penitent, to "meet the Lord in the air;
"And so to be ever with the Lord."
And being ever with Him, to advance more and more,
Even as He draws them on, from Glory to Glory.

LIX.

THE FINISHED WORK.

"*It is finished.*"—S. JOHN xix. 30.

WHAT is finished?
His Sacrifice for sin is finished:
His Sufferings are finished:
The Work of earning grace is finished:
Therein all the Types are finished:
The Prophecies are finished:
The Battle with the Devil is finished:
The Victory of right over wrong is finished:
His Example, His Instruction,
His Preparation for the Church,
All these are finished.
It remains that we ask Him to finish the rest;
To finish the application of His work to the world;
And to each separate soul.
In respect of grace and cleansing;
In respect of active righteousness;
In respect of growing Communion with Him;
In respect of knowledge of God, and of ourselves;
In respect of Heavenly joy.
We, on our part, labouring together with Him,
To finish our reformation, and good beginnings.
Lest we find at last, that we have been going backwards,
Travelling towards Hell,
Though our faces are set towards Heaven.

LX.

THE PRICE OF OUR BLESSINGS IN THIS LIFE.

"Purchased with His own Blood."—ACTS xx. 28.

YESTERDAY our Lord made and published His Will;
 To-day He signs and seals it with His Blood;
  He makes it of force by His Death.
 S. Paul argues from the first Testament,
 Which was not dedicated without Blood,
  That "wherever a Testament is,"
 There of necessity, is "the death of the Testator ⁷."
This is the difference between a promise, and a will;
  Between a Covenant, and a Testament.
 Surely the difference suggests a thought,
 To enter deeply into any affectionate heart,
  As to all the blessings we enjoy,
 That they were purchased with the Giver's Death.
  It was so even in the Old Testament,
 For He is "the Lamb slain" from the Beginning,
  Yea "from the foundation of the world."
 But it is more evidently so, in the New Testament.
  It is so in respect of our earthly blessings;
 "Let it alone this year also," is His Intercession;
"Hurt not the earth neither the sea," is His Intercession;
 But much more are our spiritual blessings His purchase,
  The price of His Blood.

⁷ Heb. ix. 16; Exod. xxiv. 5, 6, 8.

This should teach us to be very thankful;
To struggle with ourselves against a common tendency,
To take all our blessings as "matters of course."
How hard it is, for example, to say grace in earnest,
Or to mind one's prayers in church.
Yet we know that every meal is purchased for us,
Bought by the Blood of the Son of God.
Much more is this true of the Church itself;
True of the Prayer-Book;
And of the very power and leave to pray.
How seldom is Holy Matrimony rightly undertaken
In a really religious way!
How easily are religious thoughts of it disturbed!
Would it not be the best of checks and of helps,
To regard this also, as the purchase of His Blood,
Especially in that mysterious view of it,
In which the spouse symbolizes the Church[a]?
So again, when children are born, and baptized;
Or when sickness comes, is relieved, and goes;
Or when poverty is met and supported;
We do often "curse," our own "blessings[a]."
Families are not happy, because they are not holy;
They are as unlike as possible to that at Nazareth;
Where all depended on looking on to the Cross.
This is a sad pity, and a great evil;
I earnestly recommend as one way of mending it,
That we should refer all our blessings to their true Cause,

[a] Eph. v. 32; Acts xx. 28.   [a] Mal. ii. 2.

To our Lord, and to His Cross;
Marking all, as our ancestors used to mark them;
For nothing can perish which is under His custody,
The enemy of souls cannot devour what is His,
What He hath purchased;
He cannot take it out of His Hands.
With His Mark, we and ours are safe;
Without it, we are lost.
Whether we bear that Mark on us, or no,
Depends entirely on the lives we lead.

LXI.

Easter Eve.

THE PRICE OF OUR HOPES AFTER DEATH.

"Purchased with His own Blood."—Acts xx. 28.

This is the day of the Burial of Jesus:
It invites us to carry on the thought of Good Friday,
That all good is purchased by His Blood;
And to apply the thought,
To the Intermediate State of body and soul;
Both for ourselves and for our friends.
First as to the body—
Do we shrink from the changed features?
From the cold grave?
From the womb forgetting?
From the worm feeding sweetly?
He has purchased for us this privilege,
That He is with us, to keep us still;
To keep our real bodies safe,
Under all those sad appearances.
And, as a token, He went through the grave Himself,
He went through all but corruption;
He went through it, to prove His sympathy;
He saw no corruption, to warrant our trust in Him.
Let us take the corruption thankfully, as a Penance,
Not fearing to trust ourselves, and our friends, with Him,
In the grave which He has consecrated;

And remembering that this comfort is purchased for us,
As all other comforts are purchased for us,
By His precious Blood.
Next, as to the soul—
Is the thought of separation dreary?
The thought of being unclothed naturally a dismal thought?
Think not only of the future Resurrection,
But also of departing and being "with Christ."
And where was Christ in His intermediate state?
He was in Paradise, where the good thief was with Him.
He was in the regions of the dead;
With Abraham, Isaac, and Jacob,
Who saw His Day and rejoiced;
So the ancient Church taught.
And the benefit which He purchased for those separate souls,
The same He purchased for ours, and for our friends;
If, like them, we shall have rejoiced in Him.
As to the present pain of separation from them,
Let us take that also as a Penance;
Let us try and sit by their graves,
As the holy women sat by our Lord's Grave.
It is a great mercy to be admitted to such Penance;
Too great, but for the Price paid for it;
But when we look to that Price,
Then nothing is too good to be hoped for.
For "whether we live, we live unto the Lord,
"Or whether we die, we die unto the Lord;
"Whether therefore we live or die,
"We are the Lord's."

LXII.

Easter.

The Mystery of Easter.

"O Lord, Thou hast searched me out and known me: Thou knowest my down-sitting and mine uprising."—Ps. cxxxix. 1.

WHAT a wonderful time is this—
This time of Holy Week, and of Easter!
How it brings before us one Mystery after another!
One after another of God's Secrets!
Two days ago, that God should die;
To-day, that a dead Man should raise Himself,
And live for ever.
And then, the astonishing effect of these Mysteries,
By which each is connected with our own well-being,
With that of the weakest and most insignificant of us all.
And with our own doings,
With the most ordinary and natural of them all.
Consider how, every night, when we go to sleep,
We enact the mystery of Good Friday;
And every morning, when we wake up,
We go through the Mystery of Easter Day.
And so our own sleeping and waking become mysteries:
How much more, the Death and Resurrection
Of our Lord and Saviour Jesus Christ,
Of Whom it is said, "No man knoweth the Son,
"But the Father [b]."

---

[b] S. Matt. xi. 27, and S. Luke x. 22.

Observe, in connection with this saying, one special point,
  The mention of the "knowledge" of God, in the text;
    And how truly this Psalm is an Easter Psalm.
      Man may know the history of these Days;
God only knows the manner, and the mystery of them.
      So we know the outside of death, in men;
      But not really what manner of death it was.
      And we know the fact that men will rise again;
      But how they will rise, we can only conjecture.
      So in regard of our own death and resurrection;
        We know nothing as to the manner,
        Humbly therefore, leave yourselves to Him.
          But God knows all,
Behave, therefore, as one who knows at least one thing,
      That he cannot fail, except by his own fault.
      How so to behave, we know enough to help us;
    We know that when we "wake up" from our graves,
          We shall be "present" with God;
      Therefore, when you wake up from your beds,
      Remember to be present with Him, day by day.
As He kept us in the womb, so He will keep us in the grave.
        His Body is the Seed of Christian Resurrection.
          We "eat and drink" of His Flesh and Blood,
            And we " have Eternal Life,
        "And He will raise us up at the last Day[e]."

[e] S. John vi. 54.

LXIII.

THE GLORY OF THE DESPISED NAME.

"Wherefore God also hath highly exalted Him, and hath given Him a Name which is above every name; that at the Name of Jesus every knee should bow, of things in Heaven, and things in earth, and things under the earth; and that every tongue should confess that Jesus Christ is Lord, to the glory of God the Father."
PHIL. ii. 9—11.

As our Lord's doings and sufferings are a pattern for sinners,
 How they should behave towards Almighty God;
So the Father's dealings with Christ are a token and pledge,
 Revealing His dealings with us;
If we also take up our cross, we too may hope for glory.
The passage from humiliation to exaltation, is sure;
 It was a kind of proverb among Christians.
"If we be dead with Him, we shall also live with Him:
"If we suffer, we shall also reign with Him [d],"
It was to be so by the rule of God's government;
 Our Lord Himself set it forth in parables;
" Every one that exalteth himself shall be abased;
" And he that humbleth himself shall be exalted [e]."
 And now it is fulfilled in His own Person.
 Hark, how the note changes to-day!
From the mournfullest to the most joyous strain;
 As in the midnight Services of some Churches.

[d] 2 Tim. ii. 11 : see also Rom. vi. 8.
[e] S. Luke xiv. 7—11, and xviii. 10—14.

The Glory of the Despised Name.

So expressing the change this Easter Morning,
Suddenly and at an instant,
The change from Death to Life,
From Death of a few hours, to Life eternal.
In a few days more, it was a higher "Lifting up [f],"
From earth to Heaven;
From reproach, to the Songs of Angels;
From helplessness, to "all Power in Heaven and Earth [g];"
From "the contradiction of sinners,"
To the Father's Right Hand.
This change is begun now on earth,
Which was to be completed in Heaven.
During those forty days of His risen bodily Presence,
No unbeliever came nigh Him;
He taught and blessed His own people in private;
As now He grants the same privilege to sincere Christians.
He is preparing us to be exalted, even as He is exalted.
The glory of exaltation will be to "see His Face."
The preparation for it is to acknowledge His Name.
What Name? The Name JESUS.
Why that Name, rather than His other Names?
Why do we stand up at the Gospel?
Why do we make the sign of the Cross,
Rather than any other sign?
Why do we care for Bethlehem and Calvary,
More than for other places?
All these are preferred on the same principle.

[f] ὑπερύψωσεν, Phil. ii. 9.   [g] Rev. v. 12, 13.

At that Name, it is the command of the Holy Ghost,
That every knee should bow;
The Church repeats the command;
It binds the Saints and Angels in Heaven;
It binds persons on their trial on earth;
It binds those who are at rest in Paradise;
Perhaps it may include even Dæmons at last[1],
Who were obliged to confess Him when He cast them out;
And who at the last Day will own Him Lord.
By the Name of Jesus He must be honoured,
Whether they will or no,
By Saints and Angels, perfectly in Heaven;
By Souls, unweariedly in Paradise;
By men, sincerely on Earth;
Perforce, by bad men and bad Angels.
We must honour Him with body and soul,
With knee and tongue and heart;
With knee and tongue at the Creed,
And in every confession of our Faith and Love;
With the heart, day and night, continually;
Else we do not honour the Father;
We are as they who have no God.
Is this your way now?
Has it always been so with you?
Are you at least beginning to live to Christ,
With purpose of heart?
Do not venture to Holy Communion,

---

[1] Isa. xlv. 23; Rom. xiv. 11.

Without having asked yourself this question,
And considered it seriously,
"Am I, or am I not, really in earnest?
"Intending to please Christ, and not myself,
"As long as I live in this world?"

LXIV.

THE CHOSEN WITNESSES OF JESUS RISEN.

"Him God raised up the third day, and shewed Him openly; not to all the people, but unto witnesses chosen before of God, even to us who did eat and drink with Him after He rose from the dead."—ACTS x. 40, 41.

IT might have been expected of the Resurrection,
That it would have been very public;
Both for Christ's honour,
Whose Cross and shame were so public;
And for the conversion of the Jews,
To whom the Resurrection was the one appointed Sign.
But in fact it was kept very private;
None of His enemies saw Him;
No indifferent persons saw Him;
Only the witnesses chosen before.
This was according to our Lord's declared dispensation [k].

[k] S. Matt. xi. 25; xiii. 11—17: Ps. xcvii. 11; cxi. 2.

It was for an encouragement to the humble;
For a judgment on the proud;
For a help to those who may be touched.
But all this seems to relate to unbelievers;
How does the privacy of the Resurrection affect us Christians?
Consider: God hath indeed manifested His Son risen;
He hath shewn Him to all His people,
His Son risen from the dead;
But He hath not shewn His Son, as He is risen,
To be All in all to us,
Except to those who "eat and drink with Him[1];"
Or who are preparing themselves,
To eat and drink with Him, worthily.
To them, and in them, God revealeth His Son;
They are His witnesses chosen before;
Chosen since the foundation of the world.
All worthy Communicants are chosen of God;
"All that the Father giveth Me shall come to Me[m]."
But is not this a narrow and formal rule,
To put a man's life upon that One Ordinance?
It is not narrow,
For it presupposes a providential opportunity;
And a *worthy* Communion implies everything.
It is not formal,
For it is the work of the Spirit.
What is so spiritual as the worthily receiving Christ?
What are the conclusions of the whole matter?

[1] S. Luke xxiv. 30, 31, 41—45; S. John xxi. 13, 14.
[m] S. John vi. 37, 39, 44.

There is no really knowing Jesus Risen,
Without knowing Him in the Mystery of "Eating;"
"He that eateth Me, even he shall live by Me[n]."
Where this is done, men know Him,
Though they cannot speak of Him.
Why give up or delay such a Blessing for trifles?

LXV.

Easter Illumination and Reproof.

"*Did not our heart burn within us, while He talked with us by the way, and while He opened to us the Scriptures.*"
S. Luke xxiv. 32.

This verse will express what all good Christians feel,
Not only on special occasions,
Such as sometimes happen in most men's lives,
But in general, when they look back on their past lives,
From their beds of death,
And still more from the other world.
Two things will strike them concerning Jesus:—
His talking with them by the way,
Through His many providential hints;
And His opening to them the Scriptures,
Whereby, as they went on from day to day,
They came to understand their Bibles better.
And surely they will also be ready to take blame to themselves,
To apply to themselves the reproofs of the Lord.

[n] S. John vi. 57.

They will own themselves "fools," ἀνόητοι, inadvertent,
As to His Providence;
And, as to His Word, "slow of heart to believe."
Consider the short histories of the Resurrection;
How they abound with allusions to these causes of reproof.
"Their words seemed to them as idle tales [o]."
"As yet they knew not the Scriptures,
"That He must rise from the dead [p]."
S. Peter "departed" from the sepulchre "wondering [q]."
They "believed not" S. Mary Magdalene [r].
"Neither believed they" the women [s].
The whole history of the walk to Emmaus is a proof of this;
It witnessed to the doubts of the two disciples;
And when they joined the rest, "they believed not for joy [t]."
S. Thomas's unbelief called forth reproof [u].
He "upbraided" all the eleven "with their unbelief [x]."
Seven of them together "knew not that it was Jesus [y]."
And were disinclined to ask Him, "Who art Thou [z]?"
There can be no doubt as to the Apostles themselves,
When they thought it over;
How amazed they were at their own dulness.
And even as to S. Mark and S. Luke,
If they were not eye-witnesses,
The same feeling would in a manner impress them,
Regarding what they had heard from S. Peter and S. Paul.

[o] S. Luke xxiv. 11.
[p] S. John xx. 9.
[q] S. Luke xxiv. 12.
[r] S. Mark xvi. 11.
[s] Ib. 13.
[t] S. Luke xxiv. 41.
[u] S. John xx. 27.
[x] S. Mark xvi. 14.
[y] S. John xxi. 4.
[z] Ib. 12.

If Apostles were thus dull,
How must not we bear with others!
If even to them it was a loss,
How must not we see to ourselves!
What sorrow it will bring to us, by-and-by,
Should this blindness prove true of us, all our lives long,
That we have been eye-witnesses and ministers of the Word,
Of both the written Word, and the Personal Word,
Within the Church,
And yet we have not really known Christ;
That He spake to us by the way,
That He would have made known to us the Scriptures,
But that our hearts did not burn within us,
As He talked with us,
Because we were occupied with other things;
Or because there was in us no reverence,
And no prayer.

LXVI.

THE TOUCH OF FAITH.

"*Be not faithless, but believing.*"—S. JOHN xx. 27.

HERE we see the extension of our Lord's appearance,
At all times, and to all sorts of men,
On the one condition of Faith.
See how it was on the First day of the week;
He ordered it so, on purpose, by His Providence,
That at the first of His two appearances,

One of His Disciples should not be there;
And he, the down-hearted, doubting one.
He also so ordered His first appearance,
That the Disciples did not touch Him then;
An excuse was thus left for S. Thomas's scepticism.
But see how it was on the second occasion:
All the circumstances were the same, except one,
The Doubter was there.
It was on Sion; in the upper Room;
The Saints were there; and Christ was there;
He came saying "Peace;"
He shewed them His Wounds;
He invited the touch;
But there was this difference,
That He also shewed them His knowledge of themselves,
Of the very secrets of their hearts;
And this is what convinced Thomas at last.
So it is with our assemblies;
Believers are there;
Doubters may be there;
Christ is there, known by His Wounds;
He permits us not only to see, but to touch, His Wounds,
By the hand of Faith, through the Sacraments;
And He confirms His Word to us, one by one,
By telling each of us what is in our hearts;
Not altogether, but one by one.
Blessed are we, if so seeing and hearing, we believe;
The more blessed, the sooner we come to Him.
S. Thomas lost a week—can we well afford to do so?

LXVII.

Providential Hindrances to Sin.

' Then the Lord opened the eyes of Balaam, and he saw the Angel of the Lord standing in the way, and his sword drawn in his hand; and he bowed down his head, and fell flat on his face."
Num. xxii. 31.

We walk in the midst of wonders, and we know it not;
   The wonders of Creation;
   The wonders of Providence;
   The wonders of Grace;
    But all of God.
The evil one, if he can, withdraws our eyes,
Lest we should see God, in these wonders.
In old times, he tried to pervert the truth of wonders;
And in other lands, he still tries to do so;
He tries to make men think of wonders,
As if they were his own doing, not God's doing.
In our time, and land, his point is to deny—
To persuade us that they are not wonders at all,
   That they come of themselves;
   Or come by the craft and device of men;
Or by a kind of Fate, called the Laws of Nature.
And so men are led, blindly for the most part;
Even those who should know better, give way to this;
   They yield themselves to the bad ways.
But God, by His Spirit, from time to time, opens their eyes;

And then, all depends on their use of His dispensation.
Balaam was just a case in point;
He was not ignorant like the Heathen,
He knew the true God;
But he was like the unstable Christian;
He had not learned to realize God—
To see His Divine Presence, and His Will, in all things.
He thought he might take liberties;
He thought he might go very near to the edge of sin,
And do what was not, in so many words, forbidden;
And so, when his ass was restive,
He thought it was merely an accident;
And he treated it as an accident;
But we know what it was in reality.
Thus it happens to us, when we are bent on our own way,
Bent on what, in the bottom of our hearts, we know to be wrong,
And we are cheating ourselves,
And behaving as if we could cheat God;
Hindrances occur;
We may fancy them to be accidental;
But let us be sure they are of God.
Such times are times of trial;
It will be of the greatest consequence how we behave.
Let us take heed not to lose our temper,
Not to be angry at the course of things, like Balaam,
When he was violent, and smote the ass;
This is in fact to be angry with God;
Rather let us consider what we should see,
If our eyes like Balaam's were opened;

Let us remember that we should see what Balaam saw,
And so, that we should do as Balaam did, in the letter;
We should literally obey what we know to be God's Will.
Balaam did this in the letter, he offered to go back;
And he said what was to be said [a].
But we must not do as Balaam did, in spirit,
Whose obedience was with reluctance;
Whose hankering was after sin [b];
Lest we should come to Balaam's end;
Lest we be found deliberately conspiring against God.
Contriving what, we know, He most hates.
Happy they who use themselves to watching,
And earnestly take all the Lord's hints.

LXVIII.

THE RESPONSIBILITY OF BELONGING TO GOD.

"*Lo, the people shall dwell alone, and not be numbered among the Nations.*"—NUM. xxiii. 9.

WHAT people? The Children of Israel,
Whom Balaam was viewing from the top of a mountain.
He breaks out into impassioned speech;
And what is it that strikes him?
That Israel was separated from all other people;
Separated, not only by isolation in the wilderness,

[a] Num. xxii. 34, 38.   [b] Num. xxiii. 1, 13, 27.

But, much more, by the wonders of Divine Power,
With which they were encompassed.
Led through the water;
Taught by the Voice;
Living on Manna;
Drinking of the Rock;
Guided by the Pillar of Fire:
Visited from time to time by the Glory:
Supported with miracles of Mercy;
Chastened with miracles of Judgment;
Having a different law from other Nations;
And a law with different sanctions;
With every thing marking them off,
For God's own and special People.
That was the great point in their existence,
To be continually acknowledged in their worship,
And witnessed by their life.
Therefore God's enemies hated them,
And did all they could to crush or to seduce them.
But, worst of all, they wearied of it themselves;
They could not bear the restraint;
They wished to be like the rest of men.
This impatience was the main thing visible,
In all their outbreaks against the Will of God.
In their worship of the golden calf;
In their lusting for flesh;
In their murmuring at the spies;
In their complaint of the length of the way;
In their rebellion in the matter of Korah.

This is a figure of what was to be always;
All this is fulfilled in Christians[e].
We have our Privileges, with persecutions;
The Holy Spirit, the Holy Bible,
Holy Baptism, Holy Communion.
The Church, as a Witness and Guide.
And all these in a supernatural condition,
In which we are all very blessed;
The world, all the while, hating it all.
So also we have our hindrances and trials;
Too likely the sins of our forefathers;
Certainly our own worldly minds;
Our fleshy lust and fretfulness;
Our impatience and rebellion.
All these very dangerous.
The dangers must be encountered;
The blessings may be secured;
But it will never do to trifle with either.
You cannot be as the Heathen, do what you will;
A Christian you are;
And a Christian account you must give.

[e] 1 Cor. x.

LXIX.

THE UNRULY WILL.

"Ye will not come unto Me that ye might have life."
S. JOHN v. 40.

Our Lord had just been referring to the Holy Bible;
His hearers were Jews who professed to believe the Bible;
But they were not only to believe there is such a Book,
And that the Holy Bible is true,
But they were also to read it, and to hear it;
And not only that, but to search it;
As men seek for gold or silver in a mine.
How could they trifle with such a Thing as Eternal Life?
So searching, they would surely find Christ;
They would find Him in Prophecies;
They would find Him in Types;
They would find Him in the view of their natural misery;
In the manifestation of God's gracious purpose;
In all the pictures of themselves, and of Him.
Their not so finding Him was their own fault;
Not the fault of the Book;
Not the fault of their untoward position;
Not the fault of their inward frailty;
But the fault of their own will;
They cared not for "Life,"
For that kind of Life which was promised them;
They disliked the way to that Life.

Is there no fear of something of the same sort now?
There is much sad unbelief;
Yet I trust it is still true of Englishmen generally,
That they believe the Bible,
That they believe it to be the Word of God,
And that therefore they may depend upon it.
They believe that there is a Saviour there preached,
On Whom all must believe.
But they will not really "search" these Scriptures;
The task would take trouble;
The occupation would interfere with other work.
By what little they do know of the Scriptures,
They are aware of the effect of searching further,
That it would interfere with them,
And hinder the things on which they are bent.
For the same reason, they will not mind the Church;
They would be glad indeed to avoid Hell;
But they have no taste for Heaven;
For the sort of Heaven to which they are invited.
So they go on in their self-indulgence,
Yielding to their unruly wills and affections.
But what is to become of them?
We all know — and they know it themselves,
Yet they have not the will to change.
And if they had the will to change,
Of themselves they have not the power.
Then, what is to be done?
They must get help—but from Whom?
From Him Who can and will change them.

Who alone can "order the unruly wills of sinful men;"
Here then is your appointed remedy:
First, wish to have a good will;
Next, pray continually to have a good will;
Then, be with those who will help, not hinder you;
Finally, arm yourself against the next trial,
And, if you can, avoid it.
So doing, sooner or later, you may be sure,
That He will give you a new heart.

LXX.

Rogation Tide.

Failures in Prayer.

"*The effectual fervent prayer of a righteous man availeth much.*"
S. James v. 16.

How is it that the Bible is so full of promises,
The world so full of disappointments?
The Bible abounds with encouragements to Prayer—
"O Thou that hearest prayer, unto Thee shall all flesh come [d]."
"It shall come to pass that before they call I will answer,
"And while they are yet speaking, I will hear [e]."
Our Lord Himself urges to Prayer,
"Ask, and it shall be given you [f]."
"What things soever ye desire, when ye pray,
"Believe that ye receive them, and ye shall have them [g]."
"Every one that asketh receiveth [h]."
"If ye shall ask anything in My Name, I will do it [i]."
"Whatsoever ye shall ask the Father in My Name,
"He will give it you [k]."
Yet who does not seem, somehow, to pray in vain?
The question must strike every one,
But the answer also is quite plain.

---

[d] Ps. lxv. 2. [e] Isa. lxv. 24. [f] S. Matt. vii. 7.
[g] S. Mark xi. 24. [h] S. Luke xi. 10. [i] S. John xiv. 14.
[k] Ib. xvi. 23.

People do not fulfil the conditions,
Our Lord's own conditions of Prayer.
They do not pray as He would have them—
"In My Name [1];"
"Abiding in Me [m];"
"Believing [n];"
"Believing that they receive them [o];"
"Nothing wavering [p];"
"According to His Will [q];"
"Keeping His Commandments [r]."
So men go on, for a shorter or for a longer time;
But the hour will come, when they will wish it otherwise.
And then, if they are still in this world,
They will cry, "Pray for me."
Were it not better to be wise in time,
And before it is too late, to seek a good Intercessor,
Even "Jesus Christ, the Righteous,
"Who ever liveth to make Intercession for us."

[1] S. John xiv. 14.　　[m] Ib. xv. 7.　　[n] S. Matt. xxi. 22.
[o] S. Mark xi. 24.　　[p] S. James i. 6.　　[q] 1 S. John v. 14.
[r] Ib. iii. 22.

LXXI.

THE PREVAILING INTERCESSOR.

"The effectual fervent prayer of a righteous man availeth much."
S. JAMES v. 16.

WHY does the Church speak of Prayer at this time?
Because of the fruits of the Earth.
Sowing-time is pretty well over;
We have committed the seed in faith to God;
At such a time, how can we help praying?
Therefore the old Perambulations were made,
And the Litanies were said.
There are times when those Prayers are specially needed;
As when we have famine, pestilence, or war.
Such things, be sure, are in God's Providential Hand,
Although He orders them by great laws.
Even as He is Almighty, and yet there is free-will in man.
Therefore pray: for great is the power of Prayer;
But of whose Prayer? And how offered?
The "fervent prayer—of a Righteous Man"—
Plainly this points to our Lord, the Perfect Man.
But as it is in other things, so it is here;
If our prayer is to be united to His Intercession,
It must, in our measure, have the conditions of His.
Therefore, if you would avert any evil,

Or if you would do any good to any one,
You must try at least to imitate Him in His ways.
First, to be good, or "righteous," after His likeness,
Then, to be "fervent" in prayer, as He.

LXXII.

THE TYPIFIED INTERCESSION FULFILLED.

" The effectual fervent prayer of a righteous man availeth much."
S. JAMES v. 16.

THERE is a second reason for speaking of Prayer,
For meditating upon it especially at this time.
According to the course of the Church's Creed.
Now is the time, when, to the Eternal Father,
Human Prayers began solemnly to be offered up,
By the Incarnate Son in Heaven,
By Him Who is declared to be Just, by His Resurrection,
And to be our Intercessor, by His Ascension.
Before that time indeed, He heard Prayer ;
But that solemn Service had not yet begun,
Which He is now perpetually celebrating—
As God, receiving Prayer,
As Man, presenting it to His Father,
With sweet incense,
Even with the virtue of His own most precious Blood.

This could not be done until Ascension Day,
And therefore Ascension Day is so precious;
It is the greatest event that we know of,
In the history of Prayer.
Then three great Types began to be specially fulfilled;
First, the Day of Atonement,
On which only the Priest entered the Holy Place;
And he only once a year, and with blood,
And that, the blood of a Victim slain without;
All the holy things were to be sprinkled with blood,
And among them the Altar of Incense, that is, of Prayer.
Secondly, the Intercession of Moses,
Going up the second time into the Mount,
Interceding for the fallen people,
And obtaining their pardon.
So now, "If any man sin,
"We have an Advocate with the Father,
"Jesus Christ the Righteous."
Thirdly, the Intercession of Elijah,
Praying against, and for, rain.
So now, our Intercessor obtains all things from the Father,
Both Judgments and Mercies;
For all such as shall be heirs of Salvation.
All this Christ does, as our Head;
And He invites and teaches us to take part with Him.
How great and blessed a thing is Prayer!
God forgive us for dealing so unworthily with it!

LXXIII.

WAITING IN PRAYER.

"The effectual fervent prayer of a righteous man availeth much."
S. JAMES v. 16.

THESE are times of waiting for a blessing;
And they must be times of prayer,
If we are to have faith at all.
So we have yet a third reason for these Rogation Days,
That we are looking on for the Holy Ghost,
Who shall improve our Easter Blessings.
Our Lord goes away on purpose to send Him;
Therefore His going is ever joy to His best friends.
The Coming of the Holy Ghost is all good gifts in One;
For He is the Gift of God.
But we are yet, and shall be yet, in our frailty;
What if we were to abuse this Gift of God?
We know something of the consequence;
We have too much reason to fear it,
Considering our abuse of so many good gifts.
And take notice of what is really true,
Concerning our Whitsundays;
They are not mere Commemorations,
They are Repetitions of the Blessing.
The Holy Ghost really comes down then,
As if He had never come before.
He comes to you, as if He had never come before,
To the Apostles, or to any one.

Yes, it is Pentecost all the year to you,
If you do not forfeit it.
How much reason, now therefore, more than ever, to pray,
As well as ever we *can* pray,
And to get the best Intercession we can,
Even the Intercession of Jesus!
Pray to Him to teach you how to pray.
The Church, this week, has put words in your mouth,
Say them to-night with all your heart,
And see if you are not the more ready for to-morrow,
And for Whitsunday.

LXXIV. 𝔄scension 𝔇ay.

ASCENSION JOY.

"Looking unto Jesus, the Author and Finisher of our Faith; Who, for the joy that was set before Him, endured the Cross, despising the shame, and is set down at the Right Hand of the Throne of God."—HEB. xii. 2.

THIS is eminently the Feast of Congratulation,
And of mutual joy.
First, of joy on earth:
The Apostles "returned to Jerusalem with great joy[s]."
Our Lord had so directed them;
He had made their joy a sign of love[t].
And we may understand His purpose,
By observing the feeling of good Christians,
When any one, dearly loved, is taken from them.
Their feeling is of joy and grief mingled together[u].
So when the Apostles came to believe, and to know,
What His Absence meant for them,
That it was more needful for them than His earthly Presence,
By reason of the Presence of the Comforter;
By reason of His Intercession; and of His Kingdom;
Their joy would keep growing more and more,
Till it should be time for Him to return, and to perfect it.

---

[s] S. Luke xxiv. 52.   [t] S. John xiv. 28.
[u] κλαυσίγελως, see Phil. i. 23, 24.

Would it might be thus for us, every year more and more,
Instead of being as it is now, when Ascension Day comes!
Next, it is a Feast of joy in Heaven:
The Angels congratulate our Lord, and each other[x];
Our Lord exhibits His own joy;
Not joy in His own deliverance;
Not joy in His own triumph or exaltation;
But joy "over one sinner that repenteth[y];"
Joy in the blessing won for the meek and humble[z];
Joy in the children of Adam, brought to Him one by one,
Becoming, and continuing, members of Him[a].
By-and-by, when He shall give joy to each one separately,
Saying, "Enter thou into the joy of thy Lord,"
Where they shall, each one, have his joy,
Have it fulfilled in themselves,
Then His delight will be made perfect in them.
This is "the joy set before Him,"
For the sake of which "He endured the Cross,
"Despising the shame."
His meat and drink was the joy
To do His Father's will, "and to finish His work[b]."
What was that Will?
That "of all which the Father hath given Him,
"He should lose nothing."
"That every one which seeth the Son and believeth on Him,
"May have everlasting Life[c]."

[x] Ps. xxiv.: Rev. v. 6—13; xii. 10—12. [y] S. Luke xv. 7, 10.
[z] Ib. x. 21. [a] S. John xv. 11. [b] Ib. iv. 34.
[c] Ib. vi. 39, 40.

To Him, the Eternal Son, we are to look;
Towards Him we are to work;
As His joy is to have us with Him [d],
So our joy must be to be with Him.
It is said by some to be a mean and base motive,
To work for the hope of Heaven, or the fear of Hell;
That we ought to be good for the sake of being so;
Not for reward, nor yet for dread.
We must not listen to such opinions;
For no man knows better than Christ knew;
And He distinctly taught people,
To desire Heaven, and to fear Hell.
His Parables of the Tares, and of the Net, shew this.
And more—He was an Example in His own Person;
He worked for a certain "joy set before Him;"
The joy of perfecting our salvation.
Therefore the joy we seek, is the joy of being with Him;
And the ill we dread, is the ill of losing Him for ever.
If we love Him, we must care for these two things;
And if we seek Him, though at first but for fear,
He will teach us both to seek, and to find Him, for love.
But while we wish one another joy,
Of the infinite blessings of this Day,
Conferred on us by our Lord's outstretched Hand;
Let us not forget that there was a word spoken on it,
Which has a stern meaning for us all—
" He shall so come,

[d] Prov. viii. 31.

"In like manner as ye have seen Him go."
With His Wounds in Hands and Feet, and Side,
To condemn the hardened;
To pardon and to heal the penitent.
May we labour continually there to be, in heart and mind,
Where He is, in Person;
That when He comes again,
We may be found worthy to be with Him for ever,
In body and soul.

LXXV.

THE POWER OF THE ASCENDED CHRIST.

"And Jesus came and spake unto them, saying, All power is given unto Me in Heaven and in earth; go ye therefore, and teach all nations, baptizing them in the Name of the Father, and of the Son, and of the Holy Ghost."—S. MATT. xxviii. 18, 19.

THIS is our Lord's Coronation Day;
In these words, spoken apart to His chosen,
He instructs them how to keep it.
We know what the ordinary feeling would be,
When men were told, of their Head and Patron,
That he was going to be made a great King.
We see what it was, when, after His miracle of feeding them,
The people sought to make Jesus a King by force [e].
As then He withdrew from them into a mountain,
So now He leads His Disciples to a mountain of Galilee;

[e] S. John vi. 15.

He would keep His Glory a secret;
His Transfiguration, His Resurrection, His Ascension,
All were accomplished in private;
While His Humiliation and Crucifixion were public.
The very word concerning His Glory,
That it was "given unto Him¹"
Betokens the humiliation which had gone before.
We may well believe concerning the Apostles,
That they had got above mere earthly ambition;
Their question, "Wilt Thou at this time restore the Kingdom?"
Probably implied no more than their patriotism.
Still we may imagine them to have been very sanguine,
As young people are when they read the History;
And that, knowing that "all power was given" to their Lord,
They might think—"God will do His own work,
"We have only to attend on Him and to rejoice."
For, although He had often warned them,
And foretold what they would have to go through,
They never could quite take it in.
But see what follows:
"All power is given unto Me—go ye *therefore* and teach."
The mightier He is,
The more must you exert yourselves;
The more believe yourself to be nothing,
And yet work, as if all depended upon you.
This is spoken to us, and not only to them;
And to each of us, one by one;

¹ ἐδόθη.

To all of us in our common calling as Christians,
And to each of us in his own calling.
There have been, and are, persons who take no pains,
Who think it useless to take any pains,
Because God is over all.
But here, as in all the Bible,
God tells us that He works by means.
In our earthly concerns we must be hopeful,
We must say, "All power is with Jesus,
"In the hands of our best Friend;
"We will do our best, and trust Him with the result."
There must be no despondency, no laziness, no fretting.
Still less may we despair of spiritual grace;
"All Power is given" to Him Who is our Life.
You *can* subdue this lust; you *can* form this good habit,
If you *will* to subdue the one and to form the other.
Be not disheartened, if things do not go forward,
Either in your own little world, or in the Church.
Remember the words of the great Preacher of the Ascension,
"Thou hast put all things in subjection under His Feet;"
"He left nothing that is not put under Him.
"But now we see not yet all things put under Him,
"But we see Jesus, Who was made a little lower than the Angels,
"For the suffering of death,
"Crowned with glory and honour [g]."
Have patience, and you will find it so, in your own case.

[g] Heb. ii. 8, 9.

LXXVI.

THE KINGDOM AND THE PRIESTHOOD.

"*He hath made us Kings and Priests unto God and His Father.*"—REV. i. 6.

IN what condition was the person who wrote these words?
A forlorn old man,
In poverty, banishment, and solitude;
He was one of those thought to be in a manner "mad [h],"
For this sort of saying,
And yet nothing can be more true than his words.
They describe the very Blessing provided for us to-day,
By the miracle of the Ascension of our Lord.
For the Man Christ Jesus was declared to be a King [i],
By His glorious Ascension.
The Angels are described as worshipping Him [k];
The Devils as fearing Him, and giving up their prey [l].
All manner of good gifts are showered down by Him,
Showered down upon His servants on earth [m].
The people acknowledge Him with tributes [n];
And His Kingdom is to grow more and more,
Until He is owned by all as King [o].
Observe also that He was made a Priest,
"After the order of Melchisedec," who was also a King,

[h] Acts xxvi. 24.   [i] Ps. cx. 1, 2.   [k] Ib. xxiv.   [l] Ib. lxviii. 18.
[m] Eph. iv. 8—12.   [n] Ps. cx. 3.   [o] Ib. cx. 1, 5, 6, and Phil. ii.; compare Isa. xlv. 23.

To offer the "Bread and Wine,"
Which are His own Body and Blood p;
To offer them continually—"a Priest for ever q;"
Not to suffer again r;
But now to appear in the Presence of God for us;
To be our Advocate with the Father in Heaven,
As He was our Propitiation for sin, on the Cross.
And so He "hath made us Kings and Priests;"
He hath made us so many Melchisedecs.
He had made the Jews to be Priests and Kings s;
And yet they had a separate Priesthood,
With which it was deadly sin to interfere;
As shewn by the fate of Korah, of Uzzah, of Uzziah.
And they had divinely-chosen Kings,
Whom they were bound to obey;
Who were "the Lord's Anointed."
S. Peter says the same thing of us;
That we are "a chosen generation, a royal Priesthood."
S. John bears witness of the Kingdom—
"To him that overcometh will I grant to sit with Me
"In my throne."
S. Peter testifies of the Priesthood—
"Ye are built up, a spiritual house, an holy Priesthood."
And yet we too have our separate Kings,
The "higher powers" to whom we must be subject t;
And we too have our ordained Priesthood,
To whom our Lord spake the words

p Heb. ix. 11, 12. q Ib. vii. 24. r Ib. ix. 25, 26.
s Exod. xix. 6. t Rom. xiii. 1.

"Do this in Remembrance of Me:"
"Whose sins ye remit, they are remitted,
"And whose sins ye retain, they are retained."
In spiritual things they are our Judges;
"As My Father hath sent Me, even so send I you."
This grant of the Priesthood and the Kingdom,
Took place, as it should seem, at this Season,
When the Lord restored the Kingdom to Israel;
Though not as the Apostles expected.
In His own Person it took place, on His Ascension.
In His Church it took place, derivatively, on Whitsunday.
Each member of the Body of Christ is partaker with the Head.
Each is, in his measure, what the Head is.
If then we are Kings, where is our justice?
Where is our generosity, and our disregard of trifles?
If we are Priests, where is our purity?
Where is our zeal for souls?
Where is our devotion, and sacrifice?
Shewn in devout attendance at Holy Communion.
If we are both Kings and Priests,
Where is our seriousness?

LXXVII.

Praise the Key-note of the Ascension.

"*And they worshipped Him, and returned to Jerusalem with great joy; and were continually in the Temple, praising and blessing God. Amen.*"—S. Luke xxiv. 52, 53.

What did the Apostles after our Lord was gone?
They worshipped Him;
Their whole souls were swallowed up with one thought,
With the thought of Him in Glory.
And they did the one thing that He bid them do;
They "returned to Jerusalem."
And they were full of "joy;"
Though they had lost Him out of sight.
And "they were continually in the Temple;"
Their whole life was a solemn Service,
And that, a Service of Thanksgiving;
They were "praising and blessing God."
We should take them for our examples,
First, we should try to realize His Glory,
To forget ourselves in it, and in Him;
And yet not be disheartened if we fail;
We should still offer Him all homage.
Next, we should do the thing which He would have done,
Not minding disappointment,
If His Promise should keep us waiting.
Ten days might seem to the Apostles a long time.

Then, we should try to rejoice in Him always;
Even when He withdraws Himself,
However sadly, either as to earthly or spiritual favours.
And our whole life should be dedicated to Him;
The world should be to us a Temple, and we the Priests.
This need not interfere with the set Services of the Sanctuary,
Which are, in fact, the necessary expression of it.
The Apostles abode in the Upper Room for prayer,
Yet they are here "continually,"—punctually, "in the Temple ⁿ."
And our Service should be all praise and blessing;
Thanksgiving is not against, but for contrition.
He who thus spends his short ten days here,
Will be ready, when our Lord comes again,
To pass from the earthly to the Heavenly Jerusalem,
There continually to dwell,
"Praising and blessing God."

LXXVIII.

MOSES A TYPE OF CHRIST.

"I will raise them up a Prophet from among their brethren, like unto thee."—DEUT. xviii. 18.

MOSES is that Prophet whom our Lord was to be like;
Like as a Deliverer;
Like as a Legislator;
Like as a Worker of wonders;

ⁿ *Formicæ Dei.*

But like especially as a Mediator.
To this last our attention is drawn by the Prophecy,
Which promises to "raise up a Prophet like" Moses[x];
Which again refers us to Moses' Ascension,
And warrants our regarding it as a type,
A type of the Ascension of Christ.
I call it the "ascension" of Moses,
Though Moses did not go out of this world,
But only to the top of the mountain;
Yet from the mountain, he went to God.
He went as the type and representative of God's people;
So Christ, our Head, went to prepare a place for us;
Our Head, so near to us,
That in Him we are said to have ascended[y].
Moses went as the leader and deliverer of Israel,
To complete what had been begun at the Red Sea;
So our Lord went, as our Leader and Deliverer,
To do what was needful for applying Redemption to us.
Moses made two ascensions into the Mount,
So prefiguring the twofold work of our Ascended Lord.
First, to receive a Law for us;
Secondly, to plead for us when we have broken that Law.
Yet not so as that we might venture to disregard it in future;
For that Law was re-enacted.
Moses' first going up was to receive the Law written,
Which had before been spoken.
So our Lord's Ascension was to receive Gifts for men,

---

[x] Compare Deut. xviii. 15—19, and Exod. xx. 19.   [y] Eph. ii. 6.

To send the Spirit,
Who should write the same laws in men's hearts,
Which before, He Himself had spoken in their ears;
First on Sinai,
And afterwards on His own Mount.
Moses went not up without sacrifice[1];
Nor our Lord without the Blood of the New Testament.
Moses went not up without Joshua[a];
Our Lord went up in the power of His own Name JESUS,
That Name which is above every name.
Moses had been preparing for his ascent long before,
Ever since he had seen the burning Bush in Horeb;
Our Lord had been preparing for His Ascension,
From the very moment of His Incarnation;
Preparing in the Power of the Holy Ghost,
Of which His Baptism was a remembrance;
He was "He that baptizeth with the Holy Ghost."
Moses prepared himself by a forty days' fast,
So did our Lord prepare for His new Law,
The Law of Pentecost,
By forty days' fasting in the wilderness.
But the Children of Israel rebelled,
At the very time of its delivery;
They sadly broke that Law.
And Christians, alas! too sadly resemble Israel,
And break continually the Gospel Law.
Therefore, as Moses went up a second time,

[1] Exod. xxiv. 5—8.   [a] Ib. 13.

To plead for the people who had sinned;
So our Lord is at His Father's Right Hand,
Not only as our Lawgiver, but as our Mediator.
As Moses devoted himself,
So our Lord pleads His own Passion.
As Moses took up the earthly tables
To receive the writing of God,
So our Lord, as the Head, takes up the hearts of His people,
The hearts which form His mystical Body,
And He submits them to the action of His Spirit.
As Moses obtained pardon for Israel,
So also, and much more, our Lord obtains pardon for us.
But as Moses took back the Law,
And re-enacted it, under stronger obligations,
So the new Law is more stringent than the old,
And the Law of Christ more spiritual than the Law of Moses.
As Moses brought down a system of government and worship,
Of rites and civil rules;
So our Lord sent down a system of Government and Worship,
Of Sacraments, and Discipline.
As Moses might not see God's Face,
So the very Gospel is but a type of the Beatific Vision.
As Moses stayed with God in the Mount,
Interceding during all those forty days;
So our Lord pleads with the Father,
During the whole time of our trial here.
Consider what thoughts the Israelites must have had,
When Moses came among them, the second time;
How near they must have felt to God.

Do you try to keep up the same thoughts;
Remember S. Paul's appeal [b],
"Ye are not come unto the Mount that might be touched,
"And that burned with fire,
"But ye are come unto Mount Zion
"And unto the City of the living God,
"The heavenly Jerusalem."
And try to live accordingly, as in a supernatural state.
This is no counsel of perfection;
It is plain common sense, for every one desiring to be saved.
"Wherefore, receiving a Kingdom which cannot be moved,
"Let us have—or hold fast—grace,
"Whereby we may serve God acceptably
"With reverence and godly fear."

LXXIX.

ELIJAH A TYPE OF CHRIST.

"And Elijah went up by a whirlwind into Heaven."
2 KINGS ii. 11.

AFTER Moses, Elijah is the great type of our Ascending Lord;
Pointed out by the Service of the Day.
Indeed he is the more exact type of the two;
For Elijah went really out of the world,
And has continued out of sight;
In going up he provided for himself a successor;

[b] Heb. xii. 18—28.

As our Lord provided the Church.
Elijah had designated that successor beforehand,
By casting his mantle upon him;
As our Lord had chosen His Apostles,
And breathed on them.
Elijah took care to have Elisha with him,
At the time when he was to go up;
So our Lord went up while His Apostles were looking on.
Elijah dropped his mantle,
As a token of the Gift of Whitsunday.
As Elisha did the miracles of Elijah,
So the Church did, and does, miracles of grace.
As Elisha smote the waters,
So the Church baptizes with water.
As Elisha healed the waters,
So the Church ministers sanctification.
As Elisha punished the children,
So the Church uses excommunication.
Observe how the people who were with Elisha feared him.
So ought we to fear before the Lord God,
Who is always with His Church.
We should never forget how near us He is,
Nor how surely He will come again.
Observe how this is marked by what is said of Elijah's coming [c],
Whether that is to be in person, or in spirit only.
How He will then try us Christians,
Especially in the matter of reverence to parents,

[c] Mal. iv. 5, 6.

Both our natural and spiritual parents;
"He shall turn the hearts of the children to their fathers."
How He will try the fathers, in the matter of loving fidelity,
Turning "the hearts of the fathers to the children."
As He proved Israel on Mount Sinai,
So now, at Ascension, and Whitsuntide,
God cometh to prove us,
"That His fear may be before our faces, that we sin not."
May He of His mercy grant us to stand the proof!

LXXX. Whitsunday.

THANKSGIVING THE GRACE OF WHITSUNDAY.

"*Thanks be to God for His unspeakable Gift.*"—2 COR. ix. 15.

"A JOYFUL and pleasant thing it is to be thankful."
Who does not feel this, if there is any good in him?
In us, as fallen, it is the last relic of Eden;
In us, as renewed, it is the sure foretaste of Heaven;
For what is Heaven but the perfection of thankfulness?
If we may assign certain graces to certain days,
As Love seems to suit Christmas;
As Contrition seems to suit Good Friday;
As Faith seems to suit Easter;
As Hope seems to suit Ascension Tide;
So Thankfulness would seem to belong to this Feast.
For it is the conclusion of all the Feasts;
It is the crowning Feast;
It is that which brings our Saviour home to each one;
It is that which makes Him your Saviour and mine.
And this is accomplished by a New Gift;
A Gift over and above all that had gone before;
A Gift altogether free, as indeed all His Gifts are;
And a Gift so vast as to be "unspeakable."
For it is "The Gift of God [d]."

[d] S. John iv. 10.

It is the "Free Gift[e];"
It is the "Gift by Grace[e];"
It is the "Gift of Righteousness[f]," the "Gift of Grace[g],"
"According to the measure of the Gift of Christ[h];"
It is the Heavenly Gift;
And all these mean one thing;
They mean the Holy Spirit,
Who enters personally into the man,
To make him what God would have him to be.
And therefore this Gift is all gifts in One;
It is God giving Himself.
Not only God *with*, but God *in* us,
To be our Life[i], as joining us to Christ[j];
Not only entirely doing away original sin,
But also doing away the result of many transgressions[k],
Conveying to us a Kingdom, not only of Life, but of Glory[l].
It is a Gift sealing our pardon;
It is a Gift continuing our justification;
And it is a Gift quite free, as you know;
Free in Holy Baptism;
Free in Confirmation;
Free in Holy Communion;
Free in Prayer;
Free in every "holy desire, good counsel, and just work."
If you have any good thought in you this Sunday,
You know from Whom it comes;

---

[e] Rom. v. 15, and see Acts viii. 20.   [f] Rom. v. 17.   [g] Eph. iii. 7.
[h] Ib. iv. 7.   [i] See Nicene Creed.   [j] S. John iv. 14, and vii. 38, 39.
[k] Rom. v. 18.   [l] Ib. 17.

How fearful to slight or to forfeit it [m]!
If you have none such to-day,
This must be from hitherto slighting it.
But God forbid it should be so;
We will hope better, and rather exhort you,
See that you answer to the grace you have received.
And that, especially, by Thanksgiving.
"I will give thanks unto Thee, O Lord, with my whole heart,"
How sweet to make these words your own!
Thanks, not only with your lips, but in your lives.
Now then make a thank-offering.
Behold our Lord comes to you,
In the persons of His destitute brethren;
For they are all His brethren and His redeemed.
You who communicate, make your Blessing larger,
By denying yourselves a little.
You who do not communicate, yet offer,
That you may entitle yourselves to prayers,
Which in time may help you to be "worthy."
Perhaps if the rich man had helped Lazarus,
When Lazarus lay at his gate,
Lazarus' prayer might have helped him,
Helped him to repent, and to escape Hell-fire.

[m] Heb. vi. 4—6.

LXXXI.

THE PENITENT'S WHITSUNTIDE.

"Create in me a clean heart, O God; and renew a right spirit within me. Cast me not away from Thy Presence, and take not Thy Holy Spirit from me. Restore unto me the joy of Thy salvation, and uphold me with Thy free Spirit. Then shall I teach transgressors Thy ways; and sinners shall be converted unto Thee."—Ps. li. 10—13.

This Psalm is our Psalm;
We are as David;
Our sins as his sins;
Our hope as his hope;
Would that our repentance were like his!
But now observe especially these verses of David's prayer;
"Make me a clean heart, O God,
"And renew a right spirit within me.
"O cast me not away from Thy Presence,
"And take not Thy Holy Spirit from me."
See, he asks not only for pardon, but for conversion;
He asks not even for comfort,
For he would have his "sin ever before him;"
But he wants God's Presence,
He wants His good Spirit restored to him.
May one not say,
Here is a penitent sinner keeping his Whitsuntide?
Good Friday and Atonement,

Easter Day and Justification,
Ascension Day and Intercession,
All these are not enough;
No, nor Whitsunday and Sanctification,
Unless he have a reasonable hope of himself sharing in it.
He wants to be free from the power of sin,
As well as from the punishment of sin;
From the power of his own sins.
He wants the Holy Ghost;
The ever-present Friend,
Comforter,
Confirmer,
Teacher,
Guide,
Intercessor;
He wants Him for others also.
He wants the sense of God's Presence and Sympathy;
He wants the sense of liberty, and of usefulness;
He wants joy and grief at once;
He wants, in one word, Contrition.
Is this your mind?
Is this your personal feeling toward God the Holy Ghost?
Then come to Communion;
Come to Christ;
Come to His Spirit;
Offer yourself to Him once for all;
Repeat your offering night and morning;
Do nothing all day towards recalling or unsaying it.
Who knows but you too may be allowed,

Even as David was, to do some good work?
To build Sion,
At least in your own heart and home.

LXXXII.

THE WHITSUNTIDE SELF-EXAMINATION.

"Teach me to do Thy will; for Thou art my God: Thy Spirit is good; lead me into the land of uprightness."—PS. cxliii. 10.

THE Creed is a great Hymn of Praise for Gospel Mercies.
When we have got so far as to our Lord's Return,
To "judge the quick and dead,"
What is so natural as our longing to know more,
How we may shew our gratitude,
How we may ensure our blessing?
Then comes the Whitsun Truth—
"I believe in the Holy Ghost."
His Spirit is good;
He will teach; He will guide.
I will suppose you addressing yourself,
As Christians are bound to do,
To the Whitsuntide Self-examination:
Begin with this serious thought—
To trifle with your work is trifling with the Holy Ghost.
It is *a* sin against Him;
Who knows but it may be—or lead to—*the* sin,
The sin against the Holy Ghost?

Pray earnestly to be kept from this sin of trifling;
That you may not go to your work lightly,
And as it were a "dissembler."
Pray to the Son, to intercede with the Father,
To pour upon you the Spirit.
Pray to the Father to give you the Spirit;
Pray to the Spirit to come and help you;
Pray to Him to help you to pray;
Without His help, we know not what to ask;
Pray to Him to shew you your faults;
Especially your besetting fault;
And to shew you how to mend every fault;
"Teach me to do the thing that pleaseth Thee."
Pray to Him to let you know the worst,
The amount of your sin;
Not to let bad habits deceive you;
Nor the customs of others;
Nor the whispers of the Devil.
If you are in deadly sin,
Pray to Him to let you know it, and to give you courage,
Courage to confess it, where you ought;
And to break from it—at any cost;
And not to come to Holy Communion,
Till you have a reasonable hope about it,
That it is in a way to be subdued.
Pray to Him to help you on;
To give you so much of comfort and reasonable Hope,
As is necessary to please God,
And to do your duty in a plain and even way.

Expect no perfection, in yourself or in any other.
Never be content without sincerity,
Which cannot be, if you allow yourself in wilful sin.
All your way along,
Commit yourself to your Blessed Redeemer,
And have no hope but in His Cross.

LXXXIII.

THE HOLY GHOST OUR ADVOCATE.

"We know not what we should pray for as we ought; but the Spirit itself maketh Intercession for us with groanings that cannot be uttered."—ROM. viii. 26.

IT is now the time of giving—the time of Gifts—
The time of the Great Gift, Which is all in One.
All God's Gifts are promised to prayer;
The Gift of the Holy Ghost is especially promised.
"We know not what we should pray for as we ought,"
But the Holy Ghost is our Paraclete;
He is our Advocate—not as our Lord is our Advocate,
But, as coming into our hearts,
Teaching us what to ask for, and how to ask;
He puts the right meaning into our words;
He sheds the love of God in our hearts;
Causing unspeakable, silent yearnings,
Dove-like moanings of the heart;

By these He is our Advocate,
Pleading in us and for us.
And He is our Comforter,
Warning, cheering, quickening our hearts.
As Parents teach their children, and pray with them,
Or ever the children can understand,
So it is here with the Holy Ghost.
And not in prayer only,
But in holy Hymns, and in all good behaviour.
Simple Christians are, by Him, far better than they know;
He will "ordain peace for us,"
For He also hath "wrought all our works in us[n]."

[n] Isa. xxvi. 12.

LXXXIV.
Trinity Sunday.

THE GRACE OF INCORPORATION IN THE BLESSED TRINITY.

"*The grace of the Lord Jesus Christ, and the love of God, and the communion of the Holy Ghost, be with you all.*"—2 COR. xiii. 14.

THE Holy Trinity thought on us from the beginning;
Taking counsel about the making of us;
And thought of each one of us, in our own beginnings;
Causing us to be baptized into the Holy Name—
The Name of the Father, and of the Son,
And of the Holy Ghost.
Consider what that saying imports;
For we seal ourselves with that Holy Name,
When we recite the Creed;
Especially when we are confirmed;
And when we join in Holy Communion;
We confess It in litanies, and in psalms;
It is pronounced in the end of sermons;
We receive benediction from It;
Benediction in dismissals;
Benediction on great occasions, like marriage;
Benediction in the Visitation of the sick;
Benediction at the end of each Communion;
And a special benediction at the last.
What a pity to make It but a form!
O commit yourself to this Holy Name,

Take the most Holy Trinity with you,
When you go out of church.
See what the Threefold Grace is;
How can you spare It?
First, It is the free favour or grace of Christ,
Making Himself one of us;
Dying for us; interceding for us;
Not for the whole Church only, but for each one of us.
Next, It is the Father loving us, as in Christ.
Lastly, It is the Holy Ghost communicating Himself to us;
And, through Himself, communicating the whole Trinity.
We partake of a Divine Nature.
This Gift is for all, and it is for evermore.
O who can think enough of it?
Who can love, fear, trust Him enough?
If God the Son is so free in His grace towards you,
Why are you so selfish?
If God the Father loves you so dearly,
Why are you so apt to trust the world?
If you have the Fellowship of God the Holy Ghost,
Are you not afraid to drive Him away from you?

LXXXV.

THE CHRISTIAN SACRIFICE. I.

"*This do in Remembrance of Me.*"—S. LUKE xxii. 19.

Consider one point not much thought of,
A very serious matter, which concerns every Communicant,
For it tends to "lift up" the heart;
We must pray about it.
Consider the word "Remembrance,"
As applied to the Holy Communion,
By Holy Scripture, and by the Church.
"This do in Remembrance of Me [o];"
"This do ye, as oft as ye drink it, in Remembrance of Me [p];"
"The continual Remembrance of the Sacrifice
"Of the Death of Christ [q];"
"With a thankful Remembrance of His Death [q];"
"In Remembrance of His meritorious Cross and Passion [r];"
"In Remembrance of the Sacrifice of His Death [r];"
"To the end that we should always remember [r];"
"For a continual Remembrance of His Death [r];"
"A perpetual Memory of That His precious Death [s];"
"In Remembrance of His Death and Passion [s];"
"Eat this in Remembrance [t]:
"Drink this in Remembrance [t]."
Who then are to be reminded?

[o] 1 Cor. xi. 24. [p] Ib. 25. [q] Catechism. [r] Exhortations in the Office for Holy Communion. [s] Prayer of Consecration. [t] Words of Administration.

We are publickly to remind ourselves,
And to remind one another,
And to profess before all men,
That Christ crucified is our only Hope.
S. Paul says, "ye do shew the Lord's Death [u];"
Meaning, "ye do constantly proclaim or preach It [x]."
This we all understand;
It is well we should think much of it.
Were it no more than this, how great a favour!
Think of our value for keepsakes and remembrances,
Recalling the dead or the absent.
How hard-hearted then to slight the Remembrance of our Lord;
How bad for others, who cannot think us to be in earnest!
To abuse a memory is the worst of all slights.
But the word conveys more than reminding ourselves;
The first and proper meaning of it is reminding God.
We are to "Do This" for the Reminding of God—
For that Reminding which specially belongs to Him.
It is as if He had said, "Do your part,
"In that Memorial of Me, which is made by Me."
For "Memorial," "Remembrance," "Memory,"
These are the three words;
And each of them is a sacrificial word.
S. Paul refers to the "sacrifices" "every year,"
In which is made a "remembrance of sins [y];"
And the Greek word for remembrance is not otherwise applied
Elsewhere in Holy Scripture.

---

[u] 1 Cor. xi. 26.   [x] See the same word in Acts iv. 2; xvii. 3.
[y] Heb. x. 3.

The Prophet Hosea says that Israel " shall be as the olive tree,"
"And the scent," or memorial "thereof
"As the wine of Lebanon ª."
It is not that Almighty God can forget:
But it is that He wills to be put in mind.
See how the word " Remember" is applied to Him,
In Holy Scripture;
How " He remembered His Covenant with Abraham ᵇ,"
When He would shew tenderness to Israel;
How Moses appealed to Him, against His own indignation,
When Israel fell away into idolatry—
" Remember Abraham, Isaac, and Israel Thy Servants ᶜ,"
Reminding Him of His own Mercies.
How the word of Intercession for the Priest is " Remember,"
"The Lord Remember all thy offerings ᵈ;"
How the word of intercession for the King is " Remember,"
" Lord Remember David ᵉ;"
How the King pleading for himself cries " Remember,"
" Remember me, O Lord, according to Thy favour ᶠ;"
How the Word of God Himself is " Remember,"
" I will remember their sin no more ᵍ."
How Zacharias blesses God for "remembering,"
" To perform the Mercy promised to our forefathers,
" And to remember His Holy Covenant ʰ."

ª Hos. xiv. 8; in our Eng. Ver. the verse is 7; but ver. 8, which is in the original MS., has been retained, as an incidental token that the Author was using a Hebrew Bible.
ᵇ Exod. ii. 24.   ᶜ Ib. xxxii. 13.   ᵈ Ps. xx. 3.   ᵉ Ib. cxxxii. 1.
ᶠ Ib. cvi. 4.   ᵍ Jer. xxxi. 34.   ʰ S. Luke i. 72.

How the word in our Litany is "Remember,"
"Remember not, Lord, our offences."
Prayer is a mystery: yet we must pray;
There is no more difficulty in asking God to "Remember,"
Than in praying to God to hear.
In fact we continually make Christ's Memorial in words,
In every Litany, and at the end of every Collect.
The peculiarity of Holy Communion is in the Act;
We make our Memorial There, in Deed;
"Do This in Remembrance of Me."
Therefore the Holy Communion is a Memorial Sacrifice.
In the Breaking, and in the Blessing,
In the Distributing, and in the Receiving,
The Holy Communion is a Sacrificial Act,
Reminding the Father of the Death of Christ the Son.
But, if it be a Sacrifice, there must be a Priest, and an Offering.
Who is the Priest?
What is the Offering?
These are questions full of awe;
And the answers are full of awe and of blessing.
They will be considered next.
Meantime consider this one thing:
If you wilfully neglect this Memorial Sacrifice,
You lose, it may be feared, God's Blessing,
His Blessing on any of your prayers.
How much more if you profane It!
You may be turning your best Food into deadly poison.
It would be like taking His Name in vain,
And so destroying the virtue of It.

LXXXVI.

The Christian Sacrifice. II.

"*This do in Remembrance of Me.*"—S. LUKE xxii. 19.

We have seen what the very words of Institution teach;
That they mark one great end of what our Lord was then doing,
To appoint a standing Memorial Sacrifice,
For bringing His Death and Passion
To His Father's Remembrance.
He directed the Sacrifices of the Old Testament
In the same way;
And in the New Testament, His command was explicit,
That when we pray to the Father,
We should always use our Lord's own Name [1].
But He never gave this command until just before the end,
As He was about to order the first Eucharist.
Consider the result:—if the Eucharist be a Sacrifice,
There must be a Priest, and an Offering;
As in the cases of Abel, and of Noah,
Of Melchizedech and of Aaron,
So it must be in this.
But we know what the offering was in each of those cases;
What is it here?
Let the Church Catechism answer:
First, it is "Bread and Wine,
"Which the Lord hath commanded to be received;"
And next, it is "the Body and Blood of Christ,

[1] S. John xiv. 14.

"Which are verily and indeed taken and received."
The two together make That Which is offered;
For there must be the two together,
As the account of a Sacrament shews;
The one being simply the veil and conveyance of the other;
That which is truly and efficaciously offered is One;
The Body and Blood of Christ, that is, Christ Himself;
For this is part of the doctrine of the Incarnation—
That God so joined our human nature to Himself,
As to make it for ever part of His Divine Person in Christ;
The Body and Blood offered is His Person offered;
His Person is inseparable from His Human Nature;
And by It He heals and saves us [k].
He called Himself the Son of Man;
His Body was His Temple;
In that Body He did all He did;
And when He gave up that Body on the Cross,
It was God purchasing His Church with His own Blood [l].
There is then but One Sacrifice,
The Sacrifice of "the Man Christ Jesus."
But It is offered up in two ways:
First as a Sacrifice of Blood;
A Sacrifice of Suffering, *once*, on the Cross [m];
And only in this way as a proper Expiation.
And secondly by the Commemorative Sacrifice;
By the Representation of the Sacrifice of Blood,
In Heaven before the Father,

---

[k] Gen. iii.; Ps. xl.; Isa. vii.; S. Luke i. and ii. [l] Acts xx. 28; compare S. John vi. 52, 57. [m] Ἅπαξ.

Night and day without ceasing.
Which is the perpetual[a] Memorial in Heaven;
And here on earth, under the forms of Bread and Wine.
On earth, the Memorial is, in fact, occasional,
But in theory, It is continual.
Both in earth and in Heaven the Offering is the Same;
Only the Manner, and the Presence, of It are different.
In a bloody manner, It is the Sacrifice of the Cross;
And, *virtually*, That is present to us now.
In an unbloody manner, the Sacrifice is commemorative,
With a natural and corporal Presence of our Lord in Heaven.
On earth also, Christ is present,
In an unbloody and commemorative manner;
But with a supernatural and peculiar Presence.
In all these, the Sacrifice is the Same;
And also the Priest is the Same;
For there is but One Priest;
As there is but One Baptism, and One Baptizer;
As there was but one High Priest among the Jews.
Christ offered Himself on the Cross;
He offers Himself continually in Heaven;
He offers Himself, by our hands, in the Eucharist on earth.
And still it is Christ only;
He is our Aaron,
Both in ordinary Sacrifice, and on the Day of Expiation.
He is also our Melchisedech,
According to the Psalm on Christmas Day,
" Thou art a Priest for ever after the order of Melchisedech."

[a] εἰς τὸ διηνεκές.

And in both qualities, He feeds as well as offers:
He is a Feast as well as a Victim.
This is His Real Presence.
When we are preparing for the Holy Communion,
We are preparing to be with Him.
When we are there, at the Holy Communion,
We are with Him.
When we have been there, after Holy Communion,
We have been with Him.
How should we prepare, but in cleansing?
How should we be there, but in adoring?
How should we think of It afterwards,
But in making much of Him?

LXXXVII.

THE CHRISTIAN SACRIFICE. III.

"*This do in Remembrance of Me.*"—S. LUKE xxii. 19.

HAVING tried to see what the Christian Sacrifice is,
And by Whom, as Priest, It is offered,
Literally and principally;
Consider seriously now what Holy Scripture teaches,
As to the part of each one of the Christian people,
In this great Sacrifice.
Our part in It is a great, and high, and holy Mystery;
Second only to the actual Participation of Christ,
In unspeakable blessing and graciousness.

And what is our part?
In a subordinate, but very real sense, we are all Priests;
We are all allowed to share in the Priest's office;
With Christ, and under Christ.
Not, of course, in the atoning Sacrifice of the Cross;
That "Wine press He trod alone;"
It could be no otherwise;
For "beside Him there is no Saviour[o];"
No Blood could be meritorious like His.
But in the Commemoration of that Sacrifice, we may share;
And He has graciously invited us to do so;
Not only by inviting us to pray in His Name,
And by calling upon us
To "do This in Remembrance of" Him,
But also by expressly calling us "Priests."
Consider His Words to this purpose—
"Who hath made us Kings and Priests unto God[p]."
"And hast made us unto our God Kings and Priests[q]."
"They shall be Priests of God and of Christ[r]."
"A spiritual house, a holy Priesthood[s]."
"A chosen generation, a royal Priesthood[t]."
"A peculiar treasure ... a Kingdom of Priests[u]."
"Ye shall be named the Priests of the Lord[x];
"Men shall call you the Ministers of our God[x]."
And that which relates to the Clergy especially,
"I will also take of them for Priests and for Levites[y]."

[o] Isa. xliii. 11; xlv. 21; Hos. xiv. 4; Acts iv. 10, 12; 1 Tim. ii. 4, 5.
[p] Rev. i. 5, 6.   [q] Ib. v. 8—10.   [r] Ib. xx. 6.   [s] 1 S. Pet. ii. 5.
[t] Ib. 9.   [u] Exod. xix. 5, 6.   [x] Isa. lxi. 6.   [y] Ib. lxvi. 21.

Now Holy Communion is that especial Ordinance
By Which we claim this Priesthood[a];
If we do not communicate in that Ordinance,
We reject and forfeit our Priesthood;
If we communicate unworthily,
We profane our Priesthood.
How dare men trifle with such a gift?
What would you expect a Priest to be,
As compared with a Layman?
As a Christian you are bound to be such,
As compared with a Heathen.
But if you earnestly seek to be such,
Then you may draw near with faith;
You may join in offering the Holy Sacrifice "to your comfort,"
For all the great ends of Its appointment.
Consider what those ends are:
Adoration;
As the Burnt-offering made by fire[a].
Thanksgiving;
As the Thank-offering, to be eaten when offered[b].
Propitiation, or Application of Pardon;
As the Sin-offering, for Ruler, Priest, and People[c].
Impetration of grace,
As the Peace-offering of a loving free-will[d].
Offer yourself wholly;

---

[a] Heb. xiii. 15; S. Matt. v. 23, 24. Compare the free-will offerings of the people, Exod. and Numbers, and of David, 1 Chron. xxix.; Ps. xx. 3.   [a] Lev. i. 9.   [b] Ib. vii. 15.   [c] Ib. iv. N.B. for an individual lay person, see ver. 27.   [d] Ib. vii. 16.

Offer yourself with a thankful heart;
Offer yourself with a lowly heart;
Offer yourself with a loving heart;
Rehearse this daily in your prayers;
And you will be able to realize it, in Holy Communion.

LXXXVIII.

Failure in God impossible.

"Ye know in all your hearts, and in all your souls, that not one thing hath failed of all the good things which the Lord your God spake concerning you: all are come to pass unto you, and not one thing hath failed thereof."—JOSH. xxiii. 14.

God is Truth, and in Him is no Falsehood at all;
He can neither deceive nor be deceived;
"God is not a man that He should lie;"
His promises can never fail;
When they have seemed to fail,
There was some condition which was not kept.
The conquest of Canaan is a remarkable instance of this.
See the Israelites, a tired unwarlike people,
Contending against the Anakims and their cities.
How sorely the contest tried their faith!
But Jordan shall sooner flow upward,
The walls of Jericho sink down at a shout,
The sun and moon be stayed in their course,
Than the Land not be won.

But you will say, "the Land was not entirely won,
"A good many—as the Philistines—were left,
"Who were thorns in Israel's side for hundreds of years."
This was partly to prove the People of God,
And partly to exercise them in war;
God bringing good out of evil.
But, in itself, the fact was an evil;
It was an exception to the promises;
Yet it was fully accounted for;
It was owing to the disobedience of God's People,
Who refused to keep the conditions which God had set.
Well, so also it has been, and is still,
With the Promises of Christ.
Here, Trinity Sunday has left us with "The unspeakable Gift,"
And with all our Lord's Bounty towards us,
Spoken of by the Prophets, and by Himself;
Sealed by His Miracles,
By His Death, and Resurrection,
By His Ascension, and by the Gift of Pentecost.
But when we read such sayings as these :—
"Thy people shall be all righteous [e];"
"They shall not learn war any more [f];"
"All shall know Me from the least to the greatest [g];"
"He shall guide you into all Truth [h];"
"There shall be One Lord, and His Name One [i];"
What are we to think?
The conversion of the world is like the conquest of Canaan;

[e] Isa. lx. 21.   [f] Ib. ii. 4.   [g] Jer. xxxi. 34.
[h] S. John xvi. 13.   [i] Zech. xiv. 9.

It has seemed, in a manner, to fulfil these sayings;
But how does it look now?
If they are not fulfilled, it is through our wickedness;
We have so far forfeited the Blessing, as the Jews did.
For first, those Promises did not supersede our free-will,
Any more than God's other doings.
And, secondly, *the conditions were express,*
Both to the Jews and us.
To the Jews, as set forth in Deuteronomy;
To us, as signified in our Lord's Prophecies,
Who had foretold the falling away.
Therefore the seeming failure is no offence to Faith.
You do not surely, then, doubt the Promises of the Bible;
" Ye know in all your hearts, and in all your souls,
" That not one thing hath failed :"
That when you have not made it void yourselves,
" All good things are come to pass,
" Which the Lord your God spake concerning you."

LXXXIX.

The Tokens of having been with Jesus.

"They took knowledge of them, that they had been with Jesus."
Acts iv. 13.

How many must have been struck by this saying,
  As with a sort of holy envy!
   See what it teaches:
After our Lord was risen from the dead,
The world was more than ever divided into two classes,
  Into those who had been with Him,
  And those who had not been with Him.
His Appearances were "not to all the people,"
"But unto Witnesses chosen before of God [k]."
   So it is still:
The world is still Christian and Infidel;
Only the line between them is obscured here,
On account of all having "been with Jesus" to some extent;
At least in Holy Baptism, and in outward calling.
Still the question must and will be asked,
  What token have you to shew?
It is asked now: it will be asked at the last Day.
How are men and Angels to "take knowledge" of you,
  That you have "been with Jesus?"
The first answer is plain—by your open profession.

[k] Acts x. 41.

Of this at least, you may think there can be no doubt.
But consider what it includes:—
Regular attendance on Christ's Ordinances;
The Jews would not have recognized the Apostles,
As having "been with Jesus,"
Had they been only now and then, with Him.
Distinct confession of Him on proper occasions;
What was S. Peter's denial of Him?
He denied having been "with Him."
And what if you are ashamed of Him?
Reverence for His Name;
Swearing is a sort of denial of Jesus,
And so is ribaldry, and the mockery of things holy.
These all make void His Name;
They tell every one that you have not Faith;
They are the language of those who can never be "with Jesus."
When did Peter curse and swear?
It was when he denied having "been with Jesus."
Reverence for His Day;
If you profane His Day,
You tell all the world that you care not for Christ;
For it is Christ's—"the Lord's Day."
These things therefore are necessary,
In order to the true confession of Christ,
The confession of Him before Angels and men.
But more than these is required;
Else Judas might be said to have "been with Jesus;"
As indeed he was with Him, and very near Him,
Only he was not with Him profitably.

The Tokens of having been with Jesus.

What are the signs of having been "with Jesus" profitably?
The seeking Him *early;*
The *running* after Him;
The discoursing quietly and confidentially about Him;
The haunting of places, and ways, and persons, dear to Him—
And which, therefore, put you in mind of Him:
As the Upper Room, and the Sea of Galilee.
Above all, the *exactly obeying* Him.
Do you really try to do all this?
If you want more signs of having "been with Jesus,"
You may find them in the Acts of the Apostles.
They are such as these:—
Loving one another;
Feeding His Lambs;
Caring for the poor;
Continuing in Prayer;
Rejoicing in the Cross;
All these are "as ointment poured out,"
They are His fragrance, filling the whole House.
There are other tokens of having "been with Jesus,"
Of having been with Him after His Resurrection;
As the following of His Example when risen.
Do you always meet love with love?
As He met S. Mary Magdalene.
Do you forgive those who have done you wrong?
As He forgave S. Peter.
Do you take opportunities of edifying others?
As He did, on the way to Emmaus.
Do you provide for the time to come?

As He provided the Bread of Life, in the Upper Room.
Do you consider the weak?
As He considered the weak faith of S. Thomas.
Do you care for those entrusted to your charge?
As He took care for His sheep, in His Commission to S. Peter.
Do you continue the friend of loved ones out of sight?
As He promised to be to His Disciples, on His Ascension.
Finally are you dead to sin? as He to death.
And there are contrary signs,
Signs of not having "been with Jesus,"
In the true sense of being with Him.
As the Pharisees — sealing the stone;
As the Soldiers—watching the Grave;
As the Chief Priests and Sadducees—persecuting Him;
As the common people—merely recognizing Him;
As Ananias and Sapphira—trying to deceive.
By these marks shall all men and Angels know hereafter,
Whether you have been really "with Jesus" or no.
It will be a fearful Hour; and we shall all come to it:
God grant we may be prepared for it.

XC.

Christ's Love, our Coldness.

"My delights were with the sons of men."—Prov. viii. 31.

These are the words of Wisdom;
For the beginning of them is, "Doth not wisdom cry [1]?"
If you look a little further, you will find Who Wisdom is;
The Everlasting Son of God,
"Set up from everlasting, from the beginning,
"Or ever the earth was [m]."
How were His delights with us?
Not only in that He took our nature [n],
But that He would share with us in all but sin [o].
When He shewed Himself to the world,
It was not as a Solitary;
But as one "rejoicing in the habitable parts of the earth [p]."
Compare this with what He said of Himself,
"The Son of Man is come eating and drinking [q]."
When He was to go away, and return to the Father,
He still promised His own Personal Presence;
His people were to be nearer to Him by the Comforter [r].
How does He fulfil this Promise?
In the most direct way—as to His Human Nature—
He fulfils it in Holy Communion [s].

---

[1] Prov. viii. 1.   [m] Ib. 23.   [n] Ps. xl.; Heb. ii. 16.
[o] Ib. 17, and iv. 15.   [p] Prov. viii. 31.   [q] S. Luke vii. 34.
[r] S. John xiv. 18; xvi. 7.   [s] Ib. vi. 57; 1 Cor. x. 16.

If His delight is to be with us,
What a pity that to be with Him should be our weariness!
Apply this thought to the common feeling about religion;
Especially to the common feeling about Holy Communion;
How men shrink from that Ordinance!
How then have they the love of God in them?
When we love a person truly, we rejoice to be with him;
We welcome any approaches of his;
We make the most of them.
How sad is the application to ourselves of these tests!
We seem rather to delight in having Him away from us.
One thing is certain,
We shall have our own choice in the matter;
If the choice be wrong now, it may be mended;
But it will soon be confirmed and irrevocable.

XCI.

OUR LORD'S WILL FOR HIS SERVANTS.

"Father, I will that they also whom Thou hast given Me, be with Me where I am; that they may behold My glory, which Thou hast given Me; for Thou lovedst Me before the foundation of the world."—S. JOHN xvii. 24.

WHAT can be of so much consequence to the creature,
As to know the Creator's Will concerning him?
That Creator being also, Father, King, and Master,
The Almighty, the All-wise God.

Who would not wait in deep suspense before Him,
Standing as before the Judgment Seat,
And holding his breath for what is coming?
Well, here, by the Eternal Son, that Will is declared.
It is declared in respect of all the Baptized,
Of all whom the Father has "given to" Christ;
Of all who, by God's Providence, are made Christians;
Of all who are taught of God, as His Children,
And heirs of His Kingdom.
His Will is, that all these should be saved.
And what is it "to be saved?"
It is not only to be kept from evils, bodily and spiritual;
From being with devils;
But to be saved is to be with Christ,
With our best Friend, and only Saviour;
With Him Who loved us so dearly.
We know that He is always with us;
Yea, that He is the Omnipresent God;
And by His Spirit, that He is not only *with* us but *in* us;
By special love delighting to be with us.
We know also what He does for us by His Sacraments;
We know it as matter of faith and hope.
But to be actually happy, *we* must be with Him.
Consider how plainly in Holy Scripture this is taught:
We shall rejoice to be with "them that are asleep[t];"
How much more to be with Him,
Who is All in all, both to them, and to us,

[t] See 1 Thess. iv. 15—17.

And to be with Him for ever!
"If any man serve Me, let him follow Me,
"And where I am, there shall also My servant be;"
"If any man serve Me, him will My Father honour [u]."
At first His servant serves Him, perhaps, from fear, or custom,
But in order to serve Christ, he must follow Him;
And so, after a little while, His servant will get to love Him;
It will be impossible not to love Him;
And this love will be the servant's greatest reward.
"Where I am there shall My servant be."
"If I go and prepare a place for you,
"I will come again, and receive you unto Myself;
"That where I am, there ye may be also [x]."
He prepares a Place for His servants;
He sends His Spirit to prepare them for that Place;
He comes again to receive them.
"What more could have been done to His Vineyard,
"That He has not done in it?"
Lastly, His servants do not merely see His Face with joy,
But they behold His Glory,
"The Glory which He had with the Father."
And He will honour them,
"And they shall sit with Him on His Throne."

[u] See S. John xii. 26.　　　[x] Ib. xiv. 3.

XCII.

Obedience better than Sacrifice.

"I spake not unto your Fathers, nor commanded them in the day that I brought them out of the land of Egypt, concerning burnt-offerings or sacrifices: But this one thing commanded I them, saying, Obey My voice."—Jer. vii. 22, 23.

In what sense is this to be understood,
Seeing the Law speaks so much of burnt-offerings and sacrifices?
Surely the difference is one of comparison;
As where a thing is denied because it is nothing in comparison.
Consider such examples as these,
"Your murmurings are not against us, but against the Lord [y]."
"They have not rejected thee; but they have rejected Me [z]."
"Neither in this Mountain, nor yet at Jerusalem,
"Ye shall worship the Father [a]."
"It is the Spirit that quickeneth,
"The flesh profiteth nothing [b]."
So also David—"Thou desirest not Sacrifice [c]."
Isaiah—"To what purpose is the multitude of your Sacrifices [d]?"
Samuel—"Hath the Lord delight in burnt-offerings [e]?"
Solomon—"To do justice .. is more acceptable than sacrifice [f]."
Micah—"Shall I come before the Lord with burnt-offerings [g]?"

---

[y] Exod. xvi. 8.   [z] 1 Sam. viii. 7.   [a] S. John iv. 21.   [b] Ib. vi. 63.
[c] Ps. li. 16.   [d] Isaiah i. 11.   [e] 1 Sam. xv. 22.   [f] Prov. xxi. 3.
[g] Micah vi. 6.

All these are examples of God's estimate of Sacrifice,
In *comparison* with justice, judgment, and obedience.
The same is pointed at, in the beginning of the Law,
At Marah, when "to do that which is right" is insisted upon[h];
And at Sinai—"if ye will obey My Voice indeed[i];"
The Law of Sacrifice came afterwards.
So we Christians are to understand the like distinction;
Great, and blessed, and necessary as our Sacraments are,
A thousand times more so than the Sacrifices of the Jews,
They are worse than nothing,
If they are received in unbelief or disobedience.
And this is what is greatly to be feared.
Think of the Vow in Holy Baptism;
Think of the Gift in Holy Baptism;
And see how the one is broken, and the other forfeited.
Yet men are not afraid, nor rend their garments.
The same is true of Confirmation;
One generation hands on the devil's tradition to another.
And most of all, is it true of Holy Communion;
Where one shall pass on to another vain deceits,
Saying, "O you have only violated such or such a Command,
"You need not be afraid;"
And yet it is "Love" in a certain sense that is violated,
The first and great Commandment is violated;
For "walking in Love" is set against uncleanness[k],
Against that which is "not to be named" among us,
And again, when one will deliberately tempt another,

[h] Exod. xv. 26.   [i] Ib. xix. 5.   [k] Eph. v. 2, 3.

Saying, "If you want a favour from your betters,
"Go and be instructed, and receive the Holy Communion;"
And such profanity is not thought anything shocking.
So when the plainest words of our Lord are brought to mind,
His words are treated as words of course;
And men go away, and break them without scruple.
The Day of Rest becomes the day for the devil's work;
And the Day of Holiness becomes the day of impurity.
Alas! men will find out the unwelcome truth one day,
That the words of our Lord are indeed words " of course;"
That is, words to be spoken " of course" to such as they;
"Depart from Me, ye that work iniquity;"
And they will be forced then to obey.
Even as there are other, most blessed words,
Which will be spoken " of course" to many humble souls,
Who now hardly dare to think of them;
Even to all faithful and simple ones,
Who really make it their rule to obey their Saviour.
You scorn such humble souls now;
How will you then wish to be like them!
And how will parents then wish for their children,
That they had made them obedient;
Not obedient upon poor worldly motives,
Which will never save any soul;
But obedient because they are a Trust,
A precious Trust from Christ, for this very purpose.
Are there not many houses in most Parishes,
The heads of which may well tremble for their account,
What they shall answer when the question shall be asked—

Asked of them, by the Great Shepherd Himself,
"Where is the Flock that I gave thee,
"Thy beautiful Flock?"

XCIII.
NATIONAL CALAMITIES.

"All the people sat in the street of the House of God, trembling because of this matter, and for the great rain."—EZRA x. 9.

THERE are times when the weather preaches:
Compare what took place in the time of Samuel,
When God sent thunder and rain in Harvest-time,
"And all the people entreated Samuel,
"Pray for thy servants unto the Lord."
Observe the part of Samuel, and of Moses,
How they were patterns of prevailing intercession.
The history in Ezra gives another instance,
How God's judgments help people to a better mind;
But this case is not so much out of the ordinary course.
The purpose here was to correct the people for bad marriages.
The rebuke in Samuel's time was for wanting to have a King.
Are we not sometimes under a like sign?
Is not our peril great?
Are not our sins great also?
For though the promises made to us individually,
Are not so much of the life that now is;

Yet, to us, nationally, they must relate to this life.
And the Nation's sins are made up of the sins of each one.
Look inward then;
Look not to other men's sins, but to your own;
Ask yourself, "What have I done,
"To draw down this plague on the land,
" Or that visitation on my country?"
Each one will have his own sins to think of;
But, in a general way, one answer is plain for all;
And it is contained in one word—Unbelief.
We want to be as the Heathen,
That we may take Heathen liberties.
Men want to do wrong, and yet to be comfortable;
And so they put up with a low standard,
A low standard of faith, and of duty;
And they are angry if any surpass it.
So it is in Church-going; so it is in Communion;
So it is in scrupulous reverence;
So it is in honesty, in good temper, in contentedness, in truth.
And for a like reason, men would escape from the Faith;
They are glad to be rid of the Doctrine of Christ;
They are vexed at the consequences of belief—
At finding themselves so very near to our God.
Therefore they are, in good measure, unbelievers;
They will not own God's Love to themselves,
How good He is to them;
Because such a confession makes one thing needful,—
They must be good to Him.
This has been your fault, perhaps, and mine:

What if it be the common fault?
The fault of the whole Country?
Then you may well suppose the result,
That it must draw down some visitation from God.
How sad to think of such chastisements and of their cause!
But the remedy is plain:
Each one indulging himself in wrong ways was the mischief.
Each one correcting himself must be the cure.
So it was, or might have been, in Ezra's time;
So it may be, now again, if you will.

XCIV.
THE LONG-SUFFERING OF GOD.

"*The Long-suffering of our Lord is Salvation.*"—2 S PET. iii. 15.

THE Long-suffering of God may be considered as two-fold.
As shewn to the whole world, or the whole Church;
And as shewn personally to ourselves.
Let us now think of this last.
Think how long Christ has borne with us;
So many years, since we were baptized,
Have we made our vow in heart?
So long, since we learned the Lord's Prayer,
Have we yet learned to say it devoutly?
So long since we first came to Church,
Have we learned how to behave there,

So long since we were confirmed,
Have we come to Holy Communion?
So long since we first communicated,
Have we done so worthily?
And yet He bears with us.
How many Advents, how many Christmases will this year make?
How many warnings have we had individually?
Consider the admonitions of friends;
Can you remember those given you when a child,
Words and deeds, of which you knew not the meaning then,
But have come to know now?
You slighted them then, but they are doing you good now.
Consider the calls of Conscience,
To do this, or to leave that undone;
Especially if tempted to a great step in any deadly sin.
Consider sudden deaths, or accidents to others;
Hair-breadth escapes of your own.
Consider great falls of others;
Falls into the very kind of sin to which you are given;
Falls after warnings received.
Consider temptations taken out of the way;
Things happening which hindered your sinning.
Consider good examples presented to you,
Examples in books, or in reality.
We may use these warnings; or we may despise them.
But whether we use them, or despise them,
They are alike instances of God's Long-suffering.
O let us use them to our Salvation!

XCV.

THE SERVICE OF GOOD-WILL.

"With good-will doing service, as to the Lord, and not to men."
EPH. vi. 7.

THIS is the duty of servants towards their masters:
But you are not, any of you, so simple as to confine it to them;
To restrict it to those slaves to whom S. Paul first wrote it.
No: it expresses a great principle,
A principle running through all life, even the lowest,
To do things for love;
And the higher the love, the higher the service.
But now see the perverseness of men!
We are tempted just to invert this principle;
And to make Divine Service drudgery.
We are tempted to do so in matters of charity;
In nursing and waiting upon the sick, and such like;
And the temptation here is so far stronger,
As things are more out of sight.
We read of this kind of temper in Scripture;
As when the People of God said of His Service,
"Behold what a weariness is it!"
"What profit is it that we have kept His Ordinances?"
But see the fearful sentence upon this temper of service,
God refuses their offering:
"Should I accept this of your hand? saith the Lord[1]."

[1] See Mal. i. 10, 13, and iii. 14.

Such too was the temper of the Children of Israel,
  When they loathed the Manna in the wilderness.
    See which way it tends in Balaam, and Gehazi;
      See it in Demas, and in the Church of Laodicea;
        See it even in those Disciples of our Lord,
Who "went back, and walked no more with Him;"
See it at this day, in persons who serve God outwardly,
  But only when they can get something by it.
    See it in those who serve Him grudgingly,
      Who are always counting the cost;
    Who shew this temper by taking no pains,
No pains to serve Him regularly, and as perfectly as they can.
  See it in those who turn away from Church Services,
      When outward charms are wanting;
        When there is no music,
      Or when the music is harsh, and so on.
        But what is the cure for this temper?
          Good-will is the cure;
    When it comes natural to men to serve God,
          Because they love Him so well;
  When they cannot take their thoughts off from God,
        Because they reverence Him so much;
      When there is one great thought pressing upon them,
          "I am with Him, and He with me,"
And when this thought swallows up all other thoughts.
        You cannot come to this at once;
      You must come to it by constant Prayer;
    You must come to it also by dutiful Obedience.
        Consider how God is watching you all the time,

That He may have something to set down in your favour.
He is not like an earthly King, though ever so bountiful,
Who cannot know all the loyalty of his servants.
When you thus use yourself to think of God,
And of His loving remembrance of you,
It will be hard indeed for you not to love Him a little.
Then your service will begin to be of "Good-will,"
A practice of perfect freedom,
A preparation for Heaven.
Remember Joshua's choice of a Service for life,
"As for me, and my house, we will serve the Lord."
Think what it will be in that Day,
So to look back with humility and confidence,
To recollect the hours which we have spent here,
In God's Service of "Good-will."
God grant it to us.   Amen.

XCVI.

The Field of our Hidden Treasure.

"Where your treasure is, there will your heart be also."
S. Luke xii. 34.

Our treasure is Christ;
But Christ is in Heaven;
Therefore our hearts should be in Heaven.
And by the help of the Holy Spirit, they may be There.

Now see what Means He has given you,
To teach you this in a wonderful way,
And to exercise you in the practice of it.
Consider the Holy Communion:
How There is the Field of your hidden Treasure.
You have no need to buy this Field;
Christ has freely given It to you.
As surely as you were baptized and live in Christ's Church,
So surely He gives Himself to you in Holy Communion.
He gives Himself as your Sacrifice, and your Priest.
For there is His Altar,
Whereon He is offered for you.
There is His Table,
Whereon He is your spiritual Meat and Drink.
There is His Throne,
Whereon He sitteth as our King,
To be prayed to; to be thanked;
To receive all our homage.
And all this is by the power of the Holy Ghost,
Who both prepares the Sacrifice for you, and you for It.
Your Treasure therefore is doubtless on the Altar;
Is your heart there?
Is it there before coming to the Altar?
Is it there in the Service of the Altar?
Is it there after the Service of the Altar?
Are you always preparing, dressing yourself for Him?
Getting ready to appear before the Beloved?
Marking what He likes and dislikes,
And ordering yourself accordingly?

Are you vexing yourself for your unreadiness?
And accepting punishment for your neglect?
And for your wilfulness in so great a matter?
Then draw near with faith and penitence;
Come with your mind raised towards your God;
Come as if you had been invited,
To look and to listen at Heaven's Gate.
The Spirit is your Helper,
Who will also be your Comforter;
He may not comfort you in the way of joyous hope,
Yet He will do what, for most, is probably better,
He will help you in the way of humble loving faith.

XCVII.

The Woman of Sarepta: her Anticipation of Judgment.

"Art thou come unto me to call my sin to remembrance, and to slay my son?"—1 Kings xvii. 18.

Consider the story of the Woman of Sarepta,
How it implies more than the remembrance of her sins;
Not only that some grievous judgment from God would follow, .
But that this judgment would find her out;
And would strike her in the tenderest part.
And this was, with her, no special Revelation;
It was a part of true, natural Religion.
True natural Religion teaches one thing plainly,

That God and sin never did, and never can agree.
How could we wish it otherwise?
To do so were to wish that there were no God.
Holy Scripture is very plain on this point;
While, at the same time, it speaks plainly of Redemption.
Pass on to your own experience, and see how this is.
God provides for us all;
For some with more, for others with less, visible abundance.
We trifle with our Blessings;
And we imagine that it will be all the same by-and-by.
For a time, life's current closes, as it were, over our sin;
And it seems to make no difference.
Too probably this encourages the repetition of sin;
And so, sins become deadly and habitual.
By-and-by, the decree goes forth;
The evil of our hearts and lives is revealed;
It bursts out suddenly upon us;
We wake,—and find ourselves on the edge of the pit;
And then we see too plainly our danger;
What an inch there is betwixt us and Death!
What shall we do in such a case?
For Christ's sake, do not despair,
Though you will be greatly tempted to do so.
Do not listen to the false comfort of the world;
Be not deceived by the error of Antinomian teachers;
Submit yourself wholly to God;
Expect your punishment with patience;
Let it take what form it may please Him to give it.
Pray to have this submission real;

Pray to have it united to the Sufferings of Christ.
See how this frame of mind will last you through life;
How it will support you in the hour of death;
Who knows how it may be in the Day of Judgment!
And so, at last, the Mystery may be realized,
The Mystery of sinful souls entering into union with God,
And, in Him, becoming pure in Eternity.
God the while, though all-knowing, ceasing to remember,
Nay, forgetting, the sins of those who truly repent.
The corrupt united with the Holy,
And all rejoicing in His immediate Presence.

XCVIII.

THE PHARISEE AND THE PUBLICAN.

"*Two men went up into the Temple to pray, the one a Pharisee, and the other a Publican.*"—S. LUKE xviii. 10.

THIS is called a Parable;
But for aught we can tell to the contrary,
It may have been a true history.
So may have been other histories in the Gospel,
Specially by S. Luke.
The history of the rich fool; or of Dives and Lazarus;
Or of the unjust Judge;
Or of the good Samaritan;
Or of the Prodigal Son.

What if it be true of the events of life generally,
That they are all meant to be Parables,
If only we would so take them?
It is an awe-inspiring thing to think of.
In this case, at any rate, there can be no question;
We are told plainly who are concerned;
Those who "trust in themselves that they are righteous,"
And who, thus trusting in themselves, "despise others."
Who, among us, is quite free from this?
Only consider men's ordinary talk—
How they speak of themselves, and how they speak of others.
You may think it a trifle,
But here our Lord tells you plainly about this fault,
That it will spoil your prayers.
Common sense would shew how certain this is;
That if you indulge a temper of judging,
Comparing yourself with others, as you go about the world,
You cannot expect it to leave you when you pray;
And Christ confirms this verdict of common sense.
Mark the particulars:
The Pharisee and the Publican both go into the Temple;
So far they are alike; and both are right;
For the Temple is God's House,
And they could not be right if they forsook It.
But there are some even who do forsake God's House,
Who yet bring on themselves the curse of the Pharisee;
Who may be heard boasting of themselves,
Boasting that they are no "Hypocrites," no "Formalists."
However in the Parable both were in the Temple,

And both behaved outwardly well, as far as we are told.
If no eye but of their fellow-men had been on them,
Both might have gone home "justified;"
Both, that is, might have been well thought of.
And if they thus acted day by day,
Both might live and die in great favour,
With a high character for devotion;
And this record of them might be set alike on both their tombs.
Until the last Day, therefore, nothing is certain;
There can be no positive knowledge about men's prayers,
In what manner they have been praying.
We can only hope about them humbly;
And the better a man's life, the more hope.
Even the words men use are no sure sign;
For mark how it was in this case;
God judged the two men by the thoughts of their hearts.
Thoughts are, to Him, words.
Both men seem to have prayed silently;
At least the Pharisee prayed "πρὸς ἑαυτὸν [m],"
And one can hardly fancy putting such thoughts into words,
And accounting them prayer;
But one can very well imagine the use of the best of words,
Even the "God be merciful to me a sinner,"
Which have been adopted by the Church,
To the Publican's honour,
The Pharisee's thoughts being, all the while, indulged.
It is not said that his boasts were untrue;
Nor even that his censure on the other was unjust;

[m] "With himself," verse 11.

And, in a way, he ascribed to God what was good in himself.
What then was the difference between him and S. Paul,
Who, in a manner, does praise himself[n]?
It was this—the Pharisee was dishonest,
His thanking God was not sincere;
He was inwardly giving himself the credit,
As if God had been, in a way, partial to him,
And had made him, at first, better than others.
S. Paul says all along—"not I, but the grace of God;"
The Pharisee praised himself, and despised the Publican;
S. Paul called himself "the chief of sinners,"
And added that he was "not meet to be called an Apostle."
Learn we then our lesson of S. Paul;
Or if we think, as well we may, that he is too high,
That such an example is almost beyond us,
Learn we of this blessed Publican,
To come before God simply as "miserable sinners;"
Not comparing ourselves with other men,
Except it be to humble ourselves the more;
And suiting our lives to our prayers,
By all lowly and loving watchfulness.

[n] See 1 Cor. xv. 10; Epistle for Eleventh Sunday after Trinity.

XCIX.

The Secret of Ingratitude.

" Were there not ten cleansed, but where are the nine?"
S. LUKE xvii. 17.

We require our children to say " Thank you ;"
We expect favours to be acknowledged ;
We count ingratitude a detestable sin ;
Yet how very common a sin it is !
Ingratitude towards men ;
The ingratitude of children to parents ;
The ingratitude to old friends, and the like ;
So that men of the world have made a proverb,
" Gratitude is a lively sense of favours to come."
Gratitude towards God has gone out of men's thoughts.
Observe them in ordinary times ;
At their meals, on their journeys, after escapes.
In seasons of sickness and trouble,
Many, in their fright, feel truly ;
But they feel very imperfectly, and only selfishly ;
And so, when things mend, they are unthankful.
Take for example, a recovery from sickness ;
How few come to Church, or to Holy Communion ;
How few keep other promises, which they made in trouble.
And yet they have a kind of faith,
As those nine Lepers had ;
But their faith does not work in them by love ;

They are lukewarm and slothful;
They take everything easily.
The cause of this union of faith with ingratitude is Pride.
Men have a sort of notion, which pride fosters,
That prosperity is their natural right;
They own their sin, but they do not feel its ill deserts;
They do not realize what sin is;
They do not take in what a thing it is *not* to be in Hell.
For the same reason, many are wanting in Resignation.
Religious after a sort, they yet go fretting to their graves.
Jonah seems to have been like this; and Saul at first.
But if men are not resigned, they will not be thankful.
This Samaritan is an instance of the contrary;
So is the woman of Canaan:
There was no heartlessness in them,
Because they knew they had not deserved such a favour.
The same spirit made S. Paul a Saint,
While others sought their own.
The Samaritan leper was made whole;
He was made whole both inwardly and outwardly;
The rest were only outwardly healed.
Take good care then not to think too well of yourself,
If you do, you will lose the comfort of being thankful °,
And you will lose, with it, the joy of Salvation ᴾ.
Of all things, therefore, use yourself to be lowly;
Think much of your sins, and little of your virtues.
This is the way to take the best out of this world,

° Ps. cxlvii. 1.   ᴾ Ib. li. 12.

To feel yourself unworthy of it, and thankful for it.
And it is the way to prepare yourself for the next world.
Remember that humble gratitude supposes faith;
That it is not mere animal cheerfulness;
But with faith, it is a perfect school of heavenly love.
God give us all grace, to learn our lesson in that school,
And to learn it perfectly.

C.

FEARLESSNESS UNDER WARNINGS.

"*Yet they were not afraid, nor rent their garments, neither the King, nor any of his servants that heard all these words.*" JER. xxxvi. 24.

OVER and over we hear of persons rending their garments;
Rending them in dismay and horror,
As Joseph's Brethren, when convicted by conscience [q];
As Jehoram when appealed to by Naaman the Leper [r];
As the High Priest, at the words of Jesus [s].
And especially when they heard of God's judgments,
Rending them in mere dread,
As Ahab at the words of Elijah [t];
Rending them in religious dread,
As Job [u] and Joshua [x], and Hezekiah [y] and Josiah [z];

[q] Gen. xliv. 13.   [r] 2 Kings v. 7.   [s] S. Matt. xxvi. 65.
[t] 1 Kings xxi. 27.   [u] Job i. 20.   [x] Josh. vii. 6.   [y] 2 Kings xix. 1.
[z] Ib. xxii. 19.

As also S. Paul and S. Barnabas [a].
But observe one example, in contradistinction to all these,
Jehoiakim and his servants did not rend their garments;
They were "not at all afraid."
Yet there was everything to make them afraid.
First, the words of Jeremiah were themselves enough;
The loving words at the beginning [b];
The awful words as he went on:
"Reprobate silver shall men call them,
"Because the Lord hath rejected them [c];"
"Pray not thou for this people [d];"
"Shall I not visit for these things [e]?"
"So will I break this people, as one breaketh a potter's vessel [f]."
Next, the sort of person who spoke the words;
And the time that had elapsed, no less than twenty-four years;
And the fact that some of the Prophecies had been fulfilled;
For example, the judgment on Samaria,
And the defeat of Pharaoh's army.
The Captivity had already begun in Jehoiakim's own person,
After the roll had been read the first time.
Then again, they were keeping a fast, at that very time,
In remembrance of this very thing;
And God had caused His judgment to be written,
To mark the certainty of it [g].
The Princes of the Court had been alarmed;
But the King was utterly reckless;

[a] Acts xiv. 14.   [b] See Chap. ii. &c.   [c] Chap. vi. 30.
[d] Ib. vii. 16; xi. 14; xiv. 11.   [e] Ib. v. 9, 29; ix. 9.   [f] Ib. xix. 11.
[g] Rev. xxii. 18, 19.

When he heard the Book read,
He cut it in pieces and burned it.
It was a case of utter hardness and fearlessness;
You can hardly imagine one going farther;
And dreadful was the judgment that came upon him.
Perhaps you think yourself in no danger of the same:
You never wilfully burned a Bible, or cut it in pieces.
Well—so far, perhaps, you are not like Jehoiakim.
But consider this:
When God's Providence orders circumstances for you,
So that such and such a Lesson is read,
That such and such a Sermon is preached, in your hearing,
Bidding you mind how angry He is with this or that,
With some sin, of which you know yourself to be guilty,
Or with some person, for whom you are to answer;
Then, you are in the same trial with Jehoiakim.
There are many ways of meeting that trial;
A man might take it to heart, and thoroughly repent;
He might repent for himself, like David;
He might repent for his People, like Joshua or Josiah.
Or he might make believe to be shocked;
He might pretend to repent, like the High Priest;
Or he might be struck, for a time, like Ahab, or Herod;
Or he might be altogether unfeeling and unbelieving.
One or other of these must be the case of every one,
At least of all who come to Church, or read the Bible.
Which of them is your case?
Sometimes one, perhaps—sometimes another.
Not to dwell on the rest for the present,

FEARLESSNESS UNDER WARNINGS.

Ask yourselves one question:
Have you never been hard and reckless under warnings,
When you knew, in your heart,
That the words were meant for you?
A man may be in the way of keeping no guard over his senses,
Yet he may hear S. Matt. v. 28 read, and not be afraid.
Is that so impossible?
Or he may be in the way of tempting others,
And he may hear Chap. xviii. 6 read without fear.
Or he may be a covetous man,
And the sixth Chapter may have no effect upon him.
Alas! what a sad habit that will be for you,
To use yourself to go home unwarned, after such warnings,
Admiring the Church, perhaps, or the Sermon,
But not fearing for yourself.
There is a Proverb about those who say they "don't care,"
About those who boast of letting nothing daunt them,
That they are sure to "come to a bad end."
You may make yourself easy for the present, in that way,
But "the bed is shorter than a man can stretch himself upon,
"The covering is narrower than a man can wrap himself in."
Rather one may say, You are making your own bed,
A bed of fire and brimstone;
And you will have to lie in it for ever.
The words of the Holy Ghost are plain,
"He that hardeneth his heart shall fall into mischief."
But the same Spirit has a word of comfort,
"Happy is the man that feareth always."
Happy the ear and the heart which are always open,

Open to the words of Holy Scripture,
And most of all to those which tell him of his own sins.
Happy the man who, when told of other men's sins, is afraid,
Who seeing them perhaps with his eyes, gives himself to prayer,
Prays both for his sinful brother, and for himself.
Happy he who so loves the Lord Jesus, as to be always afraid ;
Who shrinks in very deed, and continually, from sin,
From all that which, he knows, the Lord Jesus hateth.
He that so fears God, need have no other fear,
Neither in this world, nor in the world to come.

CI.

ABSOLUTION.

"*Have I any pleasure at all that the wicked should die? saith the Lord God: and not that he should return from his ways, and live?*"—EZEK. xviii. 23.

WHAT say you to this gracious question?
Is not the proof of its truth everywhere around you?
How is it that we are in being?
How is it that we are now alive, and not in Hell?
Why did God give us His Law?
When we had broken it, why did He send His Son,
To make Himself one of us,
To preach to us, and to do us good?

And, above all, to die for us?
Why did He send His Holy Spirit, after His Beloved Son?
Why did He institute His Church, and His Sacraments?
Why did He ordain that gift of Absolution,
Which the Church tells us of, and offers, morning and evening?
What is Absolution?
Absolution is the Presence of " the Son of Man" upon earth,
With "power to forgive sins."
And to those who are as Himself on earth,
He has committed His own power.
When you go into Church, and confess with a good mind,
Who is it that speaks to you by the Priest's mouth?
It is "the Son of Man" Who is pardoning and absolving you.
He absolves all who "truly repent and unfeignedly believe."
What a pity to miss this Absolution!
To miss it by absence, by inattention, or by worse!
When you kneel to confess at Holy Communion,
The Son of Man is interceding for you,
And the Absolution is a token of His Intercession.
When you confess privately, as the Church directs,
Either in times of health, or of sickness,
In times of deadly sin, or in times of trouble,
The Son of Man is there to comfort you,
As He comforted the woman at His Feet,
As He comforted her who touched the hem of His garment,
Saying, "Thy sins are forgiven thee, go in peace."
Pray think of this provision of His Love;
He says to *all*, " Come unto Me;"
And, by His Church, He says "Come unto Me," in this way;

"Come" all who are troubled for deadly sin.
Are there none here who are, or ought to be so troubled?
If there are, here is Absolution for them;
Here is consolation for them; why will they scorn it?
How can it be safe, right, or loving,
To turn our backs upon the Son of Man,
Coming to us with so blessed an offer?
Remember of what these earthly Absolutions are tokens;
They are tokens of the great Absolution, by-and-by.
Beware how you slight these,
Lest you be found to have slighted that.
Are you afraid of the private Absolution?
Then try greatly to value and improve the public Absolutions;
It is the least you can do.

CII.

SELF-LOATHING.

"And there shall ye remember your ways, and all your doings wherein ye have been defiled; and ye shall lothe yourselves in your own sight for all your evils that ye have committed."
EZEK. xx. 43.

THOSE passages in Holy Scripture are most comfortable,
Which are also the keenest and most searching.
It is so with this Chapter of Ezekiel;
Under the figure of the Jewish People, the Prophet witnesses,

First, to God's great mercy towards us;
Next, to our extreme unworthiness of that mercy;
And then, to our chances of penitence;
To the tokens of our penitence;
And to God's promise to accept it.
Among those tokens, here is this of self-loathing;
More or less, self-loathing is known to all sinners,
To all sinners, that is, who are at all penitents;
They know that they must bewail themselves,
Must confess and forsake their sins, in some sense;
But they do not always remember the conditions;
That this contrition must continue through *all* their time;
That it must be felt for *all* their sins;
That it must be a principle, not an occasional exercise;
And that it must be shewn in constant self-denial.
Many might think such a life of penitence to be miserable,
But they will find it, on trial, to be the only way of peace;
He Who commands it, will sweeten it.
Such a life makes all crosses and mortifications welcome;
It takes off the danger of prosperity and praise;
It makes us feel how little we deserve praise;
It keeps us close to the Lord,
Our "Strength and our Redeemer;"
It makes us feel that we are on His Shoulders,
That we are being carried by Him, as the lost sheep.
It is the very mark of the Righteous, at the last Day.

CIII.

PARDON AND PEACE.

"*Go in Peace.*"—S. LUKE vii. 50.

THREE precious things come together,
In the Collect for the twenty-first Sunday after Trinity.
Faith on our part; Pardon and Peace on God's.
Rather all three belong to God;
For it is His Spirit Who puts Faith in our hearts,
And without Faith, neither Pardon nor Peace can be.
As these three things come together in the Collect,
So they come together in the gracious dealings of our Lord,
In His gracious dealings with "the woman that was a sinner."
She shewed herself one of His faithful people;
And he gave her first Pardon—" Thy sins be forgiven;"
And then He said to her, "Go in Peace;"
And, if this woman was S. Mary Magdalene,
We know that she was "cleansed from all her sins,"
And that she "served Him with a quiet mind,"
All the rest of her time.
The same words, and the same things came together again
In the case of the woman diseased with the issue of blood;
Her Faith, and His Forgiveness, were implied in the cure;
And His Blessing went with her, when she went away.
How very striking is this Blessing as used by our Lord!
In itself, it was but the common Oriental compliment,
Generally used on the departure of a friend;

It might be used as a mere form;
It might be most unreal, as in the mouth of S. Paul's jailor[h];
But in the Mouth of Jesus, how full of deep meaning!
In the Old Testament it often had a real meaning;
It was so used by Jethro to Moses; and by Eli to Hannah;
By Jonathan to David; and by David to Abigail;
By Achish to David; by David to Absalom;
And by Elisha to Naaman.
It is like our own "Good-bye" or "God be with you."
Think what a word to be spoken by God to His creatures!
What a word of new Creation!
Spoken by the Judge, beforehand,
To those who must give account;
An earnest, if so be, of acquittal.
How it must have sounded to people who had faith;
To those who knew that He read their hearts;
How they must have gone forth to their work!
With what gratitude, faith, hope, courage, humility, love!
Just as we know the Apostles did go forth,
Sealed with the same word—"Peace be unto you[i]."
Jesus is continually saying the same word to us;
He says it in Confirmation, and in Absolution;
He says it after every Communion,
And when we leave the Church.
Take you care how you go out;
See that you have the same mind as those true Penitents had;
The same mind as the Apostles had;

[h] Acts xvi. 36: see also S. James ii. 16.
[i] S. John xx. 21, 26.

That so you may "depart in Peace," when your time is come;
And in Eternity may never hear the word "depart,"
But only, and always, the word "Come,"
"Come ye blessed."

CIV.

The Citizenship of the Christian.

"Our conversation (πολίτευμα) is in Heaven, from whence also we look for the Saviour, the Lord Jesus Christ."—PHIL. iii. 20.

This is a short description of a Christian;
His home, or city, is in Heaven;
There are his nearest and dearest relations;
His Father;
His Saviour;
His Comforter;
There he has all the means needful to fit him for the place;
There he has his laws and rules of conduct—
The love of God, and of his neighbour;
There he looks for rest, and establishment;
There also he may look for support and redress,
During the time of his absence from Home.
For his absence is not banishment;
It is only the time of his trial;
He has still the privileges of a Citizen [k],
Only his City is in another Country [l].

[k] Eph. ii. 19.   [l] Heb. xii. 22.

He may expect therefore that God will befriend him;
Will be angry with his enemies;
Will hear his complaints;
Will furnish him with what is necessary;
Will receive him when recalled;
Upon condition of sincere loyalty of heart on his part.
He may *not* expect the same privileges as if he were at Home,
To be as much respected,
To have as many comforts,
To understand things as well,
As if he were in his Father's House.
But he knows how to make up for all deficiencies;
He "looks for the Saviour, the Lord Jesus Christ."
If we would only live by any one of these truths,
How different a face of things should we see,
In the Christian world!
If we lived as Citizens of Heaven,
Could we be so carried away with trifles?
Could we be so deluded by base pleasures?
If we considered ourselves as not at home,
Could we be so astounded at discomforts?
If we remembered to "look for" our Saviour,
Could we help preparing ourselves for Him,
By purity and brotherly kindness?

CV.

THE DIVINE USE OF DISTRESS.

"*Whence shall we buy bread that these may eat?*"—S. JOHN vi. 5.

By how many, and how often, is this question asked!
By some, every night and morning of their lives,
In care and in fear.
By many in heart-breaking agony.
But who asks it here?
Is it some poor father or mother of a family?
Some captain of a ship at sea?
Some leader of a caravan?
The commander of an army?
The governor of a besieged city?
Is it Hagar in the wilderness?
Or Jacob in Canaan?
Or Moses before the Manna came?
Or the woman of Sarepta?
Or King Joram in Samaria?
Or the Jewish mothers when Jerusalem was besieged?
Nay, it is the Great God, Who here asks it,
The Creator and Owner of all things,
He Who daily "openeth His Hand,
"And filleth all things living with plenteousness."
Why does He make as though He had no power?
It is not simply because He is one of us,

Because He is True Man also, as well as True God,
For that would be a reason more why He should help us ;
When it became His delight to be among the sons of men,
He felt for their hunger also ;
For every one of His Brethren, in such a state,
He does feel, with the true feeling of a common Nature,
With the true natural touch of brotherly love and pity.
Thus He had true compassion for this multitude,
Even in their small and temporary need ;
And can you think He does not feel for our brethren,
In their present great distress [m] ?
Why then does He permit it ?
For the reason which this Gospel gives,
To prove them ; *that* we understand.
But the text leads us to feel something more ;
That it is also permitted, in order to prove *us*.
The Almighty God made us without ourselves ;
But He does not ordinarily preserve us without ourselves,
He does not save us without ourselves.
So He condescended here to call in His creatures' aid ;
He made as though He had need ;
Need of means, and need of the Disciples' counsel.
And when Philip seemed to despair,
Pointing out how much was needed,
He bade them, at any rate, go and see what they had.
Then S. Andrew answered Him,
Who is, in a sense, the first of the Apostles,

[m] The Sermon of which this is the outline, is thought to have been preached at the time of the potato famine in Ireland.

Whose delight it was to bring others to Christ,
To bring to Him those of whom,
And that of which, He had need;
S. Andrew told Him of the lad,
"There is a lad here which hath five barley loaves,
"And two small fishes."
And He made as if He had need of "the lad,"
And as if He had need of the loaves;
It was probably their frugal meal for that day,
Got ready for Him and for them;
That little they gave up, and see how it was multiplied!
Imagine the feeling of the Apostles when they were bidden
"Make the men sit down."
Picture the scene to your minds, and dwell upon it.
If you count the Apostles favoured then,
Consider that the like favour is offered to you now;
He says to you in effect, what He said to them:
"Here are so many for whom I died,
"Whence shall we buy bread that they may eat?"
You may answer, as Philip answered at first,
Or as Andrew answered afterwards;
You may grudge the loaves, as Nabal did;
Or you may say, "It is the Nation's work to do this;"
Or, "It is the work of so-and-so to do it;"
Or, "They did nothing for us, and we owe them nothing;"
Or, "I have nearer claims on my help;"
And so you may save your money.
But if your brethren should starve, how would you feel?
And if they should not starve, how would it be?

What a loss you would have, even in this world!
You would lose the comfort of having shared in a good work,
A work which, we hope, will prove a great bond among classes;
And in the other world,
You would lose your share of the blessing.
Almighty God needs these distressed brethren,
Else He would not so visit them;
He needs you and your help,
Else He would not put them within your reach.
How much He needs both, you will not know,
Till you hear Him say it Himself,
From His Throne of Judgment.
Had you not better put by all your doubts,
And set yourself to this task of work for Him?

CVI.

ENDURING LOVE.

"Having loved His own which were in the world, He loved them unto the end."—S. JOHN xiii. 1.

THIS Scripture suits very well with the time;
We are coming once more to the end of the Church's year;
We have, so far, proved the truth of this saying;
For we are among His own;
He hath loved us in years past;
Hath He not loved us this year also?

He hath known the evil in our hearts, as in Judas,
Yet He waiteth on us.
As it was in His Incarnation,
So it was in His act of washing the disciples' feet.
The latter was a type of the former;
He humbled Himself, in His Love, knowing all things.
He humbled Himself to S. Peter,
Whose denials He knew beforehand.
He humbled Himself to Judas,
Whose treachery was in His Mind.
Such is His Love: and what doth He ask of us?
He asks, first and chiefly, that we consent to be loved;
"If I wash thee not, thou hast no part in Me."
He asks, next, that we wait on each other;
That we "love one another, as He hath loved us."
How will it be with us, in these respects, by-and-by,
When the Church's year comes round again?
No doubt *He* will have loved us;
How shall *we* have loved Him?
Perhaps the question will be asked of us in another world;
How sorry shall we be, then,
If we have put off thinking, now!
How confounded and amazed when we meet our Saviour!

CVII.
THE LAND OF BLESSING.

"Dwell in the Land, and verily thou shalt be fed."
Ps. xxxvii. 3.

WHAT Land is that?
Concerning which the Holy Ghost bids us—
"Dwell in the Land?"
Is it not His own Land—"the Land of Righteousness [n]?"
Into which He leads us, as He led Abraham;
As He led the Children of Israel,
"Out of the land of darkness, and of the shadow of death."
It is Paradise restored to us again [o].
Here we are to dwell in quiet obedience;
We are not to break our bounds.
And well we may "dwell in the Land,"
For here God delights to dwell;
He comes to bless us in it.
His eyes are upon it from the beginning of the year to the end.
It is His Shechinah.
It is Immanuel's Land.
Here He will feed you with spiritual Food;
With His Word; with His Grace; with His Body and Blood.
Keep within these bounds, and He will feed you,
As He fed your fathers.
Though you have wandered from it, yet if you turn towards it,

[n] Ps. cxliii. 10.   [o] Isa. xxxv.

He will bring you back to it,
According to His own words in the Epistle P.
Nor will He let you starve in it;
Rather He will work a miracle.
Consider the miracle recorded here,
In the Gospel for the Sunday before Advent.
And remember the gracious promise,
"Seek ye first the Kingdom of God, and His Righteousness,
"And all other things shall be added unto you."
Has it not been so, all your life long, unto this day?
Has it not been so, this year?
Consider—even in temporal things, how it has been:
Did you ever find Him fail you,
When you have trusted in Him?
And in spiritual things, if you have not been fed,
Was it not that you did not abide "in the Land?"
Here was your Food prepared for you;
Either you did not come to partake of It,
Or, coming, still you wandered from It, in your heart.
How can those who never come to the Feast, expect to be fed,
Or those who come now and then,—come only to feed,
But hardly ever come to pray,
Or those who shew no plenteousness in bearing fruit,
How can they be profitably dwelling in the Land?
How can it answer to continue to be lukewarm,
While they are close to so great a Fire?
To go on asking for "a sign,"
When Christ has given them His Church?

P For Sunday next before Advent, Jer. xxiii. 7, 8.

How can it be safe to turn back from the blessings of the Land
Because they find that the blessings are wholly spiritual?
"Be not deceived—God is not mocked;"
As you plough, so you must reap.
According to the land will be your food;
The Tree of Life, if you abide in the New Paradise;
Apples of Sodom, bitter ashes, if you abide with the wicked.
Your prayers, your Sacraments—all—will be as your lives.

CVIII.   S. Andrew's Day.

Conversion.

"And they straightway left their nets and followed Him.
"And they immediately left the ship and their father, and followed Him."—S. MATT. iv. 20, 22.

"Immediately"—"Straightway"—"Forthwith,"
These are the emphatic words.
God has indeed much patience with men;
He goes on for years, "rising early and sending,"
Whether men "will hear, or whether they will forbear."
But there is a limit, and we know not where it is set.
And His bright crowns, His special favours are reserved,
For whom?—For those who seek Him early.
Moreover, what would true love teach us?
Come then early;
If possible, come early in age;
If too late for that, still come early;
Early, in the sense of "coming when called."
And come at once;
Give yourself up at once to God;
Whenever He gives you serious convictions,
Spread your sail to the wind.
Come at once;
Refrain at once, when Conscience pulls you back,
Saying, "O do not this thing which God hates."

Come at once;
Act at once, when Conscience says, "wait no longer,"
Set about your duty, as you know you ought.
The sum is—Remember the words,
"Immediately"—"straightway"—"forthwith."
Remember there is such a sin as sloth.
Time and tide are short, and wait for no man.

CIX.

S. Thomas's Day.

LOVE THE KEY OF FAITH.

"Whom having not seen, ye love; in Whom, though now ye see Him not, yet believing, ye rejoice with joy unspeakable, and full of glory."—1 S. PET. i. 8.

ALL Christians are very much in the condition of S. Thomas,
When he was told of our Risen Lord, without having seen Him.
By whom was S. Thomas told?
First by good women;
As Christians are told by their mothers,
Or by those in the place of mothers to them;
By women, who were themselves told by Angels,
That is, by the Church, and the Holy Scriptures;
And afterwards told by the Risen Lord Himself,
As He shewed Himself to them.
Next, as S. Thomas was told by the other Apostles,
So were we, ourselves, told by the Church.
And as the two disciples from Emmaus alleged Holy Scripture,
So did the Church to us.
And there were penitents there, like S. Peter;
And chaste lovers, like S. John;
Yet S. Thomas felt as if he could not believe.
And so perhaps may some of us feel;
The Mystery seems too far, too high for us.
So it was with him; yet he wished he could believe.

LOVE THE KEY OF FAITH.

Why? because he loved;
And therefore he soon had relief and blessing.
Many others, as the Pharisees, felt like S. Thomas,
As if they could not believe,
And, so far—were like him.
But these wished to have it so;
Because they had no love.
Try your own feelings by this;
If you cannot believe the deep Mysteries of Faith,
If you cannot set your mind on these things,
Ask yourself, "Do I wish to do so?"
If you do, it will be because you love;
And therefore you will pray, as S. Thomas prayed;
And you will obey, as S. Thomas obeyed;
You will keep away from the world;
You will abide in the "Upper Room" with the Apostles;
And your Lord will come to you;
He will shew you His Wounds;
And you will be happy.

CX.
S. Paul's Day.

THE TEST OF CONVERSION.

"They had heard only, That he which persecuted us in times past, now preacheth the faith which once he destroyed. And they glorified God in me."—GAL. i. 23, 24.

S. PAUL's case, seems, at first, far removed from common life;
But, on nearer consideration, perhaps it is not so much so.
When one considers, what is true, after all,
That there is but one great division in the world:
To be against Christ; and, to be for Him;
And whoever passes from one to the other,
Of him it may be said, that he is like S. Paul.
But there is one case more distinctly like S. Paul's;
The case described in the Exhortation before Holy Communion,
Of "hindering or slandering God's Word."
This relates, of course, very much to doctrine;
But I do not intend now so to consider it;
I want you to consider it, as it relates to persons,
In whatever respect, or measure, doing wrong,
Who pertinaciously set themselves in opposition,
Against those who would set them right.
Sometimes it is the custom of the neighbourhood,
Or of some whom they look up to;
Sometimes it is their own habit, which makes them do this,
And pride backs them up in it.

The Test of Conversion.

When their own ways are disturbed,
And they have a dim consciousness that they ought so to be,
They yet set themselves against being disturbed;
They make the most of little objections,
Of personal faults and errors;
They hinder others, by scorn and unkindness;
And think how a word said may endure!
They catch up whatever they hear,
And slander it;
This, both in respect of omission, and commission.
Sometimes they die in this imperfect way;
Sad, anxious case!
Sometimes they repent;
And then S. Paul may be their guide.
He began with suffering and penance;
He spared not his own shame;
He was very zealous the other way;
But with great consideration.
This is encouragement to win the "hinderers of God's Word,"
To induce them to turn and repent.
It will test their humility,
Whether they not only abuse themselves,
But take the abuse and ill-treatment of others quietly.
If conversions were true,
Should we not see more zeal?

CXI.
Feast of the Purification.

HOLY EXACTNESS.

"The Parents brought in the Child Jesus, to do for Him after the custom of the Law."—S. LUKE ii. 27.

CONSIDER the history of the Presentation of our Lord,
How often " the Law " is referred to.
" The days of her purification,
" According to the Law of Moses [q]."
" As it is written in the Law of the Lord [r]."
" A sacrifice, according to that which is said in the Law [s],
" A pair of turtle doves, or two young pigeons;"
The one, for purifying the Mother,
The other, for redeeming the Child [t].
" To do for Him after the custom of the Law [u]."
" When they had performed all things,
" According to the Law of the Lord [x]."
The idea of the Law runs through the Chapter.
Now the Law is abolished,
But the spirit of it remains.
Accordingly the Church purifies Mothers,
And dedicates children.
And it would be thought scandalous,
If either of these were omitted.

[q] S. Luke ii. 22.   [r] Ver. 23.   [s] Ver. 24.   [t] Lev. xii. 8.
[u] S. Luke ii. 27.   [x] Ver. 39.

But Mary and Joseph were exact in all things;
So were Simeon and Anna, in the Temple worship.
See how great was their reward, in meeting Christ,
"The Desire of all nations [y],"
"The Lord whom they sought, coming suddenly [z]."
See also the reward of Mary and Joseph,
In receiving such testimony concerning the Holy Child;
And such a warning.
But, most, in the blessedness of His "increase
"In wisdom, and stature, and in favour with God and man."
Perhaps this is why Christian families suffer,
In not being more blessed, in the like way,
That they neglect holy exactness;
That they put up with light excuses;
So contrary to the way of Joseph and Mary.
Or if they do come to the House of God,
And, so far, are obedient,
They may be wanting in purity or humility;
Two graces which shine out in the blessed Virgin.
Let as many of us as have yet the chance,
Try these ways;
That we may be holy and happy families.
Let not those whose time is too far spent, despair,
For they may have the blessing of Simeon and Anna;
Only let them dutifully seek Christ,
At home, and in Church.

[y] Haggai ii. 7.   [z] Mal. iii. 1.

CXII.

THE UNION OF OFFERING WITH PURITY.

"When the Days of her purification according to the law of Moses were accomplished, they brought Him to Jerusalem to present Him to the Lord."—S. LUKE ii. 22.

THERE are two ideas connected with this Festival,
Inseparably joined together;
The idea of Presentation,
Suggested by the Presentation of Christ for us;
The idea of Purification,
Suggested by the Purification of the Blessed Virgin,
The Mother of Him Who knew no sin.
Consider the various Presentations to the Father,
And how Purification belongs to each:
The Presentations, looking forward,
Of the First-born in the Jewish Rite;
Of Samuel, and Samson, and such as they.
The Presentation, to-day, of the Eternal Son,
Whom all types prefigured.
His continual Presentation of us, in all Church offices;
In Holy Baptism, and in Confirmation;
In Ordination;
In Dedications and Benedictions and Vows;
In daily Prayers;
But most in the Holy Communion;
On earth, by His Priests, from time to time;
In Heaven completely.
Last of all, at the Great Day,
When He shall present His Bride to the Father.

CXIII. S. Matthias' Day.

THE ETERNITY OF HELL.

"It had been good for that man if he had not been born."
S. MATT. xxvi. 24.

"LET us not abuse the goodness of God."
These words are from the Commination office,
And are sounded in our ears every Lent.
But the Goodness of God is abused,
By those who will not think of Hell;
And by those who may think of Hell,
But will not believe that it is for such as they are.
Therefore this Feast of S. Matthias comes in well now;
It harmonizes with the beginning of Lent.
It shews that some will be lost;
Else, how could it be "better for them,
"Never to have been born?"
Some will be lost; even as the Devil;
God made not him for ruin; but he chose it;
And they who hold with the Devil, do the same.
It is their doing, not God's.
If you ask, "why is it allowed?"
The answer is, "This is God's secret;"
Even as the existence of pain is His secret.
The Devil among Angels, and Judas among men,
These are tokens of Hell, to keep us all in fear.

But you will say, "I am not like them."
Nay, consider:
What was the damning circumstance in the Devil?
His sinning *in Heaven*.
What was it in Judas?
His betraying our Lord, when *so near* Him[a].
Be sure, it is the same kind of sin,
Whenever a Christian wilfully turns from His Saviour.
And if he dies in this sin,
It has the same effect, though in different degrees[b].
Not to take Christ at His word will never do.
If we refuse to believe an Eternity of misery,
We must give up a happy Eternity as well.
This is especially a Lent warning,
And a warning for those who have Christian privileges;
For, by how much nearer these are,
The more danger they are in.
These very alarms, slighted, make the case worse.
If S. Matthias had followed Judas,
He would have been worse than Judas.

[a] S. John vi. 70, 71. [b] S. Luke xii. 47, 48.

CXIV.

The Annunciation.

How?

"How shall this be?"—S. LUKE i. 34.

THIS is the greatest Day in the year,
For, in one sense, it is the Beginning of the Gospel.
So great a Thing implies an immense need,
And therefore a great change,
To which fallen nature demurs.
And the common way is to refuse to notice it;
And, when you cannot help that, to undervalue it;
And when you are pressed with the full Truth,
To ask the question—" How?"
It is much the same with the Holy Eucharist,
Which is the application of the Incarnation to each one.
Observe then about this word " How,"
That it is used in Holy Scripture, rightly and wrongly,
When the question is of God's doings.
It has three uses;
First—there is an unbeliever's use:
Sometimes in scorn,
" How is it that He saith, I came down from Heaven[c]?"
" How can this Man give us His Flesh to eat[d]?"
Sometimes in mere doubt and wonder[e],

---

[c] S. John vi. 42.   [d] Ib. 52.   [e] Ib. iii. 9.

As by Nicodemus, "How can these things be?"
Sometimes in cowardice;
"How can I dispossess them[¹]?"
Secondly—there is a believer's use:
As by Blessed Mary, "How shall this be?"
Or where there are conflicting duties.
Thirdly—there is a Divine use:
Where God's mercy is, as it were, in suspense,
Contending with His Truth and Justice;
"How shall I pardon thee?"—"How can ye escape?"
This third use is dimly copied in loving hearts,
When, humanly speaking, they are in despair about any one,
And they go on, hoping and praying, against hope.
Sometimes God answers this "How,"
Sometimes He answers not.
"How can this Man give us His Flesh?" He answers not.
In, "How can a man be born again?" He gives an analogy.
In, "How can I dispossess?"
He refers to His own Almightiness.
In, "How shall this be?" "With God nothing is impossible."
So He quiets the scruples of the Blessed Virgin;
But He also adds a sign.
In the other places, He just expresses His Will to save;
Which is warrant for our hope,
That in each case, He may save.
Apply these thoughts to daily trials;
To a strong temptation; to a deep affliction;
To a wrong, which seems unpardonable;
To a habit, which seems incurable.
Take this medicine, and the cure will be certain.

[¹] Deut. vii. 17.

CXV.

SS. Philip and James's Day.

STRICTNESS AND SEVERITY.

"After that, He was seen of James."—1 COR. xv. 7.

THERE are four persons mentioned in the Divine Record,
To whom our Lord is said to have appeared singly,
After His Resurrection.
Two of them were Penitents;
The other two were S. James, and S. Paul.
We see plainly the moral of three of them;
What is that of the fourth?
S. James was the "Brother" of our Lord;
And this recommends to us family affection.
He was remarkable for self-denial;
And this recommends hard living.
He was Bishop of Jerusalem;
And this may seem the most probable reason of all.
We see how he was distinguished afterwards [g];
We see how much the people thought of him,
So that his testimony, at his Martyrdom, was very valuable.
Who can tell about his interview with our Risen Lord,
What effect it had, upon his life, and upon his Martyrdom?
Again, his Epistle is of a peculiar character;
It is more like our Lord's own words than any other;

[g] See Acts xii. 17; xv. 13; xxi. 18: Gal. ii. 9.

It does not please those who do not like strictness;
They are apt to pass slightly over it.
It is for them, perhaps, that two events are specially recorded,
His conferences with our Lord, and with S. Paul.
Many things might be said on this:
But I will only say one thing:
Beware of prejudices against strictness and seriousness;
Love those who practise a holy severity;
Love them for our Lord's Sake,
Whose brethren they are.
With such an one He had His last private conference,
Before He went up into Heaven.
With such we should consort in spirit,
That we may be ready to keep His Ascension.

CXVI.
S. Barnabas' Day.

KINDLINESS AND STEDFASTNESS.

"Who when he came, and had seen the grace of God, was glad; and exhorted them all that with purpose of heart they would cleave unto the Lord."—ACTS xi. 23.

S. BARNABAS was a very genial and popular person,
As his very name denotes;
He was brave, and free in giving, and of noble presence [g].
He always looked at the favourable side of men,
As in S. Paul's case [h];
As also in S. Mark's case, though that was a mistake;
Even that might be attributable to his family feeling [i].
He was full of sympathy,
And liable to be carried away;
As indeed he was, in the question of circumcision [k].
He was the very man to be a Missionary Bishop,
Especially when joined with S. Paul.
Of course such an one would be glad,
When he saw the Grace of God,
When he saw goodness generally;
But especially glad when he saw conversion.
Perhaps you might pass this over,
You might take it as a thing of course.
But are *you* always glad, when you see the grace of God?

[g] Acts xiv. 12. [h] Ib. ix. 26, 27. [i] Ib. xv. 37. [k] Gal. ii. 13.

Is there no such thing as vexation,
When you perceive people to be better than yourself?
Is there no disposition to carp at them,
To think them too strict, or worse—hypocritical?
To grudge others the credit and comfort of helping them?
To be a little glad when they prove inconsistent,
And to say—"I thought so?
Or are you not inclined to pass the signs of Grace by,
Which is still more common,
Either as not caring for such things,
Or as though it were "very well for those who like it?"
Is not this true especially in respect of devotional virtues?
And of humility, patience, and the like?
Forgetting the revelation to "babes[1]."
Consider that it is a great part of the Christian character,
To practise the contrary of all these dispositions.
And, remembering men's instability,
To encourage them, not only by congratulation,
But also by "exhorting them all,
"That with purpose of heart they would cleave to the Lord."
"Cleave," and persevere, that is the force of the word:
Genial people do not always think of perseverance,
As gravely as they ought to think,
Either for others, or for themselves.

[1] S. Matt. xi. 25.

CXVII.
S. John Baptist's Day.

Energy and Strength.

"*The child grew, and waxed strong in spirit.*"—S. Luke i. 80.

The Lord God shall come with a strong Hand;
As God's work does not falter,
So it must be with those whom He chooses for συνεργοὶ,
They must work with energy and constancy;
Zion must lift up her voice "with strength."
It is a great work which has to be done;
" Every valley shall be filled,
"And every mountain and hill brought low [m];"
And feeble means cannot do it.
Accordingly, what is the first thing told of S. John Baptist,
Who was raised up to do this great work?
That he was a boy of energy and constancy;
When he had a good thought he laid strong hold of it,
And he kept that hold steadily.
The Providence of God led him to be in the desert,
He led a hermit's life;
He was steady in resisting temptation;
For example, to be delicate in meat, clothing and the like,
Which therefore we see to be a great point.
Then, as he had to preach repentance,

[m] Isa. xl. 4.

So he was strong in reproving all sorts of people;
Having been strong against himself,
He was also strong against others.
Then his success would tempt to self-reliance;
But he owned himself to be, still, only "a voice [n]."
Having been thus faithful in life,
It was, for him, no great thing to die as he did.
He added the glory of his death to his other glories,
For he was the nearest Martyr to our Lord,
Of all those who went before Him.
Observe well how his foundation was laid;
In not being selfish, but ready to deny himself,
In meat, and drink, and clothing.
Yet if he had not persevered in his course,
It would have come to nought.
Remember the proverb about intending and not doing,
"Hell is paved with good intentions."

[n] S. John i. 23.

CXVIII.
S. Peter's Day.

The "Apostolic Church."

"*I say also unto thee, That thou art Peter, and upon this rock I will build My Church, and the gates of hell shall not prevail against it.*"—S. MATT. xvi. 18.
"*And that Rock was Christ.*"—1 COR. x. 4.

CONSIDER a great event in this day's Gospel,
That our Lord gave a new name to one of His Apostles,
To the great Apostle of this day—S. Peter.
When the Omniscient is pleased to give names,
Or to change them, by special revelation,
There is always some deep mystery;
Some mercy for us, and some lesson to us.
The mercy is always in Christ;
The lesson is always to Christians.
What, for example, is contained in the name Abraham?
The mercy *for* us is our universal adoption as children of God;
The lesson *to* us is Faith.
What is signified by the name Isaac?
The mercy—that we are children of promise, by miracle;
The lesson—joy after waiting.
What do we find in the name Israel?
The mercy—that each Christian is made a "Prince of God;"
The lesson—that, as a Prince, he must struggle "and prevail."

So here the name Peter is to us a token—
A token of Christ's being our Rock.
Christ is our Rock in the sense of a sure Foundation,
In the sense of the wise man's house,
Which he built upon a rock,
As described in the Sermon on the Mount.
For so our Lord goes on with the Parable,
"'Ἐπὶ τῇ πέτρᾳ—upon this rock:"
Now we know that "other Foundation can no man lay
"Than that is laid, which is Jesus Christ [o]."
He Himself is the sole "Corner-stone" of His Church;
Its creed is grounded on faith in Him, as "the Christ,"
And to that one, all the other articles are bonded;
Upon Him the Church is all built;
And to Him it is all cemented;
So that His Eternity is the pledge of ours.
But, in a way, the Church is also built on Peter,
As being the first, in order, of the other foundation-stones,
Who are bonded on to the Coin-stone.
It was S. Peter who first added souls to the Church,
Both Jews and Gentiles;
This was the reward of his confession;
But the other Apostles took up the confession;
And S. Peter spoke for them, as well as for himself;
They were real Foundation Stones, as well as he.
S. Paul speaks of them
As "the Foundation of the Apostles and Prophets [p],"

[o] 1 Cor. iii. 11.   [p] Eph. ii. 20.

And in the vision which S. John saw,
"The City had twelve Foundations,
"And in them the Names of the twelve Apostles of the Lamb [q]."
The power of binding and loosing was the same in all.
What, in short, is the promise made to S. Peter?
In it, our Lord seals His love to His Church;
He makes it "Apostolic," as the Creed calls it;
He ensures to it His perpetual Presence,
His Presence with those whom He commissioned,
As He commissioned S. Peter and the rest.
What an encouragement to us to hold fast our inheritance,
The holy Creeds, the Ministry, and the Sacraments,
All the great things of our most holy Faith,
Which all who hold to the ancient Doctrine, believe alike.
That would be the way to perfect union;
"The gates of hell shall not prevail,"
Neither in judgment nor in persecution.
Only "hold that fast which thou hast,
"That no man take thy crown."

[q] Rev. xxi. 14.

CXIX.

S. Michael and all Angels.

THE MINISTRY OF THE ANGELS.

" Then the devil leaveth Him, and behold Angels came and ministered unto Him."—S. MATT. iv. 11.

OUR Blessed Lord "took on Him the seed of Abraham;"
He condescended to be like us in all things;
Amongst the rest, He subjected Himself to the changes of life,
And He welcomed the changes which God sends;
As, joy after sorrow; rest after toil;
And, as in the text, Angel ministrations,
After diabolical temptations.
This He did, for our sakes,
To sanctify innocent refreshment after times of pining;
All discontent and faithlessness being overcome;
Imparting the sense of special favour,
Without the danger of presumption.
Granting us to enjoy all the best of this world,
As well as of the next,
Without covetousness, and without ambition.
And how is all this, in part, accomplished?
Through the ministry of the Holy Angels;
The Angels fulfil a great part of our Lord's Dispensation;
So great that they are specially mentioned by S. Paul,
In his summary of the Mystery of Godliness [*],

[*] 1 Tim. iii. 16.

"Great is the Mystery of Godliness;
"God was manifest in the Flesh,
"Justified in the Spirit,
"Seen of Angels."
As then we should be very serious in our temptations,
Knowing *from* whom they come,
So we should be very devout in our refreshments,
Knowing *through* whom they come.
We should not take them as "of course;"
Nor as an "occasion to the flesh;"
Nor as any such great thing in themselves;
But as children take keepsakes;
For a token and earnest of love,
The love of the good Angels themselves,
And the Love of their Lord.
And we must not depend on them;
For even from Christ the devil did not go altogether,
He only "departed for a season."

CXX.

S. Luke.

S. LUKE AN "IMAGE" OF OUR LORD.

"*Himself took our infirmities, and bare our sicknesses.*"
S. MATT. viii. 17.

WHAT are the Saints of God?
They are but faint images—each one— of the Holiest.
"But, we all, with open face,
"Beholding, as in a glass, the glory of the Lord,
"Are changed into the same Image from glory to glory[t]."
The Saints are images,
Reflected as it were in a mirror.
But how does a mirror reflect an object?
By shewing only one side of it at a time;
Even so is it with the several Saints;
They reflect their Lord in some one special aspect.
It is easy to see in what aspect S. Luke reflects Christ.
He was a Physician,
Healing first by drugs,
Then by the wholesome medicine of Doctrine.
He was also ὁ ἀγαπητός:
Thus he represents Him Who "took our infirmities,
"And bare our sicknesses."
True, these words mean much more;
Principally they mean something incommunicable,

[t] 2 Cor. iii. 18.

They point to our Lord's Atonement.
Still, we are taught thus to apply them.
They express the Divine sympathy,
Which is, so to speak, the first motion
Towards the Atonement.
Our Lord came to heal;
And how did He heal?
He took the burden on Himself;
He took it in deed, and in fact.
As to the diseases of our souls,
He took it, by His Humiliation and Passion:
As to the diseases of our bodies,
He took it, in mysterious compassion and trouble;
And the one is the type of the other.
Consider the word ἐσπλαγχνίσθη;
"He was moved with (or had) compassionᵘ,"
How it is applied to both soul and body;
And it is never otherwise applied in either Gospel
Than to our Blessed Lord Himself.
Such are the yearning tender mercies of our God!
See in three places of the Holy Gospelᵛ,
How He yearns upon sinners,
How He heals them with His *word*, and with His *touch*.
And what are the Physicians of souls,
But tokens of His Presence doing the same?
When you read S. Luke's Gospel,
And learn the precious "doctrine delivered by Him,"

ᵘ S. Matt. ix. 36; xiv. 14; xviii. 27; xx. 34: S. Luke vii. 13; x. 33; xv. 20.   ᵛ S. Matt. xiv. 14; xx. 34: S. Luke vii. 13, 14.

The doctrine of Sacrifice and Remission,
Know that it is Christ come to heal **and** to raise you;
Be as thankful, and as fearful of rejecting Him,
As if you saw and **heard** the Lord Himself,
And **felt** the touch of His Hand.

CXXI.

THE GOOD PHYSICIAN AND THE GOOD PATIENT.

"*Luke, the beloved Physician.*"—COL. iv. 14.

In His appointment of disciples,
Our Lord had, frequently, respect to their former calling.
S. Peter and S. Matthew are examples of it.
It is easy to see it in S. Luke;
And to trace the analogy between his two offices,
Wherein, as all Saints do, he especially represented our Lord,
His medical office being the type of his Evangelical.
What therefore is one leading thought for this day?
That the Church's work is a healing work;
Consider how near it comes home to each one of us;
For each one is trusted with his own soul,
Each one is, so far, his own Physician,
As well as a Patient of the Church.
What, then, is a good Physician to do?
His heart must be in his work;
He must not spare himself;

He must be very watchful;
He must be very tender;
He must be open to reasonable hints;
He must be very truthful,
How irksome soever the truth may be;
He must have a mixture of fear and hope,
But hope must prevail, because of faith and love.
What, again, are the signs of a good Patient?
Obedience;
Trusting, cheerful, punctual obedience;
Not wishing to have things explained.
And both, Physician and Patient, must refer all to God.
As this is the way to make the best of an illness,
So it is the way to make the best of this mortal life.
We can wish no better for ourselves;
We can wish no better for one another;
We can ask no greater blessing of our God.

CXXII.

SS. Simon and Jude.

Railing Words.

"*Yet Michael the Archangel, when contending with the devil he disputed about the body of Moses, durst not bring against him a railing accusation, but said, The Lord rebuke thee.*"—S. Jude 9.

These two Saints, Simon and Jude, are patterns of zeal.
What is zeal?
When it is a positive pain to see God dishonoured.
These brothers would feel it *naturally*,
Because they were our Lord's brothers;
But they would also feel it *spiritually*,
Because they loved Him.
That they did feel it, we know,
By S. Simon's name, and by S. Jude's Epistle.
And, certainly, unless we feel it,
We are none of us quite consistent Christians.
But such pain is like other strong feelings;
It is akin to natural excitement,
And it gives much room for self-deceit.
Whoever is inclined to indulge it, must take care;
He has need to be applying continual tests of reality.
This is the great lesson of the Epistle for the Day;
And the text applies the lesson to our words;
We are apt to speak sharply of others,
When we think they are dishonouring God;

Or when they are against us in any good work;
And we count it almost necessary so to speak,
In order to shew ourselves in earnest;
But can we be more in earnest than the Angels?
Than the Seraphim—the flaming fires?
Than Michael the Archangel?
Yet how guarded, how serious, how calm was his rebuke!
He left the matter to God;
He called no hard names;
Yet he distinctly indicated his horror at the sin,
And his fear for the person;
And that, though he was greater in power and might.
When there are exceptions in Holy Scripture,
It is either God *Himself* passing sentence,
As on Elymas the sorcerer:
Or it is apologized for, as by S. Paul,
When he had called the High Priest "a whited wall[x]."
But you say, "I find it hard to refrain;
"Saying the names relieves me."
Still refrain:
Remember the third Commandment.
"But must I not contend for the truth?"
You do it more effectually, by gentleness[y];
Gentleness is more according to your calling;
We are called by a common invitation to a common Blessing;
Therefore keep yourself down,
When you are, yourself, reproached.
Or when a friend is reproached;

---

[x] Acts xxiii. 5.　　　　　[y] See Bp. Butler.

Much more, when God is reproached.
"Sanctify Him in your hearts,"
As Moses once forgot to do,
And paid so dearly for it.

CXXIII.

THE PERIL OF KNOWLEDGE WITHOUT LOVE.

" But now have they both seen and hated both Me and My Father."
S. JOHN xv. 24.

In the Creed we confess " One ... Apostolic Church."
What does this mean?
Not merely that we teach the doctrines of the Apostles,
Nor merely that we are of the same Society as they;
But that we are joined to our Lord,
By grace transmitted through them.
The Collect for this day recognises this distinction.
Acknowledging the union of the Church,
It prays for unity of doctrine among ourselves;
That the Church, and each one of us, may be a holy Temple,
Wherein Christ may delight to dwell.
Unity tends to holiness;
Division is against charity;
It interrupts prayer.
Heresy always lowers the Christian standard,

"Turning the grace of God into lasciviousness;"
But the Creed is the pledge and means of unity;
For the Creed, then, we must earnestly contend.
We must neither add to it, nor take away from it;
We must say it night and morning;
We must live by it all day long.
Live by it—else the effect will be worse than all.
What does our Lord say of the Jews in the Gospel for the day?
"If I had not come and spoken to them they had not had sin,
"But now they have no cloke for their sin."
"If I had not done among them the works
"Which none other man did,
"They had not had sin;
"But now they have both seen and hated both Me
"And My Father."
It is more especially true of wicked Christians,
That they are in the way to hate Christ and the Father;
If this thought is too horrible,
Take we care to be good Christians.

CXXIV.

All Saints' Day.

The Note of Holiness.

"It is written, Be ye holy, for I am holy."—1 S. Peter i. 16.

Where is it so written?
It is written three times in the Old Testament [a].
And each time, in connection with the same Law,
The Law of meats, and other distinctions,
Which were appointed to separate the Jews
From the Canaanites.
The Jews were to be holy, as being nearer to God.
Much more is this true of us Christians,
Who are so much nearer to God than the Jews.
"We are partakers of the Divine Nature [a],"
Partakers of It even in our very bodies,
By Christ's Incarnation [b];
And by the indwelling of the Holy Spirit [c].
What then is this Holiness,
Standing above all God's Attributes, perhaps alone,
As That which we are to endeavour after?
We think of it as of a Divine Goodness,
A Heroical goodness, beyond our comprehension.
But there are two things in this Holiness,

---

[a] Lev. xi. 45; xix. 2; xx. 7.　　[a] 2 S. Pet. i. 4.　　[b] 1 Cor. vi. 15.
[c] 1 Cor. iii. 16.

The Note of Holiness.

In both of which we can follow it.
First, it is "perfect;"
And we are to be "perfect [d]."
But in this world, we do not reach perfection,
We can but aim at it [e];
And aim at it by love, especially [f].
Therefore, sanctity is not actual perfection;
Sanctity is the constant aiming at perfection.
Next, God loveth goodness for its own sake, essentially;
He does not love it for what comes of it;
For, He is altogether blessed;
And neither we nor any angel can *give* to Him [g].
Therefore, Disinterestedness is a great point of sanctity.
And we can but aim at this too, with constancy.
Thus aim at Disinterestedness;
Aim at doing right;
Not for earthly rewards [h];
Not for the spiritual comfort of it [i];
Not with a view of meriting Heaven [k];
But in order to please God;
In order to come nearer to God;
In order to be with God [l];
In order to see the Face of God [m];
In one word—for *Love* of God.
And this reconciles the different motives recommended;

[d] Rom. xii. 2; S. Matt. v. 48.   [e] 1 Cor. xiii.   [f] 1 S. John iv.
[g] Job xli. 11; Rom. xi. 35; Ps. xvi. 2;
[h] S. Matt. vi.; S. Mark viii.   [i] Isa. l. (our Lord's agony).
[k] S. Luke xvii. 10; Gal. ii.   [l] Phil. i. 23.   [m] Rev. xxii. 4.

U

They are but aspects of one and the same Truth;
Love of God is love of Holiness;
For God is Holiness [n].
And love of Heaven is love of His Presence;
For His full Presence is Heaven.
What then does God say when He enjoins us, "Be ye holy?"
He says in effect, "Be not contented with yourselves,
"Until you are as good as ever you can be."
And what say we to this,
We who are so wilfully imperfect?
God says, "Be holy, for I am Holy:"
"Let your motive be, to come as near Me as you can:
"To love Me so well as to keep Me ever before you,
"To have My Will and My Example always in mind."
What say we to this?
We, who so continually forget Him for earthly motives?
We admire the Saints; can we help it?
We wish to know and to resemble them:
Here are two plain ways to do so:
First—to seek and to pray always for *the best*.
Secondly—to set God always before you.
"He will be on your right hand;"
And, in time, you will have your wish.

[n] 1 S. John iv. 16.

CXXV.
Fellowship with the Saints.

"And these all, having obtained a good report through faith, received not the promise; God having provided some better thing for us, that they, without us, should not be made perfect." HEB. xi. 39, 40.

  A HOLY and happy season is this of All Saints,
    For all good Christian people.
   For it teaches this comfortable truth,
 That the great doings and sufferings of our God
Are brought home to us in the Communion of Saints.
   It tells us of our "fellowship with the Father,
    "And with His Son Jesus Christ."
And that, having *that*, we have fellowship with one another;
   Fellowship, not only with those now living,
    But with those who are gone before;
  And with those who are yet behind, with us.
    The dead in Christ live;
They live unto God; they think of us; they pray for us.
   Consider how near we must be to each other,
When the dead are said to be imperfect without us.
A truth in unison with what we read of Christ Himself.
    "The Lord hath need of them o."
   "The Church which is His Body,
"The fulness of Him that filleth all in all p."
   All are imperfect until Christ shall come.
   Even the best are so, till the Resurrection.

o S. Matt. xxi. 3.   p Eph. i. 22, 23.

And this is true of the Christian Saints [q];
The ancient Liturgies preserve the token of this doctrine;
The very highest of the Saints used to be named in them;
Christ interceding, both for them and for us, in Heaven.
See then, how great and holy we all are!
You think no one cares for you;
While Apostles, Patriarchs, Prophets, Martyrs, care for you;
They are leaning down, as it were, to watch you;
They are a "cloud of witnesses" beholding you;
They long for your company.
How can you choose such company as you do,
And care for such sympathy as you do,
In preference to the company and sympathy of the Saints?
You think you are left alone and helpless,
While the air is full of Angels,
And Heaven is full of prayers.
How can you fret and grumble here,
While you have such a Home, and such Friends there?
How can you say you want encouragement in goodness,
When you know what we are taught by S. Paul,
That "the Heavens and all the Powers therein" wait for you,
Do not count themselves perfect without you.
That Apostles wish "your perfection;"
That the Son invites you to be perfect as the Father is?
May God grant us in good time to know ourselves;
And to know Him that is within us,
That we may, at least, begin His work before we die!

[q] Compare Rev. vi. 9.

CXXVI.

THE SAINTS' NEARNESS TO CHRIST.

"*That we may grow up unto Him in all things, which is the Head, even Christ.*"—EPH. iv. 15.

THIS time is a time of building;
It is also a time of growing;
For we are limbs of Christ [r].
Attend to this; for what is the Mystery of the Season?
"The Communion of Saints."
And this being a Mystery of the Creed,
Let all Catechumens attend particularly.
How are we limbs of Christ?
Christ has, so to speak, two Bodies:
His natural Body, born of the Blessed Virgin Mary;
His mystical Body, made up of all His Elect.
We are engrafted into His mystical Body, by His Spirit,
Entering into us at our Baptism [s].
We are kept alive in His mystical Body,
And we grow in It, by the gift of the same Spirit,
Through participation of His true Body,
In the Blessed Eucharist [t].
Thus, "of His Fulness have all we received,
"And grace for grace [u]."

[r] S. John xv. 5 : 1 Cor. xii. 12, 13 : Col. i. 18; ii. 19.   [s] Rom. vi. : Gal. iv. 6.   [t] S. John vi. 53—57 : 1 Cor. x. 16.   [u] S. John i. 16.

We are therefore of the "Elect" in the first part of the Collect.
We are chosen and called out of every nation,
Called to share the Communion of the Holy Ghost.
We enter into the Communion of Saints,
By being "partakers of Christ."
Only we must "hold the beginning of our confidence,"
Hold it "steadfast unto the end, while it is said to-day[x]."
But now, being limbs, we may grow;
Being souls, we may improve.
And since it is of "His Fulness" that we receive,
The process is by grace answering to His grace,
And there need be no limit to our progress;
Nor will there be, if all be healthy and right;
For it is said, "Be ye holy, for I am holy."
But He Who gave this command, foreknew all men;
He knew that some would obey the call
More early than others;
Some more unreservedly, more intensely, than others;
And He prepared for them Crowns and Thrones accordingly[y].
These are the "Saints" in the latter part of the Collect.
These are the First-fruits, in the Vision of S. John[z];
The Saints who shall come with the Lord[a];
The Saints who shall judge the world[b].
And with all these we have Communion,
As well as with others, who are not so high,
Even with all "who have departed this life in faith and fear."

[x] Heb. iii. 14, 15. [y] S. John xiv. 2; 1 Cor. xv. 41. [z] Rev. xiv. 4.
[a] Zech. xiv. 5; S. Jude 14; Rev. xix. 14.   [b] S. Luke xxii. 30;
1 Cor. vi. 2.

There are several tokens of this Communion;
One is our commemoration of the Saints at the Altar;
We have another in the Burial Service;
Every Saint's Day brings us another;
But we have a special token in this Feast of All Saints,
And in the Collect for this Festival.
We are not to pray to the Saints to pray for us;
Far less are we to worship them.
But we may have this comfortable thought,
That they do remember us.
And we may ask this petition of God,
That the prayers of the Saints being offered for the Church,
May be effectual for our personal good.
And we may honour them by following them,
By treading in their steps,
By walking in all virtuous and godly living,
By setting our hearts on the Joy into which they have entered,
The "Joy unspeakable,"
The Joy of being with Christ, Whom they unfeignedly love.
Be sure this is what they would wish.
Transporting thought!
That a place may be, even now, prepared for us,
At the feet of some of the Saints!
And more, in His Presence Who is crowning them,
And Who will crown us also, according to our measure,
The measure in which we have "grown up unto Him,
"In all things."
Never fear then, being *too* good;
Never fear that, either for yourself or for any one else;

Since every degree in goodness is a new Crown in Heaven,
A new Eternity of Joy and Glory,
A step nearer to Christ.
He that loves Christ, must desire one thing above all,
To be as near Him as he can.

The Penitential Psalms.

I.

Psalm VI.

v. 1. Consider how the soul, looking back on its past doings and present condition, feels that it must be rebuked and chastened, and only prays that this may not be in wrath, and heavy displeasure [c].

vv. 2 and 3. And what does the soul plead? Its affliction [d]. It is so "languid," and in such pain, even in the "bones," (the strongest bodily part,) "trembling and quivering."

Why should this be a reason? Because of Christ's sympathy [e].

v. 3. For the "soul" also, and not only the outward "bones," is sore troubled; it appeals to the time already endured; it asks, "how long?"

But this is of God's mercy, that the deliverance may be valued and complete; as the woman of Canaan had her patience tried, and as the Church is kept waiting still.

v. 4. "Turn Thee, O Lord,"—that is, "do not pass by; take some notice of me [f]." As it is written, "Return unto Me, and I will return unto you [g];" "so turn, as not to turn away," but so as to "save" me; and that, not for our merits, but "for Thy mercy's sake."

---

[c] Cf. Rev. iii. 19; 1 Cor. iii. 12—15.   [d] Cf. Ps. xxv. 18.
[e] Heb. iv. 15; Ps. xxii. 16.   [f] Ps. lxxxvi. 16, 17.   [g] Cf. S. Jas. iv. 8.

v. 5. Yea, for Thine own glory[h], Death and the grave must come to an end, before Thou canst be worthily praised[i].

v. 6. But still, weariness, sighing, intense weeping, restlessness go on. The eye is wearing and wasting, as a garment, or as in consumption, from continually looking on to God's anger; and it is growing old and weak (like Jacob) in the consciousness that all things are against it.

These are the symptoms of true sorrow for sin; and they are most blessed in the end.

How unlike to most of us! and if so, how unsatisfactory our condition!

O let us try to pray with all our hearts that He would give us godly sorrow.

v. 7. Consider here who are our enemies, and how wearing their presence is to us.

They are the bad spirits tempting us with thoughts, suggestions, fancies, interruptions of good; and so taking occasion by the flesh.

Or they are worldly friends, who, even unintentionally, even with kind intentions, prove to be our enemies. As it is said, "a man's foes shall be they of his own household."

Remember Job's wife; and think of our Lord's caution, "If any man come to Me, and *hate* not his father and his mother, he cannot be My disciple."

But, not to dwell on such extreme cases, how many have those, at home, or among their relations and companions,

---

[h] Cf. Isa. xxxviii. 18, 19.   [i] Rev. xx. 14.

who teach them lightness, selfishness, impurity, vanity; by example, or by ridicule, by scornfulness, by flattery, or by misrepresentation! Not minding the threat addressed to those "who shall offend [k]" His "little ones;" or by rejoicing in iniquity; and so doing the devil's work.

These are they who help the ill-inclined to ruin; and are a wasting, wearing trial to the penitent.

v. 8. Fancy then the joy at final deliverance from all such dangers. "Away from me, all ye that work vanity, for the Lord hath heard 'my prayer.'"

This release may be understood of the Church, or of each special soul; at the last Day; or in partial deliverance here on earth.

For even here, the good are made aware of their being kept out of reach of evil; as grain and chaff lying together on the floor, waiting for the great Wind. As S. Paul was aware, when the word was spoken to him, "My Grace is sufficient for thee."

Of all this mystery we have the type and earnest, in the devil "departing for a season," to return, and to be bruised finally on Mount Calvary.

And so, "He that is begotten of God keepeth himself, and that wicked one toucheth him not." And a great step towards such deliverance is made when, from our heart, we can say, "Away from me all ye that work vanity;" in other words, when we are really convinced of the nothingness of things here.

v. 9. And what joy and gladness, when our minds are made

[k] S. Matt. xviii. 6.

up, and God speaks to our hearts accordingly: a *threefold* joy—because of the joy in Him: "Glory be to the Father, and to the Son, and to the Holy Ghost!" Joy for reconciliation, as the misery was from alienation. Joy which those who have tried can never forget—joy which makes them ready to die, with the feeling that they never can be happier in this world; and joy which makes them wish to live, that they may shew themselves thankful.

v. 10. And this joy is the fruit and the seal of His reconciliation—the witness that those, who are corrigible, are converted; and that the incurably evil ones depart, according to the old notion, when the Sign of the Cross is made, or the Holy Name is spoken; as in the miracles of our Lord and the Apostles.

This witness too has its beginning, when we overcome temptation. Would you know what it means? Try in earnest the next time a bad thought comes over you.

Resist the tempter in Christ's Name: he will be ashamed; he will tremble; he will turn away disappointed. And by the joy then, you will be able to guess the last joy[1].

When will that Joy be? The Psalmist says "suddenly"—"in a moment—in the twinkling of an eye;" for so all our great changes are. Birth, Marriage, Baptism, Orders, Death, Resurrection, all are suddenly effected. Only think of the vast, entire, unspeakable change!

Or the word may mean shortly; and so it will seem at the time, however long may be the days and years which we count first.

[1] Rev. xx. 10.

Therefore, have patience, and endure, if it must be so, even the presence of the enemy; until he shall depart from you and from the Church altogether. And then this Psalm, with the other Psalms, will perfectly become a "new song" indeed; we singing, as we never yet have sung, "Glory to the Father, and to the Son, and to the Holy Ghost."

II.

Psalm XXXII.

This second Penitential Psalm has a special mark put upon it, in that the Holy Ghost, by S. Paul, has declared it to contain the Christian doctrine of Justification, not by merit of our works, but entirely by God's free grace.

We all, of course, acknowledge this in words; but how is it with us in fact?

This Lent, and every Lent, will help us to judge ourselves on this point, if we will try in earnest. For it is a *time* of confession: And so will this Psalm help us; for it is a *Psalm* of confession.

The misery which it especially mentions, as connected with sin, is the burden of concealment; and the relief is a full and true confession.

Let us go through it, and we shall see how, in helping us to Repentance, it also teaches us the true doctrine of Justification.

The Psalm supposes a sinner admitted to Penance, as sinners are at the beginning of Lent; and as he calmly and deeply considers in his mind the unspeakable mercy he has in view, the Holy Spirit teaches him to say to himself—

v. 1. "Blessed is he," (and only he, among men), "whose unrighteousness is forgiven, and whose sin is covered."

Observe the words; for each one has deep meaning.

Blessed with "all blessings"—thoroughly blessed—having nothing *but* blessings [m]—is he—not "who is without spot of sin," but whose sin, even the worst ἀνομία, is borne for him, as a burden [n]; who is himself borne—cross and all—as the sheep by the Good Shepherd.

And, whose errors are "covered"—who has Christ's Skirt spread over him—"The wedding garment" put on—whose sins are out of sight; the Lord casting them behind His Back. This takes off the shame; as the other takes off the punishment.

v. 2. Again, "Blessed is he"—not, who was never in debt, but whose sins are not imputed to him; whose debt is cancelled from the Book.

Yet observe the necessary sign of this blessing,—"in whose spirit there is no guile."

We must not put God's Name to a lie; we must use no fraud, no hypocrisies, with our Lord; else we destroy the virtue of the only Name Which can save [o].

And this agrees exactly with what comes afterwards about confession, and must be borne in mind all through the Psalm.

v. 3. As for thinking to stand upon our own goodness, such presumption will cause not only a sullen silence in the way of faith and confession ("I held my tongue"), but a good

---

[m] Cf. Gen. xlix. 25, 26.   [n] Cf. Ps. xxxviii. 4; S. Matt. xi. 28.
[o] Cf. Rev. xiv. 5.

deal of wasting and disturbance, through the noise made by worldly discontent, "through my daily complaining."

Or again, in better dispositions, it will be a wearing thought if people reserve things unconfessed; it will weaken the "bones" of the Christian character.

v. 4. God's Hand is heavy upon such, and His Grace dries up; a result bad enough if it comes through timidity or ignorance; but if it comes in unbelief, it is yet worse.

vv. 5, 6. We have seen the trouble; now see the remedy—

"I will make the Lord know my sin," my bad condition altogether; and "I will not hide my iniquities"—my special sins. Not that hiding is possible, but that it is here, as in Prayer. "I said"—I thoroughly made up my mind—thus to "confess" to the Lord; and forgiveness came at once, even before the confession was complete P.

But you must go on with your confession, just the same q.

And it must be "to the Lord," and therefore in the way which He appoints. Some confessions are made to His Ministers; others need not so be made. The distinction pointed out by the Church, is in her words "a weighty matter."

It must, above all, be quite true.

Observe here how it answers to telling one's case to the Doctor; one's general decay; one's occasional and one's chronic symptoms; one's want of grace.

v. v. 7. Your confession must also be in a time acceptable.

---

p Cf. Isa. lxv. 24; S. Luke xv. 18—21.   q Cf. S. Luke xv. 21.

All who are ὅσιοι, who by virtue of sanctifying grace find mercy, will come in time. If they do, no great "waters," neither of sin, nor affliction, nor false doctrine, will be able to come nigh them. His Hand will draw them out: His Love will guard them[r].

Let your confession be thus, timely, true, and dutiful; and then, besides the final forgiveness which it will bring, it will be full of blessing even here.

"Thou art a Place to hide me in[s];" a Shelter from shame; a Preservation from Enmity; a World full of holy joy.

v. 8. But you are not yet safe. The Voice promises, "I will inform thee,"—edify thee in principles, as the Creeds and the Commandments, "and teach thee," in practice. "I will guide thee with Mine Eye"—by slight hints which a dutiful heart will understand.

v. 9. And the Voice proceeds—Be not wilful and unruly, like wild creatures of the desert, to need sharp discipline. Be like that gentle creature which our Lord honoured when He entered His City in triumph. Accept discipline, and judge yourself that you be not judged.

v. 10. And again, many stripes are appointed to the wicked, as many troubles to the righteous; but the latter have two advantages: first, that trusting in the Lord, mercy is around them all the while; and next, that they have the promise of deliverance out of all.

This trust is the very "faith" which is so praised everywhere; and to such the Voice ends by saying,—

[r] Ps. cxliv. 7: Cant. viii. 7.   [s] Cf. Ps. xxvii. 5; xxxi. 20; cxix. 114.

v. ~~14~~ /12. "Be glad, Oh ye righteous, and rejoice in the Lord." Be glad inwardly, be cheerful outwardly; and as the highest instance of it, "sing Psalms [t]."

But this is said only to the true and upright of heart—to those whose rule it really is, (with whatever infirmity they may keep it), to fit on their own wills to the Will of God, in doing and in suffering. Such are able to say, "We glory in tribulation also."

O great and blessed effects of that simple act, an humble, true, loving confession of sin to your loving Saviour!

Why should you draw back from it?

III.

Psalm XXXVIII.

THE complaint here would seem to be not so much for any great new sin, as for the habitual evils still returning, and prevailing, which cause a kind of *sickness* in the heart.

This is the key to the whole Psalm, from the first to the twelfth verse.

Still, as before in Ps. vi., it is the *anger* of God, more than the *pain* of punishment, which the penitent deprecates. And that *more than before;* as we see by the more distinct reference to the sin of his life in verses 3—6.

And he offers his sorrows past and present, as a sort of plea before God, that he may not incur His anger.

---

[t] S. James v. 13; Col. iii. 16.

v. 2. His "*arrows*" are the sharp stings of conscience [u], or the sharp words of Scripture [x]; and His "heavy Hand" is the aching, or wringing, of the heart, as in the Agony.

v. 3. "There is no health," that is, soundness, entireness—"in my flesh because of Thy displeasure." There is a deep sense of original sin pervading all [y], so that our best health is but deferred disease. Neither is there any "rest"—peace, "in my bones." There is a tossing to and fro—an utter restlessness of heart.

v. 4. Old wickednesses returning, and the burden heavier and heavier.

v. 5. Wounds not cleansed, putrifying sores—as in leprosy—opposed to the sweet odour of Christ and of good works: wounds intolerable to himself, and with the sense of being intolerable to others. Through "foolishness"—the provoking feeling of having been utterly mad and senseless: as with Esau, if he had repented; or as with David, after numbering the people.

Take care lest penitence should become bitter through this provoking sense of our own foolishness.

v. 6. I am bent and bowed down greatly; I go stooping, as Hezekiah and Ahab. Mourning (wearing black) becomes one's companion everywhere and at all times.

v. 7. Especially for the consciousness of carnal sins "my loins" being filled with what is loathsome.

Consider how this affects the whole body; the eye, the hand, and every thought, insensibly corrupt.

---

[u] Cf. Job vi. 4.   [x] Cf. Ps. xlv. 6.   [y] Isa. i. 5.

v. 8. I am "*feeble*," that is, benumbed; and "*sore smitten*," that is, bruised greatly (*attritus*). I have roared aloud, because of the inward moaning of my heart.

v. 9. I appeal unto God, as people do in extremity: He only knows what I suffer, and what I long for.

v. 10. My heart is giddy, restless; it has no stay—nothing to depend on—no strength; I am not as I was; the light of mine eyes is gone; I have no clear perception; all is doubt, or dim with anguish. Such is the distress.

Next, we look for relief.

But first, consider how God shews His knowledge and His sympathy, by the very fact of giving us such a Psalm as this; much more by taking our nature, and going through all the suffering for us; so that a Christian, as he reads, knows that it is Christ suffering for him.

Let us say to ourselves, but not in fretfulness, not in reproach—"God knows and regards it all." This thought will be a great relief now, and a great step towards deliverance.

Those who, with full faith, use themselves to say, "Thou considerest my trouble, and knowest my soul in adversities," are not far from the joyful hour when they shall say, "Thou hast not shut me up into the hand of the enemy, but hast set my feet in a large room."

vv. 11, 12. The general notion of this Psalm being "sickness of the heart from sin, and relief therefrom"—the first, though unuttered, relief, is here; for no Christian can read these verses without feeling that they speak of the Cross, and whatever does so, of course, leads straight to relief.

My lovers and my neighbours—the Mother of Jesus, and His Mother's Sister, S. John and the Magdalene; the other women, Salome, and the rest; Joseph of Arimathea and Nicodemus—all His acquaintance—the women that bewailed and lamented Him—all these, even if they were near in body, were far from His trouble.

So it is when we are sick; so in remorse; so when we come to die. Much more was it so in that Mysterious Death of our Lord.

Again, there were the Chief Priests and the Scribes all that day, contriving how to take Him; framing charges, suborning witnesses, wresting His words, insulting Him on the Cross.

So our spiritual enemies, and sometimes those in the world also, deal with us. Christ endured their reproaches because He made our sins His own. We must bear our share, because they *are our* sins. And O, be patient, for He bore all.

v. 13. His remedy was, to be silent—before the Chief Priests—before Pilate—before Herod; and, most part of the time, on the Cross; and this was a token of His speaking in judgment.

Much more must silence be *our* remedy: we must dispense with all excuses, and bear the reproach of conscience and of the evil spirits, and the indignation of the Lord, because we have sinned against Him.

v. 14. We must also be very unwilling to judge others; but, as for ourselves, the only thing is to renounce ourselves altogether.

v. 15. And then, if we put our trust in Him always, He will answer for us, Who is our Lord and God, as well as our Brother and our Surety. He will silence the evil one[a]: but we must wait His time.

v. 16. And in this we may pray as Moses prayed for Israel[a], and as the Psalmist prayed for preventing Grace[b], and as S. Paul prayed for the penitent[c].

(Observe here the Head, again, taking the part of the members.)

v. 17. He confesses his chronic lameness; the sad remnant and effect of his old sins: it haunts him continually. His own sin, as in Psalm li., not his neighbour's, is "ever before" him[d].

v. 18. He resolves that his whole life shall be confession, and sorrow, or trembling, for his sin.

v. 19. The rather that his enemies are still living and mighty; and his evil accusers many.

v. 20. And the enemies of Christ are against him, because he tries to be a good Christian.

v. 21. Therefore, his only hope is that his God will never forsake him; nor remove too far, or too long, away from him; not only "deliver him from evil," but not "lead him into temptation."

v. 22. His prayers are continually more and more earnest, that the number of the Elect may be accomplished, and that God's kingdom may be hastened.

---

[a] See Rev. xii. 10; Job i. 9; Zech. iii. 2. Deut. ix. 26—29; Num. xiv. 13. [b] Ps. xiii. 4. [a] Ex. xxxii. 12; [c] 2 Cor. ii. 10, 11. [d] Ps. li. 3.

And so, we have the complete cure of heart-sickness; relief for the time, enough to sustain us so that we may commit all to God, as He did in His last words; and then, no long waiting; but "after three days He will raise us up."

His full, great, entire, Salvation will be here; the waiting, long or short, will seem, then, "but a few days, for the love we bear Him."

As a token and pledge of all this, observe how God's Providence, in His Church, teaches us, every time we come to church, to use these very words of the Psalm, "O God, make haste to help us." "Haste Thee to help me, O Lord God of my Salvation."

He puts the words in our mouth; can we doubt that He will fulfil them in His own good time, if we do not contradict them by our heart and life?

IV.

Psalm LI.

This is eminently the Psalm of Confession—so used by the Ancient Church—and so used by us, in the Office of Commination.

Why is this? Because it is the fullest specimen of Evangelical Repentance; David's privileges having been so great; his sin so sad; his repentance so entire; and his sense, particularly of having grieved the Holy Spirit, so keen.

Now, for exposition, observe first, that the nine opening verses especially ask for Pardon; and the ten concluding verses ask for the renewal of Grace; and then note the following points:—

v. 1. The Penitent trusts to nothing but to God's goodness.

v. 2. He longs for cleansing more than for being spared.

v. 3. He confesses unreservedly,—and bears the sense of his sin about with him.

v. 4. He feels his sin to be, beyond comparison, greatest *towards God*, and submits entirely to be cast in the trial; using words which the Holy Ghost, in the New Testament, has taught all of us to use, to express the manner of our justification:

"Let God be true but every man a liar, as it is written, that Thou mightest be justified in Thy saying, and mightest overcome when Thou art judged [e]."

v. 5. He has a deep feeling of the effect of the Fall—which all ought to remember, in order to keep them humble.

v. 6. He has also a sense of the deep inward requirements—of Truth especially—in God's Law, enforced by Conscience and by Revelation, and implying *some* way of help.

v. 7. Accordingly, the Holy Ghost teaches him to pray for, and to depend on, pardon through the Blood of Jesus Christ; which Pardon would make him "white as snow," both referring him backward to the Law—of the Passover [f], of the Covenant [g], of Purification, of Leprosy [h], and of other uncleanness; and pointing forward to the Cross [i].

v. 8. And not only Pardon through the Cross, but comfort also, and thorough cure of all the powers of the soul and

---

[e] Rom. iii. 4.   [f] Exod. xii. 22.   [g] Heb. ix. 19.
[h] Lev. xiv. 6, 7.   [i] S. John xix. 34.

body, bringing to him the feeling of renewed health, and of special comfort, as after the bath.

v. 9. Yet still accompanied with prayer for Pardon, and inward confession, as in the case of the Prodigal, "Father, I have sinned against Heaven and in thy sight, and am no more worthy to be called thy son."

In conclusion, take, for the present, this rule:—that the Gospel Redemption is a work going on all through life; and, all through life, accompanied with a deep sense of sin, which is all the keener the more we love God.

The Notes on the latter half of this Psalm have not been found.

V.

Psalm CII.

CONSIDER into what kind of a Family you were introduced by Holy Baptism:

What therefore you lose, in losing Baptismal grace.

How this loss comes, in a measure, by all sin; and entirely, by deadly sin.

Your temptation is to disregard this loss; and to go on as if you might do well enough, with the company of the world.

You are forsaken, and do not know it.

When, therefore, you are coming to a better mind,—when God is teaching you, then you know your loneliness; you "sit alone and keep silence,"—you cover your heads and go softly.

And this so much the more as you come to think, also,

of that other invisible company with which you have thrown yourself—"Mine enemies revile me all the day long, and they that are mad upon me are sworn together against me."

There will be small help or comfort, then, to be had from friends who do not know you.

There is no comfort but in His Presence, which we know is continued "for ever, and His remembrance throughout all generations." Who knows when we feel our condition, and is ready to hear and to deliver; to offer Absolution to His Penitents, when they groan as bearing their sentence; Who "heareth the mournings of such as are in captivity, and delivereth the children appointed unto death."

Then, may we be free to praise God among the Saints— and to "declare the Name of the Lord in Sion, and His worship in Jerusalem."

Then, may we continue His for ever, by virtue of His promise to Abraham :—" The children of Thy servants shall continue, and their seed shall stand fast in Thy sight."

VI.

Psalm CXXX.

v. 1. "Out of the deep." What deep?

Jonah cried from the deep; S. Peter cried from the deep; and S. Paul; and God heard.

So it will be when we are in the deep of sin, which is such a deep as that from which Jonah's prayer was made, such as in Ps. lxix. and xlii.

v. 2. And He will hear and consider; for He came Himself

into the deep, though it could not soil Him. And He is with us in the deep, even in our hearts.

He will be "very attentive." The deep of His mercies will answer to the deep of our miseries.

v. 3. If indeed He were "extreme to mark what is done amiss," this could not be: for our iniquities are an overwhelming deep: yes, ours and all men's. None can keep his footing in such a flood. None can stand under such a burden.

v. 4. But, we are bold to plead this with Thee, for there is pardon with Thee—even He Who, Himself, is Pardon and Propitiation: first, that men may not despair; and next, that they may be very watchful.

v. 5. Therefore our word is, to "wait for the Lord[k];" and to "hope in His Word."

v. 6. Our soul must flee "to the Lord" more than they that "watch for the morning." Observe the repetition, see how it teaches the "*Patience* of Hope."

Think of sick people, and nurses; of watchmen, and shepherds; of travellers, and seamen; and of shipwrecked persons.

v. 7. And then the Name of Israel, that is, God's own people; how much more does it suggest! Even His yearning mercy; His redemption, and that manifold.

v. 8. Yea, even to the redeeming of His own people (grievous as their transgressions are) from all their sins. Redemption both from the Power and from the Punishment of their sins.

[k] Cf. Ps. xxvii. last verse.

Think how all this applies to Easter Eve, to our Lord in the grave: and to Penitents awaiting His entire Absolution.

VII.

Psalm CXXX.

HERE He seems to sympathize with a drowning man.

As in, "Save me, O God, for the waters are come in even unto my soul. I stick fast in the deep mire where no ground is; I am come into deep waters, so that the floods run over me."

"Take me out of the mire that I sink not; O let me be delivered from them that hate me, and out of the deep waters. Let not the water-flood drown me, neither let the deep swallow me up [l]."

And in, "Deep calleth unto deep at the noise of thy water-pipes. All Thy billows and storms are gone over me [m]."

And in, "Thou hast laid me in the lowest pit, in darkness, in the deep. Thy wrath lieth hard upon me, and Thou hast afflicted me with all Thy waves [n]."

And especially in, "Then I said, I am cast out of Thy sight: yet I will look again toward Thy holy temple.

"The waters compassed me about, even to the soul: the depth closed me round about; the weeds were wrapped about my head. . . . .

"When my soul fainted within me, I remembered the

[l] Ps. lxix. 1, 2, 15, 16.   [m] Ib. xlii. 7, 8.
[n] Ib. lxxxviii. 6, 7.

Lord: and my prayers came in unto Thee, into Thy holy temple º."

Observe, from this last, how infinite is the sympathy, since Jonah is a Type of Christ.

And the sympathy is not only with one drowning, but with all sudden death.

And with those who are confounded at their own sudden falls, as S. Peter.

How their heaps of sin come rushing upon them.

Their unpreparedness, though God had prepared them. What if they are cast out of His sight?

There is one thing only to be done—to look towards His Temple; to cry to Him, to cling to Him ᵖ, to grasp, like S. Peter, the Hand which He holds out to them.

And so their affright changes into a calm and humble and loving fear.

And they know that their Prayer has come into the Temple.

And they wait quietly, not impatiently, for the morning.

Observe, the true Penitent thinks of Israel as well as of himself, "O be favourable and gracious unto Zion; build Thou the walls of Jerusalem ᵠ."

And, "Thou shalt arise and have mercy upon Zion ʳ."

So here, "He shall redeem Israel from all his sins."

God grant us so to die! and that we may so die, may we pray and labour, and may He grant us, so to live!

º Jonah ii. 4—7. ᵖ See the Hymn, "Jesu, Lover of my soul."
ᵠ Ps. li. 18. ʳ Ib. cii. 13.

VIII.

Psalm CXLIII.

In this Psalm, we have the bewilderment and perplexity of the Penitent, expressed and cured.

They are expressed in such terms as these—"The enemy hath persecuted my soul, he hath smitten my life down to the ground, he hath laid me in the darkness, as the men that have been long dead. Therefore is my spirit vexed within me, and my heart within me is desolate. Yet do I remember the time past, I muse upon all Thy works, yea, I exercise myself in the works of Thy hands,"—and the following verses.

And they are cured by such words as these—"O let me hear Thy loving-kindness betimes in the morning, for in Thee is my trust; shew Thou me the way that I shall walk in, for I lift up my soul unto Thee. Deliver me, O Lord, from mine enemies, for I flee unto Thee to hide me,"—and the following verses.

The perplexity of a Penitent comes of sin; as did communion with Satan, who is now permitted to try us with it, as part of our punishment.

Such punishment must be accepted by the Penitent.

Even as it was accepted by Him, Who made Himself sin for us [a].

This is the comfort for those who try to be penitent, and are perplexed. They look to Him. They resign themselves in prayer. They rouse themselves to do what they know

---

[a] See Ps. xxii.; S. John xii. 27.

to be right, and to think of others. They remember His Promise that He will give the Holy Spirit.

O the joy—when the loving Spirit shall lead you forth, and you shall be out of the reach of your "enemies" for ever!

Printed by James Parker and Co., Crown Yard, Oxford.

A SELECTION FROM
THE PUBLICATIONS OF
MESSRS. JAS. PARKER AND CO.
OXFORD, & 377, STRAND, LONDON.

NEW BOOKS.

Hints to Preachers, with Sermons and Addresses.
By S. REYNOLDS HOLE, Canon of Lincoln. Post 8vo., cloth, 6s.

What is of Faith as to Everlasting Punishment?
In Reply to Dr. Farrar's Challenge in his "Eternal Hope," 1879. By the Rev. E. B. PUSEY, D.D., Regius Professor of Hebrew, Canon of Christ Church. 8vo., cloth, 286 pp., 3s. 6d.

The Worship of the Old Covenant
CONSIDERED MORE ESPECIALLY IN RELATION TO THAT OF THE NEW. By the Rev. E. F. WILLIS, M.A., Vice-Principal of Cuddesdon Theological College. Post 8vo., cloth, 5s.

Notes of My Life, 1805—1878.
By GEORGE ANTHONY DENISON, Vicar of East Brent, 1845; Archdeacon of Taunton, 1851. Third Edit., 8vo., cloth, 12s.

The Ancient Use of Liturgical Colours.
By CLAPTON C. ROLFE. An attempt to show that the ancient use of the Church of England is in harmony with the Levitical use, and entirely distinct from that which is now sanctioned by the Church of Rome. 8vo., cloth, 10s. 6d.
"An elaborate and learned work."—*Bishop of Lincoln.*

The Christian Ministry.
SOME REMARKS ON THE ESSAY BY DR. LIGHTFOOT, now Lord Bishop of Durham, on the CHRISTIAN MINISTRY. By CHARLES WORDSWORTH, D.C.L., Bishop of St. Andrew's. Crown 8vo., limp cloth, 2s.

An Introduction
TO THE HISTORY OF THE SUCCESSIVE REVISIONS of the Book of Common Prayer. By JAMES PARKER, Hon. M.A. Oxon. Crown 8vo., pp. xxxii., 532, cloth, 12s.

The First Prayer-book of Edward VI.
Compared with the Successive Revisions of the Book of Common Prayer. Together with a Concordance and Index to the Rubrics in the several Editions. Crown 8vo., cloth, 12s.

Church History.
PASSAGES IN CHURCH HISTORY selected from the MSS. of the late Rev. JOHN DAVID JENKINS, D.D., Canon of the Cathedral of Natal, with a Memoir of the Author, by T. J. DYKE. Edited by F. M. F. S. 2 vols. Cr. 8vo., cloth, 15s.

[980.4*50.]

The Powers of the World to Come.
SHORT SERMONS by HENRY HARRIS, B.D. Crown 8vo., cloth, 5s.

The History of Confirmation.
By WILLIAM JACKSON, M.A., Queen's College, Oxford; Vicar of Heathfield, Sussex. Crown 8vo., cloth, 4s.

Winchester College.
WYKEHAMICA: A History of Winchester College and Commoners, from the Foundation to the Present Day. By the Rev. H. C. ADAMS, M.A., late Fellow of Magdalen College, Oxford. Post 8vo., cloth, 508 pp., with Nineteen Illustrations, 10s. 6d.

Historical Tales.
TALES ILLUSTRATING CHURCH HISTORY. ENGLAND: Mediæval Period. Vol. III. of the Series. By the Rev. H. C. ADAMS, Vicar of Dry Sandford. With Four Illustrations on Wood. Fcap. 8vo., cloth, 3s. 6d.

THE ANDREDS-WEALD, or THE HOUSE OF MICHELHAM: A Tale of the Norman Conquest. By the Rev. A. D. CRAKE, B.A., Fellow of the Royal Historical Society; Author of "Æmilius," "Alfgar the Dane," &c. With Four Illustrations by LOUISA TAYLOR. Fcap. 8vo., cloth, 3s. 6d.

The Awaking Soul,
As sketched in the 130th Psalm. Addresses delivered at St. Peter's, Eaton-square, on the Tuesdays in Lent, 1877, by E. R. WILBERFORCE, M.A., late Vicar of Seaforth, Liverpool; and Sub-Almoner to the Queen. Crown 8vo., lp. cl., 2s. 6d.

The Founder of Norwich Cathedral.
The LIFE, LETTERS, and SERMONS of BISHOP HERBERT DE LOSINGA (b. circ. A.D. 1050, d. 1119), the LETTERS (as translated by the Editors) being incorporated into the LIFE, and the SERMONS being now first edited from a MS. in the possession of the University of Cambridge, and accompanied with an English Translation and English Notes. By EDWARD MEYRICK GOULBURN, D.D., Dean of Norwich, and HENRY SYMONDS, M.A., Rector of Tivetshall, late Precentor of Norwich Cathedral. 2 vols. 8vo., cl., 30s.

The Catholic Doctrine of the Sacrifice and Participation of the Holy Eucharist.
By GEORGE TREVOR, M.A., D.D., Canon of York; Rector of Beeford. Second Edition, Revised and Enlarged. Crown 8vo., cloth, 10s. 6d.

Sermons preached on Special Occasions
By JOHN MITCHINSON, D.D., Bishop of Barbados. Crown 8vo., cloth, 5s.

Daniel the Prophet.

Nine Lectures delivered in the Divinity School, Oxford. With a Short Preface in Answer to Dr. Rowland Williams. By E. B. PUSEY, D.D., Regius Professor of Hebrew, and Canon of Christ Church. *Seventh Thousand.* 8vo., 10s. 6d.

The Minor Prophets;

With a Commentary Explanatory and Practical, and Introductions to the Several Books. By the Rev. E. B. PUSEY, D.D., &c. 4to., cloth, price £1 11s. 6d.

The Fifty-third Chapter of Isaiah,

According to the Jewish Interpreters. I. Texts edited from Printed Books, and MSS., by AD. NEUBAUER. Price 18s. II. Translations by S. R. DRIVER and AD. NEUBAUER. With an Introduction to the Translations by the Rev. E. B. PUSEY, Regius Professor of Hebrew, Oxford. Post 8vo., cloth, 12s.

The Prophecies of Isaiah.

Their Authenticity and Messianic Interpretation Vindicated, in a Course of Sermons preached before the University of Oxford. By the Very Rev. R. PAYNE SMITH, D.D., Dean of Canterbury. 8vo., cloth, 10s. 6d.

A Plain Commentary on the Book of Psalms

(Prayer-book Version), chiefly grounded on the Fathers. For the Use of Families. 2 vols., Fcap. 8vo., cloth, 10s. 6d.

The Psalter and the Gospel.

The Life, Sufferings, and Triumph of our Blessed Lord, revealed in the Book of Psalms. Fcap. 8vo., cloth, 2s.

A Summary of the Evidences for the Bible.

By the Rev. T. S. ACKLAND, M.A., late Fellow of Clare Hall, Cambridge; Incumbent of Pollington cum Balne, Yorkshire. 24mo., cloth, 3s.

Musings on Psalm cxix.

"THE PSALM OF DIVINE ASPIRATIONS." By the Author of the Cottage Commentary. 150 pp. 16mo., limp cloth, red edges, 2s.

Godet's Biblical Studies

ON THE OLD TESTAMENT. Edited by the Hon. and Rev. W. H. LYTTELTON, Rector of Hagley, and Honorary Canon of Worcester. Fcap. 8vo. cloth, price 6s.

Catena Aurea.

A Commentary on the Four Gospels, collected out of the Works of the Fathers by S. THOMAS AQUINAS. Uniform with the Library of the Fathers. A Re-issue, complete in 6 vols., cloth, £2 2s.

A Plain Commentary on the Four Holy Gospels,

Intended chiefly for Devotional Reading. By the Very Rev. J. W. BURGON, B.D., Dean of Chichester. New Edition. 4 vols., Fcap. 8vo., limp cloth, £1 1s.

The Last Twelve Verses of the Gospel according to S. Mark

Vindicated against Recent Critical Objectors and Established, by the Very Rev. J. W. BURGON, B.D., Dean of Chichester. With Facsimiles of Codex ℵ and Codex L. 8vo., cloth, 12s.

The Gospels from a Rabbinical Point of View,

Shewing the perfect Harmony of the Four Evangelists on the subject of our Lord's Last Supper, and the Bearing of the Laws and Customs of the Jews at the time of our Lord's coming on the Language of the Gospels. By the Rev. G. WILDON PIERITZ, M.A. Crown 8vo., limp cloth, 3s.

Christianity as Taught by S. Paul.

By WILLIAM J. IRONS, D.D., of Queen's College, Oxford; Prebendary of S. Paul's; being the BAMPTON LECTURES for the Year 1870, with an Appendix of the CONTINUOUS SENSE of S. Paul's Epistles; with Notes and Metalegomena, 8vo., with Map, Second Edition, with New Preface, cloth, 9s.

S. Paul's Epistles to the Ephesians and Philippians.

A Practical and Exegetical Commentary. Edited by the late Rev. HENRY NEWLAND. 8vo., cloth, 7s. 6d.

The Explanation of the Apocalypse.

By VENERABLE BEDA, Translated by the Rev. EDW. MARSHALL, M.A., F.S.A., formerly Fellow of Corpus Christi College, Oxford. 180 pp. Fcap. 8vo., cloth, 3s. 6d.

Meditations on the Gospels,

Distributed for Every Day in the Year by the ABBÉ DUQUESNE. Edited by DR. PUSEY. In 4 vols., Fcap. 8vo. [*In preparation.*

A History of the Church,

From the Edict of Milan, A.D. 313, to the Council of Chalcedon, A.D. 451. By WILLIAM BRIGHT, D.D., Regius Professor of Ecclesiastical History, and Canon of Christ Church, Oxford. Second Edition. Post 8vo., 10s. 6d.

The Age of the Martyrs;

Or, The First Three Centuries of the Work of the Church of our Lord and Saviour Jesus Christ. By the late JOHN DAVID JENKINS, B.D., Fellow of Jesus College, Oxford; Canon of Pieter Maritzburg. Cr. 8vo., cl., reduced to 3s. 6d.

The Councils of the Church,

From the Council of Jerusalem, A.D. 51, to the Council of Constantinople, A.D. 381; chiefly as to their Constitution, but also as to their Objects and History. By E. B. PUSEY, D.D. 8vo., cloth, 6s.

The Ecclesiastical History of the First Three Centuries,

From the Crucifixion of Jesus Christ to the year 313. By the late Rev. Dr. BURTON. Fourth Edition. 8vo., cloth, 12s.

A Brief History of the Christian Church,

From the First Century to the Reformation. By the Rev. J. S. BARTLETT. Fcap. 8vo., cloth, 2s. 6d.

Manual of Ecclesiastical History,

From the First to the Twelfth Century inclusive. By the Rev. E. S. FFOULKES, M.A. 8vo., cloth, 6s.

A History of the English Church,

From its Foundation to the Reign of Queen Mary. By MARY CHARLOTTE STAPLEY. Fourth Edition, revised, with a Recommendatory Notice by DEAN HOOK. Crown 8vo., cloth, 5s.

Bede's Ecclesiastical History of the English Nation.

A New Translation by the Rev. L. GIDLEY, M.A., Chaplain of St. Nicholas', Salisbury. Crown 8vo., cloth, 6s.

St. Paul in Britain;

Or, The Origin of British as opposed to Papal Christianity. By the Rev. R. W. MORGAN. Second Edition. Crown 8vo., cloth, price 2s. 6d.

The Principles of Divine Service;

Or, An Inquiry concerning the True Manner of Understanding and Using the Order for Morning and Evening Prayer, and for the Administration of the Holy Communion in the English Church. By the late Ven. PHILIP FREEMAN, M.A., Archdeacon of Exeter, &c. 2 vols. 8vo., cloth, 16s.

A History of the Book of Common Prayer,

And other Authorized Books, from the Reformation; with an Account of the State of Religion in England from 1640 to 1660. By the Rev. THOMAS LATHBURY, M.A. Second Edition, with an Index. 8vo., cloth, 10s. 6d.

Catechetical Lessons on the Book of Common Prayer.

Illustrating the Prayer-book, from its Title-page to the end of the Collects, Epistles, and Gospels. Designed to aid the Clergy in Public Catechising. By the Rev. Dr. FRANCIS HESSEY, Incumbent of St. Barnabas, Kensington. Fcap. 8vo., cloth, 6s.

A Short Explanation of the Nicene Creed,

For the Use of Persons beginning the Study of Theology. By the late A. P. FORBES, D.C.L., Bishop of Brechin. New Edition, Crown 8vo., cloth, 6s.

An Explanation of the Thirty-Nine Articles.

By the late A. P. FORBES, D.C.L., Bishop of Brechin. With an Epistle Dedicatory to the Rev. E. B. PUSEY, D.D. New Edition, in one vol., Post 8vo., 12s.

Addresses to the Candidates for Ordination on the Questions in the Ordination Service.

By the late SAMUEL WILBERFORCE, LORD BISHOP OF WINCHESTER. Fifth Thousand. Crown 8vo., cloth, 6s.

A Commentary on the Epistles and Gospels in the Book of Common Prayer.

Extracted from Writings of the Fathers of the Holy Catholic Church, anterior to the Division of the East and West. With an Introductory Notice by the DEAN OF ST. PAUL'S. 2 vols., Crown 8vo., cloth, 15s.

The Ornaments of the Church, &c.

PARISH CHURCH GOODS IN BERKSHIRE, A.D. 1552. Inventories of Furniture and Ornaments remaining in certain of the Parish Churches of Berks. Transcribed from the Original Records, with Introduction and Explanatory Notes by WALTER MONEY, F.S.A. Crown 8vo., limp cloth, 3s. 6d.

On Eucharistical Adoration.

With Considerations suggested by a Pastoral Letter on the Doctrine of the Most Holy Eucharist. By the late Rev. JOHN KEBLE, M.A., Vicar of Hursley. 24mo., sewed, 2s.

Advice on Hearing Confession,

From Writings of Saints. Condensed, abridged, and adapted from the ABBÉ GAUME'S Manual. With PREFACE, embodying English Authorities on Confession, by E. B. PUSEY, D.D. 8vo., cloth, 6s.

The Administration of the Holy Spirit

IN THE BODY OF CHRIST. The Bampton Lectures for 1868. By the Right Rev. the LORD BISHOP OF SALISBURY. *Second Edition.* Crown 8vo., 7s. 6d.

S. Athanasius on the Incarnation, &c.

S. Patris Nostri S. Athanasii Archiepiscopi Alexandriæ de Incarnatione Verbi, ejusque Corporali ad nos Adventu. With an English Translation by the Rev. J. RIDGWAY, B.D., Hon. Canon of Ch. Ch. Fcap. 8vo., cloth, 5s.

De Fide et Symbolo:

Documenta quædam nec non Aliquorum SS. Patrum Tractatus. Edidit CAROLUS A. HEURTLEY, S.T.P., Dom. Margaretæ Prælector, et Ædis Christi Canonicus. Fcap. 8vo., cloth, 4s. 6d.

The Canons of the Church.

The Definitions of the Catholic Faith and Canons of Discipline of the First Four General Councils of the Universal Church. In Greek and English. Fcap. 8vo., cloth, 2s. 6d.

The English Canons.

The Constitutions and Canons Ecclesiastical of the Church of England, referred to their Original Sources, and Illustrated with Explanatory Notes, by MACKENZIE E. C. WALCOTT, B.D., F.S.A., Præcentor and Prebendary of Chichester. Fcap. 8vo., cloth, 4s.

Cur Deus Homo,

Or Why God was made Man; by ST. ANSELM. Latin and English. *[Nearly ready.*

The Athanasian Creed.

A Critical History of the Athanasian Creed, by the Rev. DANIEL WATERLAND, D.D. Fcap. 8vo., cloth, 5s.

S. Aurelius Augustinus,

EPISCOPUS HIPPONENSIS,

De Catechizandis Rudibus, de Fide Rerum quæ non videntur, de Utilitate Credendi. In Usum Juniorum. Edidit C. MARRIOTT, S.T.B., olim Coll. Oriel. Socius. A New Edition, Fcap. 8vo., cloth, 3s. 6d.

St. Cyril, Archbishop of Alexandria.

The Three Epistles (ad Nestorium, ii., iii., et ad Joan Antioch). A Revised Text, with an old Latin Version and an English Translation. Edited by the late P. E. PUSEY, M.A. 8vo., in wrapper, 3s.

Vincentius Lirinensis.

For the Antiquity and Universality of the Catholic Faith against the Profane Novelties of all Heretics. Latin and English. New Edition, Fcap. 8vo. *[Nearly ready.*

The Pastoral Rule of S. Gregory.

Sancti Gregorii Papæ Regulæ Pastoralis Liber, ad JOHANNEM, Episcopum Civitatis Ravennæ. With an English Translation. By the Rev. H. R. BRAMLEY, M.A., Fellow of Magdalen College, Oxford. Fcap. 8vo., cloth, 6s.

The Book of Ratramn

The Priest and Monk of Corbey, commonly called Bertram, on the Body and Blood of the Lord. (Latin and English.) To which is added AN APPENDIX, containing the Saxon Homily of Ælfric. Fcap. 8vo. *[Nearly ready.*

NEW AND CHEAPER ISSUE
OF

The Library of the Fathers

OF THE HOLY CATHOLIC CHURCH, ANTERIOR TO THE DIVISION
OF THE EAST AND WEST.

Translated by Members of the English Church.

Already Issued.

St. Athanasius against the Arians. 1 vol., 10s. 6d.
—————————— Historical Tracts ⎫ 10s. 6d.
—————————— Festal Epistles ⎭
St. Augustine's Confessions, with Notes, 6s.
—————————— Sermons on the New Testament. 2 vols., 15s.
—————————— Homilies on the Psalms. 6 vols., £2 2s.
—————————— on the Gospel and First Epistle of St. John. 2 vols., 15s.
—————————— Practical Treatises. 6s.
St. Chrysostom's Homilies on the Gospel of St. Matthew. 3 vols., £1 1s.
—————————— Homilies on the Gospel of St. John. 2 vols., 14s.
—————————— Homilies on the Acts of the Apostles. 2 vols., 12s.
—————————— to the People of Antioch. 7s. 6d.
—————————— Homilies on St. Paul's Epistles, including the Homilies on the Epistle to the Hebrews. 7 vols., £2 12s. 6d.
St. Cyprian's Treatises and Epistles, with the Treatises of St. Pacian. 10s.
St. Cyril (Bishop of Jerusalem), Catechetical Lectures on the Creed and Sacraments. 7s.
St. Cyril (Archbishop of Alexandria), Commentary upon the Gospel of St. John. Vol. I. 8s.
The Five Books against Nestorius, together with the Scholia on the Incarnation. *In Preparation.*
St. Ephrem's Rhythms on the Nativity, and on Faith. 8s. 6d.
St. Gregory the Great, Morals on the Book of Job. 4 vols., £1 11s. 6d.
St. Irenæus, the Works of. 8s.
St. Justin the Martyr. Works now extant. 6s.
Tertullian's Apologetical and Practical Treatises. 9s.

⁎⁎* *The 44 Vols. bound in 40, cloth, price £15.*

Works of the Standard English Divines,
PUBLISHED IN THE LIBRARY OF ANGLO-CATHOLIC THEOLOGY.

Andrewes' (Bp.) Complete Works. 11 vols., 8vo., £3 7s.
    THE SERMONS. (Separate.) 5 vols., £1 15s.

Beveridge's (Bp.) Complete Works. 12 vols., 8vo., £4 4s.
    THE ENGLISH THEOLOGICAL WORKS. 10 vols., £3 10s.

Bramhall's (Abp.) Works, with Life and Letters, &c.
5 vols., 8vo., £1 15s.

Bull's (Bp.) Harmony on Justification. 2 vols., 8vo., 10s.
————————— **Defence of the Nicene Creed.** 2 vols., 10s.
————————— **Judgment of the Catholic Church.** 5s.

Cosin's (Bp.) Works Complete. 5 vols., 8vo., £1 10s.
Crakanthorp's Defensio Ecclesiæ Anglicanæ. 8vo., 7s.
Frank's Sermons. 2 vols., 8vo., 10s.
Forbes' Considerationes Modestæ. 2 vols., 8vo., 12s.
Gunning's Paschal, or Lent Fast. 8vo., 6s.
Hammond's Practical Catechism. 8vo., 5s.
————————— **Miscellaneous Theological Works.** 5s.
————————— **Thirty-one Sermons.** 2 Parts. 10s.

Hickes's Two Treatises on the Christian Priesthood.
3 vols., 8vo., 15s.

Johnson's (John) Theological Works. 2 vols., 8vo., 10s.
————————— **English Canons.** 2 vols., 12s.

Laud's (Abp.) Complete Works. 7 vols., (9 Parts,) 8vo., £2 17s.

L'Estrange's Alliance of Divine Offices. 8vo., 6s.
Marshall's Penitential Discipline. 8vo., 4s.
Nicholson's (Bp.) Exposition of the Catechism. (This volume cannot be sold separate from the complete set.)

Overall's (Bp.) Convocation-book of 1606. 8vo., 5s.

Pearson's (Bp.) Vindiciæ Epistolarum S. Ignatii.
2 vols., 8vo., 10s.

Thorndike's (Herbert) Theological Works Complete.
6 vols., (10 Parts,) 8vo., £2 10s.

Wilson's (Bp.) Works Complete. With Life, by Rev. J. KEBLE. 7 vols., (8 Parts,) 8vo., £3 3s.

    ⁎ *The 81 Vols. in 88, for £15 15s. net.*

The Catechist's Manual;
By EDW. M. HOLMES, Rector of Marsh Gibbon, Bicester. With an Introduction by the late SAMUEL WILBERFORCE, LORD BISHOP OF WINCHESTER. 6th Thousand. Cr. 8vo., limp cl., 5s.

The Confirmation Class-book:
Notes for Lessons, with APPENDIX, containing Questions and Summaries for the Use of the Candidates. By EDWARD M. HOLMES, LL.B., Author of the "Catechist's Manual." Fcap. 8vo., limp cloth, 2s. 6d.
> THE QUESTIONS, separate, 4 sets, in wrapper, 1s.
> THE SUMMARIES, separate, 4 sets, in wrapper, 1s.

The Church's Work in our Large Towns.
By GEORGE HUNTINGTON, M.A., Rector of Tenby, and Domestic Chaplain of the Rt. Hon. the Earl of Crawford and Balcarres. Second Edit., revised and enlarged. Cr. 8vo., cl. 3s. 6d.

The Church and the School:
Containing Practical Hints on the Work of a Clergyman. By H. W. BELLAIRS, M.A., One of Her Majesty's Inspectors of Schools. Cheap re-issue, Crown 8vo., limp cloth, 2s. 6d.

Notes of Seven Years' Work in a Country Parish.
By R. F. WILSON, M.A., Prebendary of Sarum, and Examining Chaplain to the Bishop of Salisbury. Fcap. 8vo., cloth, 4s.

A Manual of Pastoral Visitation,
Intended for the Use of the Clergy in their Visitation of the Sick and Afflicted. By A PARISH PRIEST. Dedicated, by permission, to His Grace the Archbishop of Dublin. Second Edition, Crown 8vo., limp cloth, 3s. 6d.; roan, 4s.

The Cure of Souls.
By the Rev. G. ARDEN, M.A., Rector of Winterborne-Came, and Author of "Breviates from Holy Scripture," &c. Fcap. 8vo., cloth, 2s. 6d.

Questions on the Collects, Epistles, and Gospels,
Throughout the Year. Edited by the Rev. T. L. CLAUGHTON, Vicar of Kidderminster. For the Use of Teachers in Sunday Schools. Fifth Edition, 18mo., cl. In two Parts, *each* 2s. 6d.

Pleas for the Faith.
Especially designed for the use of Missionaries at Home and Abroad. By the Rev. W. SOMERVILLE LACH SZYRMA, M.A., St. Augustine's College, Canterbury. Fcap. 8vo., cl., 2s. 6d.

MEDITATIONS FOR THE FORTY DAYS OF LENT.
With a Prefatory Notice by the ARCHBISHOP OF DUBLIN. 18mo., cloth, 2s. 6d.

DAILY STEPS TOWARDS HEAVEN;
Or, PRACTICAL THOUGHTS on the GOSPEL HISTORY, and especially on the Life and Teaching of our Lord Jesus Christ, for Every Day in the Year, according to the Christian Seasons, with the Titles and Character of Christ, and a Harmony of the Four Gospels. Newly printed, with antique type. Fortieth thousand. 32mo., roan, gilt edges, 2s. 6d.; morocco, 5s.

LARGE-TYPE EDITION. Square Crown 8vo., cloth antique, red edges, 5s.

THE HOURS:
Being Prayers for the Third, Sixth, and Ninth Hours; with a Preface and Heads of Devotion for the Day. By the late A. H. D. TROYTE, Author of "Daily Steps Towards Heaven." Seventh Edition. 32mo., vellum wrapper, 1s.

ANNUS DOMINI.
A Prayer for each Day of the Year, founded on a Text of Holy Scripture. By CHRISTINA G. ROSSETTI. 32mo., cl., 3s. 6d.

LITURGIA DOMESTICA:
Services for every Morning and Evening in the Week. Third Edition. 18mo., 2s. Or in two Parts, 1s. each.

EARL NELSON'S FAMILY PRAYERS.
With Responsions and Variations tor the different Seasons, for General Use. New and improved Edition, *large type*, cloth, 2s.

OF THE IMITATION OF CHRIST.
Four Books. By THOMAS À KEMPIS. Small 4to., printed on thick toned paper, with red border-lines, mediæval title-pages, ornamental initials, &c. Third Thousand. Cloth, 12s.

PRAYERS FOR MARRIED PERSONS.
From Various Sources, chiefly from the Ancient Liturgies. Selected and Edited by CHARLES WARD, M.A., Rector of Maulden. Second Edition, Revised. 24mo., cloth, 4s. 6d.

FOR THE LORD'S SUPPER.
DEVOTIONS BEFORE AND AFTER HOLY COMMUNION. With Preface by J. KEBLE. Sixth Edition. 32mo., cloth, 2s.
With the Office, cloth, 2s. 6d.

DEVOUT COMMUNION, from HORST. 18mo., cloth, 1s.

OFFICIUM EUCHARISTICUM. By EDWARD LAKE, D.D. New Edition. 32mo., cloth, 1s. 6d.

A SHORT AND PLAIN INSTRUCTION FOR THE BETTER UNDERSTANDING OF THE LORD'S SUPPER. By BISHOP WILSON. 32mo., with Rubrics, cloth, gilt edges, 2s.
——————— 32mo., limp cloth, 8d.; sewed, 6d.
——————— 24mo., limp cloth, 1s.

Oxford Editions of Devotional Works.

Fcap. 8vo., chiefly printed in Red and Black, on Toned Paper.

Andrewes' Devotions.
DEVOTIONS. By the Right Rev. LANCELOT ANDREWES. Translated from the Greek and Latin, and arranged anew. Cloth, 5s.

The Imitation of Christ.
FOUR BOOKS. By THOMAS À KEMPIS. A new Edition, revised. Cloth, 4s.
Pocket Edition. 32mo., cloth, 1s.; bound, 1s. 6d.

Laud's Devotions.
THE PRIVATE DEVOTIONS of Dr. WILLIAM LAUD, Archbishop of Canterbury, and Martyr. Antique cloth, 5s.

Spinckes' Devotions.
TRUE CHURCH OF ENGLAND MAN'S COMPANION IN THE CLOSET. By NATHANIEL SPINCKES. Floriated borders, antique cloth, 4s.

Sutton's Meditations.
GODLY MEDITATIONS UPON THE MOST HOLY SACRAMENT OF THE LORD'S SUPPER. By CHRISTOPHER SUTTON, D.D., late Prebend of Westminster. A new Edition. Antique cloth, 5s.

Taylor's Golden Grove.
THE GOLDEN GROVE: A Choice Manual, containing what is to be Believed, Practised, and Desired or Prayed for. By BISHOP JEREMY TAYLOR. Antique cloth, 3s. 6d.

Taylor's Holy Living.
THE RULE AND EXERCISES OF HOLY LIVING. By BISHOP JEREMY TAYLOR. Ant. cloth, 4s.
Pocket Edition. 32mo., cloth, 1s.; bound, 1s. 6d.

Taylor's Holy Dying.
THE RULE AND EXERCISES OF HOLY DYING. By BISHOP JEREMY TAYLOR. Ant. cloth, 4s.
Pocket Edition. 32mo., cloth, 1s.; bound, 1s. 6d.

Ancient Collects.
ANCIENT COLLECTS AND OTHER PRAYERS, Selected for Devotional Use from various Rituals, with an Appendix on the Collects in the Prayer-book. By WILLIAM BRIGHT, D.D. Fourth Edition. Antique cloth, 5s.

Devout Communicant.
THE DEVOUT COMMUNICANT, exemplified in his Behaviour before, at, and after the Sacrament of the Lord's Supper: Practically suited to all the Parts of that Solemn Ordinance. 7th Edition, revised. Edited by Rev. G. MOULTRIE. Fcap. 8vo., toned paper, red lines, ant. cl., 4s.

ΕΙΚΩΝ ΒΑΣΙΛΙΚΗ.
THE PORTRAITURE OF HIS SACRED MAJESTY KING CHARLES I. in his Solitudes and Sufferings. New Edition, with an Historical Preface by C. M. PHILLIMORE. Cloth, 5s.

THE AUTHORIZED EDITIONS OF
THE CHRISTIAN YEAR,
With the Author's latest Corrections and Additions.

NOTICE.—Messrs. PARKER are the sole Publishers of the Editions of the "Christian Year" issued with the sanction and under the direction of the Author's representatives. All Editions without their imprint are unauthorized.

	s. d.		*s. d.*
SMALL 4to. EDITION.		**32mo. EDITION.**	
Handsomely printed on toned paper, with red border lines and initial letters. Cl. extra	10 6	Cloth, limp	1 0
		Cloth boards, gilt edges	1 6
DEMY 8vo. EDITION.		**48mo. EDITION.**	
Cloth	6 0	Cloth, limp	0 6
		Roan	1 6
FOOLSCAP 8vo. EDITION.		**FACSIMILE OF THE 1st EDITION**, with a list of the variations from the Original Text which the Author made in later Editions. 2 vols., 12mo., boards	7 6
Cloth	3 6		
24mo. EDITION.			
Cloth	2 0		
Ditto, with red lines	2 6		

The above Editions (except the Facsimile of the First Edition) are kept in a variety of bindings, the chief of which are Morocco plain, Morocco Antique, Calf Antique, and Vellum.

By the same Author.

LYRA INNOCENTIUM. Thoughts in Verse on Christian Children. *Thirteenth Edition.* Fcap. 8vo., cl., 5s.
———— 48mo. edition, limp cloth, 6d.; cloth boards, 1s.

MISCELLANEOUS POEMS BY THE REV. JOHN KEBLE, M.A., Vicar of Hursley. *Third Edition.* Fcap., cloth, 6s.

THE PSALTER, OR PSALMS OF DAVID: In English Verse. *Fourth Edition.* Fcap., cloth, 6s.

The above may also be had in various bindings.

By the late Rev. ISAAC WILLIAMS.

THE CATHEDRAL; or, The Catholic and Apostolic Church in England. 32mo., cloth, 2s. 6d.

THE BAPTISTERY; or, The Way of Eternal Life, with Plates by BOETIUS A BOLSWERT. Fcap. 8vo., cloth, 7s. 6d.; 32mo., cloth, 2s. 6d.

HYMNS translated from the PARISIAN BREVIARY. 32mo., cloth, 2s. 6d.

THE CHRISTIAN SCHOLAR. Fcap. 8vo., cl., 5s.; 32mo., cloth, 2s. 6d.

THOUGHTS IN PAST YEARS. 32mo., cloth, 2s. 6d.

THE SEVEN DAYS; or, The Old and New Creation. Fcap. 8vo., cloth, 3s. 6d.

THE LATE BISHOP WILBERFORCE.

SERMONS preached before the University of Oxford: Second Series, from 1847 to 1862. By the late SAMUEL WILBERFORCE, LORD BISHOP OF WINCHESTER. 8vo., cloth, 10s. 6d.
────── Third Series, from 1863 to 1870. 8vo., cloth, 7s. 6d.
SERMONS preached on Various Occasions. With a Preface by the Lord Bishop of Ely. 8vo., cloth, 7s. 6d.

REV. E. B. PUSEY, D.D.

PAROCHIAL SERMONS. Vol. I. From Advent to Whitsuntide. Seventh Edition. 8vo., cloth, 6s.
PAROCHIAL SERMONS. Vol. II. Sixth Edition. 8vo., cloth, 6s.
PAROCHIAL SERMONS. Vol. III. Reprinted from the "Plain Sermons by Contributors to the 'Tracts for the Times.'" Revised Edition, 8vo., cloth, 6s.
PAROCHIAL SERMONS preached and printed on Various Occasions. 8vo., cloth, 6s.
UNIVERSITY SERMONS preached between 1841 and 1855. New Edition, 8vo., cloth, 6s.
─────────────── 1859 to 1872. 8vo., cloth, 6s.
─────────────── 1864 to 1876. 8vo., cloth, 6s.
LENTEN SERMONS, preached chiefly to Young Men at the Universities, between A.D. 1858—1874. 8vo., cloth, 6s.
ELEVEN SHORT ADDRESSES during a Retreat of the Companions of the Love of Jesus, engaged in Perpetual Intercession for the Conversion of Sinners. 8vo., cloth, 3s. 6d.

THE LORD BISHOP OF SALISBURY.

SERMONS ON THE BEATITUDES, with others mostly preached before the University of Oxford; to which is added a Preface relating to the volume of "Essays and Reviews." New Edition. Crown 8vo., cloth, 7s. 6d.

REV. J. KEBLE.

SERMONS FOR THE CHRISTIAN YEAR.

Eleven Vols., price £3 6s.

FOR ADVENT TO CHRISTMAS EVE (46). 8vo., cloth, 6s.
FOR CHRISTMAS AND EPIPHANY (48). 8vo., cloth, 6s.
FOR SEPTUAGESIMA TO LENT (43). 8vo., cloth, 6s.
FOR LENT TO PASSIONTIDE (46). 8vo., cloth, 6s.
FOR HOLY WEEK (57). 8vo., cloth, 6s.
FOR EASTER TO ASCENSION-DAY (48). 8vo., cloth, 6s.
FOR ASCENSION-DAY TO TRINITY SUNDAY (41). 8vo., cl., 6s.
FOR SAINTS' DAYS (48). 8vo., cloth, 6s.
FOR TRINITY (45). Part I. Sundays I. to XII. 8vo., cl., 6s.
─────── (45). ,, II. ., XIII. to end. 8vo.,cl.,6s.
FOR VARIOUS OCCASIONS (44). 8vo., cloth, 6s.
VILLAGE SERMONS ON THE BAPTISMAL SERVICE. 8vo., cl., 5s.
SERMONS, OCCASIONAL AND PAROCHIAL. 8vo., cloth, 12s.

THE BISHOP OF TRURO.

"SINGLEHEART." Four Advent Sermons, by EDW. M. BENSON, Lord Bishop of Truro. Crown 8vo., cloth, 2s. 6d.

UNIVERSITY SERMONS

ON GOSPEL SUBJECTS. By JOHN WORDSWORTH, M.A., Tutor of Brasenose College; Examining Chaplain to the Bishop of Lincoln. Fcap. 8vo., cloth, 2s. 6d.

THE CITY OF THE LOST,

AND XIX. OTHER SHORT ALLEGORICAL SERMONS. By WALTER A. GRAY, M.A. (Π.), Vicar of Arksey;—and B. KERR PEARSE, M.A. (Φ.), Rector of Ascot Heath. Sixth Edition. Sewed, 1s.

CHARACTERISTICS OF CHRISTIAN MORALITY.

THE BAMPTON LECTURES FOR 1873. By the Rev. I. GREGORY SMITH, M.A., late Fellow of Brasenose College; Vicar of Malvern. Second Edition, Crown 8vo., cloth, 3s. 6d.

REV. E. MONRO.

ILLUSTRATIONS OF FAITH. Eight Plain Sermons. Fcap., 2s. 6d.
Plain Sermons on the Book of Common Prayer. Fcap., 5s.
Historical and Practical Sermons on the Sufferings and Resurrection of our Lord. 2 vols., Fcap. 8vo., cloth, 10s.
Sermons on New Testament Characters. Fcap. 8vo., 4s.

LENTEN SERMONS AT OXFORD.

Re-issue of the Series of Sermons preached at St. Mary's, &c.

The Series for 1857. 8vo., cloth, 5s.
For 1858. 8vo., cloth, 5s.
For 1859. 8vo., cloth, 5s.
For 1863. 8vo., cloth, 5s.
For 1865. 8vo., cloth, 5s.
For 1866. 8vo., cloth, 5s.
For 1867. 8vo., cloth, 5s.
For 1868. 8vo., cloth, 5s.
For 1869. 8vo., cloth, 5s.
For 1870-1. 8vo., cloth, 5s.

SHORT SERMONS FOR FAMILY READING,

Following the Course of the Christian Seasons. By the Very Rev. J. W. BURGON, B.D., Dean of Chichester. First Series. 2 vols., Fcap. 8vo., cloth, 8s.

——— SECOND SERIES. 2 vols., Fcap. 8vo., cloth, 8s.

RT. REV. J. ARMSTRONG D.D.

PAROCHIAL SERMONS. By the late Lord Bishop of Grahamstown. Fifth Edition. Fcap. 8vo., cloth, 5s.
SERMONS on the Fasts and Festivals. Third Edition. Fcap. 8vo., cloth, 5s.

SERMONS FOR THE CHRISTIAN SEASONS.

First Series. Edited by JOHN ARMSTRONG, D.D., late Bishop of Grahamstown. 4 vols., Fcap. 8vo., cloth, 10s.

——— Second Series. Edited by the Rev. JOHN BARROW, D.D., late Principal of St. Edmund Hall, Oxford. 4 vols., Fcap. 8vo., cloth, 10s.

THE CLERGYMAN'S
DESK CALENDAR, 1880.

THE above consists of pp. 2 to 14 and 64 of the "CHURCH CALENDAR," containing the DAILY AND PROPER LESSONS, &c., and is interleaved for Memoranda. It will be found convenient for use on READING DESKS in Churches.

Fourth Annual Issue, price 2d.

Crown 8vo., in roan binding, 12s.; calf limp, or calf antique, 16s.; best morocco, or limp morocco, 18s.

The Service-Book of the Church of England.

In this New Edition the Lessons appointed for the Immoveable festivals are printed entire in the course of the Daily Lessons where they occur. For the Sundays and Moveable Festivals, and for the days dependent on them, a table containing fuller references, with the initial words and ample directions where the Lesson may be found, is given. Where the Lesson for the Moveable Feast is not included entire amongst the Daily Lessons, it is printed in full in its proper place. Also in the part containing Daily Lessons, greater facilities have been provided for verifying the references.

There are also many modifications in the arrangement, wherein this Service-book differs from the Prayer-book: the Order for the Administration of the Holy Communion is printed as a distinct service, with the Collects, Epistles, and Gospels, which belong to the same: the Psalms immediately follow Daily Morning and Evening Prayer: the Morning and Evening Lessons also are by this arrangement brought nearer to the Service to which they belong, while the Occasional Offices are transferred to the end of the book.

Records of the City of Oxford.

SELECTIONS FROM THE RECORDS OF THE CITY OF OXFORD, with Extracts from other Documents illustrating the Municipal History: Henry VIII. to Elizabeth, [1509—1583]. Edited, by authority of the Corporation of the City of Oxford, by WILLIAM H. TURNER, of the Bodleian Library; under the direction of ROBERT S. HAWKINS, Town Clerk. Royal 8vo., cloth, £1 1s.

OXFORD and LONDON: JAMES PARKER and CO.

www.ingramcontent.com/pod-product-compliance
Lightning Source LLC
Chambersburg PA
CBHW030304240426
43673CB00040B/1057